M000317263

THE POWER OF PRAYER

Channeling Brain Waves Through Dhikr

AHMED HULUSI

As with all my works, this book is not copyrighted.
As long as it remains faithful to the original,
it may be freely printed, reproduced, published and translated.
For the knowledge of ALLAH, there is no recompense.

Copyright © 2014 **Ahmed Hulusi**
All rights reserved.
ISBN-10: 0692238379
ISBN-13: 978-0692238370

THE POWER OF PRAYER

Channeling Brain Waves Through Dhikr

AHMED HULUSI

www.ahmedhulusi.org/en/

Translated by ALIYA ATALAY

Transliteration by RASHAD ALI

ABOUT THE COVER

The black background of the front cover represents darkness and ignorance, while the white color of the letters represents light and knowledge.

The image is a Kufi calligraphy of the Word of Unity: *"La ilaha illallah; Muhammad Rasulullah"* which means,

"There is no concept such as 'god', there is only that which is denoted by the name Allah, and **Muhammad (SAW)** is the *Rasul* of this understanding."

The placement of the calligraphy, being on top and above everything else on the page, is a symbolic representation of the predominant importance this understanding holds in the author's life.

The green light, reflecting from the window of the Word of Unity, opens up from the darkness into luminosity to illustrate the light of Allah's *Rasul*. This light is embodied in the book's title through the author's pen and concretized as the color white, to depict the enlightenment the author aims to attain in this field. As the knowledge of Allah's *Rasul* disseminates, those who are able to evaluate this knowledge attain enlightenment, which is represented by the white background of the back cover.

"Prayer is the weapon of believers."

Muhammad (saw)

"Inquiry is half of knowledge."

Muhammad (saw)

"The greatest obstacle preventing man from seeing the truth is his prejudice."

Ahmed Hulusi

لَا إِلَهَ اِلَّا الله

La ilaha illAllah

There is no god, only Allah

Rabbi annee massani ash-shayṭaanu binuṣubin wa `adhaabin rabbi a`oodhu bika min hamazaati ash-shayṭaani wa a`oodhu bika rabbi an yaḥdurooni wa ḥifẓan min kulli shayṭaanin maaridin

My Rabb (The reality of the Names comprising my essence)! Satan (the internal mechanism (ego) that promotes the illusory existence of the inexistent and veils the Absolute Reality) is distressing and tormenting me. My Rabb, I seek refuge in You from the incitements of Satan, and I seek refuge in You from the presence of Satanic influences around me. And We have provided protection from all rejected Satans.[1]

A`aoodhu bi wajhi l-llahil kareem wa kalimaati l-ta'ammatillati la yujaawiz huna barun wa la fa'ajirun min sharri maa yanzilu mina s-samaa-i wa maa y`aruju feeha wa min sharri maa dhara fee-l ardhi wa mayakhrujoo minha wa min fitanil layli wan nahari illa tariqan yatruku bikhayrin ya Rahman...

I seek refuge in the face of Allah (in that which the attributes of Allah become manifest), the Karim (the exceedingly generous and bountiful), and in all His Names, nothing good or bad can attack them.

I seek protection in RAHMAN, the source of all potentials, from that which ascends to the heavens (from provocative thoughts) and that which descends from the heavens (from thoughts that conjure doubt and suspicion), from that which is produced from the plane of perceived manifestation (ardh) (that which emanates from corporeality) and grows out of it (bodily demands and desires), from the provocations of the day (our internal life) and the night (the outside world), and from that which knocks on the door at night (instinct), except if it is with good intent.[2]

---

[1] Based on verses 38.Saad: 41 – 23.Mu'minun: 97-98 – 37.Saffat: 7.
[2] Please refer to the chapter 'Beneficial Prayers' for further information.

I dedicate this book to my mother, Adalet, my most beloved, and my father, Ahmet Ekrem. May Allah bestow His mercy upon them all. Please do not forsake your prayers from their spirits.

TRANSLATOR'S PREFACE

If you were told of an exclusive technique that could extraordinarily enhance all your capabilities and enable you to create and manifest anything in your life that you desire, change or fix any situation, direct the motion of events, design and transform yourself in any way and without any limitation, and attain anything you could possibly imagine… What would you be willing to give up to possess this power?

But, what if you were told you didn't have to give up anything at all because it had already been given to you for free? What if this inherent power was the art of channeling brain waves: the power of prayer and dhikr?

If we only knew that every instance of our lives is the creation of our conscious and unconscious prayers, no doubt we would all want to master this incredible force.

Say, "If it wasn't for your introspection (prayer) my Rabb would not hold you in esteem!"[3]

Our ability to direct our brain waves towards a specific internal or external target, whether unconsciously through our random thoughts or consciously via prayer and dhikr, is what constantly creates anew our world experience.

This innate power with which we have all been endowed is the one and only master key to resolving

---
[3] Quran 25:77.

adversities and unlocking brand new potentials and experiences.

In this book, Ahmed Hulusi shares some of the most potent and unique prayer and dhikr formulas suited for specific situations and purposes.

Apply the formulas. Experience the transformation. Enjoy the outcomes.

Aliya Atalay
Antalya - Turkey
2014

CONTENTS

PREFACE

My friend,

Know that this book is one of the most valuable things you have been given in your life.

This book is the calling of your Rabb; it is a sacred door that He has opened for you.

Whoever you may be, whatever may be your occupation or religion, know that your Rabb is awaiting you and His door is wide open.

Do not ask where the door to your Rabb is. "IT" is within you, in your heart!

"IT" is beyond the door that opens from you, to you!

This door is the door of prayer and dhikr. A door that opens from your heart to your Rabb, your essential reality!

It is an act of introspective, turning to one's Rabb. It is the path of need.

So, abandon your imagined god up in the heavens and turn to Allah, the eternal and limitless One. Realize He is present at every point and within every iota of existence, and find Him in your heart!

Then ask of Him whatever you desire! Health, wealth, abundance, love, guidance, whatever you will! And know with certainty that the only thing to guide you to your desires is prayer and dhikr...

Know, my friend, that Allah, who is ever present with all of His qualities and attributes in every hint of existence, will respond to you – from you!

Know that you are His vicegerent on earth!

Now, as the vicegerent of Allah, are you aware of the incredible potential with which your brain has been endowed?

Are you aware that you can activate the power inherent in your brain through prayer and dhikr?

Do you know about the mechanism called 'prayer', your most powerful weapon?

Many weak and powerless men have overthrown and vanquished kings and emperors with prayer and dhikr!

Countless poor have attained great wealth and success with prayer and dhikr!

Many afflicted, distressed and diseased ones have reached salvation and emancipation through prayer and dhikr!

Know, my friend...

Prayer and dhikr are the world's most powerful weapons with which you have been endowed. By learning to use these forces within your brain and heart, you can reach endless beauties of the life of this world and beyond. Or, you may choose not to use them, let them rot away, and face the consequences of this for eternity!

This mechanism has been given to you for free, unrequitedly! It is a divine gift!

You neither need a mediator nor anyone's assistance to engage in prayer and dhikr. Whether you use the prayers in this book or pray in any way that you desire ... Just learn to use prayer and dhikr, your most valuable tools in this world...

You will see how your world will transform.

AHMED HULUSI

1

INTRODUCTION

My first book was called *A Guide to Spiritual Practices*, written in 1965.

The publishing industry, in those days, had a serious lack in this topic area. There were myriad prayer books available in the market, but their inadequacy made it mandatory to write and publish a new book. So, to the best of my ability, I prepared a short book on prayer according to the classical understanding and presented it to the service of my Muslim sisters and brothers.

It was printed many times over and I saw and heard it was in the hands and houses of many, for which I can never be sufficiently grateful, though I do not know the actual extent to which it spread in Turkey over the years.

Here is a paragraph from one of my readers whose children have now become adults:

"One day during my childhood my father came home with a prayer book... It was called 'A Guide to Spiritual Practices'. Being equally enthusiastic and curious as my mother, I read the book and tried to apply it according to my needs and troubles at the time. I asked for guidance and the strengthening of my faith, and I definitely saw its benefit. When I was getting married, my father gave me a copy of the same book, which I still read today..."

I am most fortunate to know this book has reached many generations and has become a classic in its own category.

However, through divine inspiration and comprehensive research, I have been able to reach many more powerful formulas and want to share these with as many Muslims as possible. Additionally, I want this book to answer the many unanswered questions in this area, in a way that new generations can understand.

Out of the inexperience of youth, I had given the copyright of my first book to a publisher, but this time, with the favor of Allah, I am donating this book to all my Muslim brethren. This book's copyright is not limited. It was not written for financial gain. So long as it remains loyal to its original, everyone can benefit from this book and distribute it for the benefit of others. The recital of three *ikhlas* and one *fatiha* will be more than enough…

The Rasul of Allah (saw) says, "To be a cause for good is the same as doing the good."[4]

I beseech that Allah enables us to be causes for good and protects us from deeds that will lead to much misery and regret in the future.

May Allah guide us to evaluate this book in the best way possible and allow us to recognize and comprehend the value of that which we possess.

---

[4] Al-Tirmidhi.

2

WHY PRAY?

The Rasul of Allah (saw) says, "Prayer is the weapon of the believer."[5] He also says, "Prayer is the essence of worship."[6]

Related to this hadith, the Quran says:

"I have created the jinn and men only so that they may serve Me (by means of manifesting the qualities of My Names)."[7]

In simple terms, servitude is prayer and *dhikr*!

In general terms, servitude is the fulfillment of an individual's purpose of existence.

"Are our prayers accepted when we pray?"

A Hadith Qudsi answers this question:

"If My servant raises his hands in supplication to Me, I would be ashamed to return them empty."[8]

Another Hadith Qudsi says:

"O son of Adam, prayer is from you, response is from Me. Repentance is from you, forgiveness is from Me. To ask forgiveness is from you, to grant it is from Me. To thank is from you, to give

---

[5] Ibn Hibban.
[6] Al-Tirmidhi.
[7] Quran 51:56.
[8] Al-Tirmidhi, Abu Dawud.

abundantly is from Me. Patience is from you, to aid is from Me… What have you ever asked of Me that I did not give?"

The following verse supports this hadith:

"Pray to Me, so that I may respond to you!"[9]

Another Hadith Qudsi that sheds light to the matter is:

"I am upon the assumption of My servant. So, let him assume as he wills!"[10]

In other words, if you believe beyond any doubt that your prayer will be accepted, then know with certainty that it will!

Based on this, one of the most eminent of saints, Imam Rabbani Ahmad Faruq Sarhandi, says, "Wanting something is attaining it, for Allah will not allow His servant to pray for something He will not accept."

When we make a prayer, we should be mindful of the verse:

"You cannot will unless Allah, the Rabb of the worlds, wills!"[11]

That is, any desire that becomes apparent in you only does so because it is the desire of Allah. Had Allah not willed it, you could not have wanted it.

Prayer is the easiest and most effective method, not to mention it is completely free! Thus, it has been said that prayer is the weapon of the believer.

How can prayer be a weapon?

To understand this, one needs to delve into the depths of Sufism.

Man, in respect to his essence, has been created with the attributes of Allah and subsists with the existence of Him.

Man is ALIVE because of the HAYY quality of Allah and has KNOWLEDGE because of the ALEEM quality of Allah. Man is able to put things into action with the quality of WILL deriving from

---

[9] Quran 40:60.
[10] Sahih al-Bukhari, Sahih al-Muslim.
[11] Quran 81:29.

Allah's Name MUREED. Thus, the extent to which man is able to manifest the meanings of these Names, which are all present within his being, is the extent to which he will be able to attain his desires and be safe from his fears.

But, what is prayer?

Is it a request made to a God far away?

Or is it to request the expression of the power of Allah, with which you exist and which is present in every cell of your being?

Prayer is no more than a technique to manifest the divine power within you!

Thus, when man is able to pray with full concentration and focus, he can reach and accomplish many seemingly impossible things.

This is why prayer is the most powerful weapon of man.

But, if we want to optimize the effectiveness of this technique, we must realize the relevance of the form of prayer, its place and time.

3

THE FORM OF PRAYER

Our motions during prayer are actually quite important...

When one is praying, the arms should be raised on both sides, high enough for the armpits to be visible, and the hands should be extended out, level with the face. It helps to direct the rays coming out of the fingertips, which should be approximately thirty centimeters away from the face, so they join with the rays that are emitted from the forehead. The Rasul of Allah (saw) says: "If one lifts his hands high enough for his armpits to be visible and prays, without rushing, his prayer will definitely be accepted..." Upon which he was asked, "How can one be in a rush, O Rasulullah?" And he answered, "By saying, 'I made a prayer, but my prayer was not accepted (and thus giving up).' This is incorrect; one should persist until it is accepted."[12]

The joining of the waves from the fingertips with the directed[13] waves that are emitted from the brain has a laser-like effect and plays a very important role in the actualization of prayer.

As can be seen, the primary force that enables the acceptance of prayer is not one that is external, but is activated completely from the Names of Allah present within the person. In short, prayer is the act of actualizing one's wants through the divine powers present within. There is, of course, a scientific explanation to this act.

---

[12] Sahih al-Bukhari, Sahih al-Muslim.
[13] More information on guided brain waves can be found in the *Mystery of Man*.

Essentially, prayer is 'guided brain waves.' Just as the dimension of knowledge transforms into energy and the quantum field to form the universe, the wants and desires of consciousness emanate from the dimension of knowledge to reveal themselves as the wants and desires of man and become actualized through the densification of guided brain waves. Due to this, the stronger the concentration level, the faster the response will be to the prayer. This is why there is a saying, "The prayer of the oppressed will not be left unheard; never will the accursed attain true success!" For a curse is made with such intense concentration that the negative brain waves that are guided directly to that person are literally inescapable. They say, "If the curse doesn't affect the grandfather, it will eventually affect the grandson." This is because the curse the grandparent receives modifies his genetic code such that, even if its effect doesn't reveal itself on him, eventually it is passed onto his children and grandchildren; hence, another proverb, "The fathers eat the sour grapes, but the children's teeth are set on edge."

Back to the motions of prayer... As I said previously, the arms have to be raised and open, and the hands in front. This is how the Rasul of Allah (saw) prayed. When a group of bandits in the desert fled after killing a group of people who attended to their needs and healed their wounds, the Rasul of Allah (saw) stood in prayer with his apostles and prayed in this exact manner, shortly after which the bandits were captured.

Praying as such; in a standing position with your arms raised high and your hands open with the palms facing your face so the rays can be freely emitted from your fingertips, is highly effective, as is praying while in a position of prostration. In particular, prayers that are made in prostration after midnight, when the sun is completely behind you and its radiation effect is minimal, are immensely effective. If you pray during the *final prostration* of the Prayer of Need (hajat) or any other salat, its effectiveness will be even more powerful.

If you perform salat during the night and in the final prostration make a prayer by first confessing and admitting your mistakes and asking for forgiveness, and repeat this for a few days, depending on what is requested and divine will, there will definitely be a response effecting the realization of the prayer. The fact the same prayer is allowed to be made persistently is in itself a sign that it will be responded to, for Allah would not allow a prayer to made persistently if it is not to be accepted. So, in other words, if you are not persistent in your prayer, its chance of being accepted and actualized is low.

But, why is a prayer made during prostration, especially after confessing your mistakes, so powerful?

When you prostrate, there is a strong flow of blood to the brain and hence the brain is abundantly nourished with oxygen and other sources of energy. This allows the brain to emit powerful waves. When you confess and admit your mistakes, an intense concentration and focus takes place, which strengthens the waves of the thing that is prayed for even more.

Another important factor, which strengthens and enables the actualization of the prayer, is that the person should be completely free of suspicion and groundless fear. Prostration is a state in which the illusory self, the ego, is completely lifted. Thus, the Rasul of Allah (saw) advises us to "pray with the certainty that your prayer will most definitely be accepted, without doubt or suspicion."

The biggest obstruction to the realization of prayer is doubt and suspicion. The extent to which this is minimized in a person determines the speed and the certainty of the prayer's fulfillment.

The reason why the prayers of those who have attained certainty (yakeen) of Allah are immediately accepted is due to their minimized suspicion. Additionally, the enlightened engage heavily in spiritual practices, which activate certain divine forces within them, also contributing to the effectiveness of their prayers.

One other important point to consider is that the jinn, who are known by satanic attributes, infuse misleading suggestions in regards to prayer in man, preventing him from using this most powerful weapon. Just as you feel an urge to pray, the jinn who are called devils due to their satanic behavior, whisper something along the line of, "What's the point of praying, I'll live whatever I'm destined to live anyway" or "Whether I pray or not, what will be will be, so why should I pray?". Hence, you stop praying and become deprived of this most powerful weapon. The implications of this deprivation, you cannot fathom. This is why the Rasul of Allah (saw) advises:

"Ask everything from Allah, from the strap of your horse to the grass of your sheep."[14]

"Ask from the bounty and generosity of Allah, for Allah likes to be asked of."[15]

"Indeed, Allah loves His servants who pray with persistence."[16]

"Consider it a prize to pray in the hours in which you feel sensitive, for this is the state of the hour of grace."

The word sensitive in this last hadith means a state of emotional sensitivity due to being completely consumed by a particular topic. Turning to Allah in such a state means the brain is focused entirely on one specific purpose, and the divine qualities inherent within the brain become activated to manifest this purpose.

The most important factor in the actualization of a prayer is for the person to nullify himself (the ego-based identity) such that the one uttering the prayer is the one stimulating the want in the brain; Allah, the Truth itself...

"When He wills a thing, He only says to it 'Be' and it is."[17]

The other crucial element, as I already mentioned above, is persistence... To pray for something a few of times and then abandon the prayer is a grave mistake. Persistence in prayer, and praying for things that will serve us in our life after death, is very important. For, if we pray for the wrong thing, we may be inadvertently causing harm to ourselves. Just as electricity is infinitely beneficial, it may well be used to cause harm or even to kill.

Prayer is the actualization of the divine powers inherently present in your being. So, the degree to which we can make conscious use of this weapon is the degree to which we may be protected from our enemies, achieve our desires and attain certainty (*yakeen*) of Allah.

---

[14] Al-Tirmidhi, Ibn Hibban.
[15] Al-Tirmidhi, al-Tabarani.
[16] Al Hakim, al-Tirmidhi.
[17] Quran 2:117.

In 1984, I had written in the *Mystery of Man* that prayer works with brainpower, that the brain has been equipped with divine power, and that using brain waves even weapons can be rendered ineffective.

Let us have a look at how the Russian scientist proffesor Dr Kaznatcheev evaluates the brain in his article published in the *Sabah* newspaper on 11 June 1991.

FUTURE WARS WILL BE TELEPATHIC

The renowned Soviet Union scientist Vlail Kaznatcheev remarked that human brains could affect wars telepathically. Prof. Kaznatcheev is continuing his research at an exclusive research facility founded in the body of Novosibirsk Academy where geniuses work.

MOSCOW – Prof. Vlail Kaznatcheev, who is one of the most respected members of the Soviet Science Academy, pointed out that the human brain could have an effect on people, thoughts and electronic equipment that are physically far away from it.

Kaznatcheev is intensely researching to prove his claim. Even though most people think his claims are nonsense, he is receiving great interest in his own country, the USSR. The government, which provided Kaznatcheev with a fully equipped laboratory and assistants for help with his research in the body of Novosibirsk Academy where geniuses are educated, expects a lot from his research.

KGB Protection

The most important aspect of Kaznatcheev's research is that he is trying to use the telepathic powers of the human brain as a weapon. According to him, using only the power of thoughts, it is possible to disable computer systems, radars at the airports, and every kind of weaponry that can be developed using modern technology.

The government, who is watching this research very closely, mobilized the most talented KGB agents to protect Kaznatcheev to prevent the CIA from kidnapping him. The famous scientist explains his views with very simple examples:

"If the computer you are using suddenly stops working, do not blame the manufacturer. If you are under stress or if you are angry, you could affect the equipment you are using because an ordinary human brain is more powerful than the most powerful computer and sometimes a person may use the powers that nature gave him without realizing it."

According to Kaznatcheev, if a person intensely thinks about someone whom he hasn't seen for a long time, and unexpectedly receives a phone call or a letter from that person, he should not consider this as chance. This act is the person directly affecting the person he is thinking about with his thoughts.

Lastly, at a Soviet television program in which Kaznatcheev participated, he displayed a plant in his laboratory for a long time and asked the audience to think for an hour only about the plant growing. The result was truly astonishing. The plant showed inexplicable growth in a very short amount of time.

The basis of Kaznatcheev's research is to capture the infinity of the power of thought.

Continuing his research by merging science and parapsychology, in which he tries to reach the human subconscious, Kaznatcheev states his findings will some day produce very important results in crippling enemy equipment. However, he would like this technology not to be used as a weapon, but to prevent wars."

For all these reasons, PRAYER is the most excellent power given to a human being.

4

THE PLACE OF PRAYER

You may well wonder, "Must there be a specific place for prayer? What does location have to do with praying?" Surely, one can pray everywhere and need not specify a special place...

This said, the human brain is closely related to the magnetic and radial field by which it is surrounded. Both the positive energy resonating from the ley lines under the earth's surface and the effect of the radial field by which the person is surrounded during the time of prayer are exceedingly significant.

Also, as the brain waves radiating from the people surrounding the person who is praying can merge with their own to form extremely strong waves, praying with a congregation can produce profound results. Thus the Rasul of Allah (saw) says:

"When three people come together and pray, Allah will not decline their prayer."[18]

Some examples of optimal places of prayer are:

The Kaaba, Arafat, the Baqi cemetery in Medina (where the Rasul of Allah (saw) is buried), House of the Virgin Mary in Ephesus, near the cemetery of the companion Ayyoub Sultan in Istanbul, and all other tombs and cemeteries of eminent saints. Praying in the presence of a saint with a congregation will also produce exceptional results.

---

[18] Abu Nu'aym, *Hilya.*

Two important factors to consider are:

1. The energy resonating from the magnetic field of that particular location.

2. The energy resonating from the spirit of the person buried there.

Thus, when one prays with the reinforcement of this field of energy, the probabilities of their prayers being accepted or actualized is much greater.

5

THE TIME OF PRAYER

Just as one may pray whenever one likes, praying on particular days and nights can also be very effective.

For example:

The time between the Friday sermon (hutbah) and asr time

The first and 15th night of the month of Rajab

The Night of Ascension

The 27th night of Rajab

The 15th day and night of the month of Shaban

The eves and nights of all Eids

The month of Ramadan

Odd numbered nights after the 20th of Ramadan (eg. 21st, 23rd, etc.)

The nights of Eid al-Fitr and Eid al-Adha

The 10th day and night of the month of Muharram

The 10th day of the month of Zilhijja

It is important to note that it is more optimal to pray during the night hours, particularly in the hours after midnight.

Two points are crucially important in regards to the time of prayer:

1. One's inner state

2. External conditions

One's inner state is the spiritual state and general condition at the time of prayer. For it is important to pray with much fervor and passion because only then does the person engage in high levels of concentration, which enables the brain force to become dense and directed towards one particular vector.

External conditions pertain completely to the state of the external environment at the time of prayer. Little or no sunlight is ideal as the cosmic rays emitted by the Sun generally impede brain waves.

Additionally, conditions for prayer are more optimal during the hours of Jupiter and Venus, when softer and more nourishing rays are emitted, rather than say the hour of Mars, when the rays may be harsher.

When events may lead to disputes and quarrels and sub-optimal results during other hours, you will be surprised at how smoothly things flow during the hours of Venus or Jupiter, and how complex issues are easily resolved.

Information on how to calculate these hours may be found via various publications and software applications.

6

PRAYER AND DESTINY

When it comes to prayer, many of us have a preconceived idea that there is no need to pray because everything is already predetermined and predestined.

This understanding is completely incorrect!

I have covered the topic of fate in light of the Quran and the teachings of the Rasul of Allah (saw) in *The Mystery of Man*. Fate is definite and none can surpass its boundaries. The Rasul of Allah (saw) makes this clear in many of his explanations. Unfortunately, the hadith that reveal this truth cannot be found in any book other than certain hadith books. They cannot write it! But the truth is always the truth whether it is written or not. Especially, if it is declared so by the Rasul of Allah (saw)!

What is important to understand is the 'technique' of fate; how it actually works.

Let us first consider some of the words of the Rasul of Allah (saw) in regards to this:

"Only prayer can change fate and only good deeds can extend one's lifespan. Indeed, bad deeds and mistakes will deprive a person of provision."[19]

---

[19] Ibn Majah.

"Accidents can only be prevented with prayer... Lifespan can be extended with good deeds."[20]

"Precaution is useless when it comes to fate, but prayer can benefit both afflictions that have already come about and ones that have not yet occurred. When affliction arrives, prayer stands in opposition to it and they battle on until Doomsday."[21]

Yes, while fate is claimed not to be subject to change in one instance, in other instances we are told prayer can change the course of fate. As contradictory as this may sound, there is in fact logic in it.

Though each person's fate is pre-destined, prayer is an integral factor of the system of fate. With prayer, one may in fact avert a destined event and prevent an accident from taking place. Nevertheless, praying is not independent from the system of fate; one can only pray to prevent a calamity from occurring if their fate allows them to. If making a particular prayer is made possible for you, then you will make the prayer before the event occurs and thus be protected from its misfortune. In other words, you cannot change what is destined by taking caution, but you may take caution and prevent a calamity if it is destined.

Hadhrat Omar (ra) has displayed a profound example of how fate works. Upon arriving at the city of Damascus with his army he hears of a plague outbreak in the city and instructs his army to retreat. Those who have not grasped the mystery of fate question him, "O Omar, are you trying to flee from the fate (qadar) of Allah?" Omar's (ra) answer is a lesson to all of us, "I am fleeing from the decree (qadha) of Allah to the fate (qadar) of Allah."[22]

This is the pivotal point of the mystery of fate. Fate is absolute and definite! And man will see the results of what comes forth from him!

Let us remember the verse:

---

[20] Al-Tirmidhi.
[21] Al-Tabarani, al-Bazzar.
[22] Sahih al-Bukhari.

"And man will only accrue the results (consequences) **of his own deeds** (what manifests through him; his thoughts and actions)**!"**[23]

This is why we must put forth all that we are able to. If you can pray, then do so immediately! If you have the chance and ability to engage in certain practices, then do so immediately! If you have the means to protect yourself, do so immediately!

Know that the things you are able to do are the things that your fate allows you to do, and you will definitely see their results. Thus, the Rasul of Allah (saw) says: **"Nothing can change the Divine decree except prayer."**[24] That is to say, the prevention of an affliction depends on your prayer. Whether or not you will be afflicted by a misfortune is directly dependent on your prayers regarding that situation. If you pray, you can prevent a misfortune from happening or enable a favorable event to take place.

The Rasul of Allah (saw) has described the expression "If only…" as the deed of Satan. It is important to ponder this and understand it well. Why has the expression "If only…" been forbidden?

Prayer is a crucial element of the system of fate. If you have the ability to pray, then do so as much as you can; the benefits you will reap are beyond fathomable in the worldly sense. Allah has made prayer the means to manifest the qualities He has ordained for His servants. Thus, it has been said 'prayer is the weapon of the believer.'

Prayer enables the ordained favors to reach you; it is the greatest blessing.

He who uses it the most efficiently and powerfully is he who will reach the greatest divine favors.

---

[23] Quran 53:39.
[24] Ibn Majah, al-Tirmidhi, Sahih al-Jami.

It is the ignorant one who does not understand the system of fate, who neglects prayer and thus deprives themself of this blessing.

Let us conclude the topic with the words of the Rasul of Allah (saw):

"To whom the gates of prayer have been opened, indeed the gates of mercy have opened, and nothing more pleasing has been asked of Allah than welfare."[25]

"Prayer is beneficial to both afflictions that have occurred and have not yet occurred. O servants of Allah, hold fast unto prayer!"[26]

---

[25] Al-Tirmidhi.
[26] Al-Tirmidhi.

7

DHIKR

Dhikr is the most beneficial thing one can do in this world.

Even though many have translated dhikr as 'the remembrance of Allah' this is in fact an inadequate definition.

1. Dhikr increases brain capacity in the direction of the meaning of the word that is repeated.

2. Dhikr enables radial energy emanating from the brain to be uploaded to the spirit, a holographic radial body, thus strengthening the spirit body to be used after death.

3. On continual practice, dhikr develops the comprehension capacity of the brain in relation to the meaning of the words that are repeated.

4. Dhikr enables reaching a state of certainty (yakeen).

5. Dhikr allows the actualization of divine meanings.

Due to these reasons and more, the Quran states dhikr is a much praised practice and warns those who fail to recognize its importance:

"And whoever is blinded (with external things) **from the remembrance of Rahman** (remembering that his essential reality is composed of the Names of Allah and thus from living the requirements of this)**, We appoint for him a Satan** (a delusion; the idea that he is only the physical body and that life should be lived in pursuit of bodily pleasures) **and this** (belief) **will become his** (new) **identity! And indeed, these will avert them from the way** (of the reality) **while they think they are on the right path!"**[27]

"Satan (corporeality; the idea of being just the physical body) **has overcome them and made them forget the remembrance of Allah** (their own reality of which they have been reminded, and that they will abandon their bodies and live eternally as 'consciousness' comprised of Allah's Names!) **Those** (who are receptive to satanic impulses and think of themselves as only the physical body) **are the acquaintances of Satan. Take heed, most assuredly, the partisans of Satan are the very losers!"**[28]

"O believers! Remember Allah much!"[29]

"And he who turns away from My dhikr (the Absolute Reality of which I have reminded him)**, indeed, he will have a restricted life** (limited by the conditions of his body and mind)**, and We will resurrect him as blind in the period of Doomsday."**[30]

"So remember (dhikr) **Me** (contemplate)**; so that I will remember you..."**[31]

"So, if My servants ask you of ME, undoubtedly I am Qarib (as close as the limits of one's understanding; remember the verse 'I am closer to you than your jugular vein'!) **I respond to those who turn to Me** (in prayer). **So, let them respond to Me and believe in Me so that they experience their maturation."**[32]

---

[27] Quran 43:36-37.
[28] Quran 58:19.
[29] Quran 33:41.
[30] Quran 20:124.
[31] Quran 2:152.
[32] Quran 2:186.

"Indeed, the dhikr (remembrance) **of Allah is Akbar** (enables one to experience Akbariyyah – Absolute Magnificence)**!"**[33]

When the Rasul of Allah (saw) is asked, "What is the most pleasing practice in the sight of Allah?" He explains the importance of dhikr with his words, "Dying while your tongue is engaged in dhikr!"[34]

Abu al-Darda' narrates: The Rasul of Allah (saw) once asked his companions: "Shall I tell you about the best of all deeds, the best act of piety in the eyes of Allah, which will elevate your status in the Hereafter, and carries more virtue than the spending of gold and silver in the service of Allah or taking part in jihad and slaying or being slain in the path of Allah? The dhikr of Allah."[35]

"Nothing is more supreme in saving one from the wrath of Allah than His dhikr."[36]

Abu Sa'id narrates: The Rasul of Allah (saw) was asked, "Which of the servants of Allah is best in rank before Allah on the Day of Resurrection?" He said: "The ones who remember him much." I said, "O Messenger of Allah, what about the fighter in the way of Allah?" He answered, "Even if he strikes the unbelievers and *dualists* with his sword until it broke, and becomes red with their blood, truly those who do dhikr are better than him in rank."[37]

"… A servant may ONLY be protected from Satan with the dhikr of Allah!"

"The best of your possessions is a tongue that engages in the dhikr of Allah, a heart that is thankful, and a spouse who supports you in faith."[38]

---

[33] Quran 29:45.
[34] Ibn Hibban, al-Tabarani.
[35] Al-Tirmidhi, Ibn Majah, Malik's *Muwatta'*, the *Musnad* of Ahmad and the *Mustadrak* of Hakim. Al-Bayhaqi, Hakim and others declared it *sahih*.
[36] Ibn Majah.
[37] Ahmad, al-Tirmidhi, al-Bayhaqi.
[38] Al-Tirmidhi.

Abu Musa reported, "The likeness of the one who engages in the dhikr of Allah and the one who does not is like that of a living to a dead person."[39]

"Remember (dhikr) Allah as much as you want, until people call you crazy and foolish."[40]

"Engage in the dhikr of Allah so much so that the hypocrites claim you are doing it for show."[41]

The Rasul of Allah (saw) said, "The *mufarridun* have taken precedence." They asked, "Who are the mufarridun, O Rasul of Allah?" He said, "Those who remember Allah often and whose burdens dhikr removes from them so that on the Day of Resurrection they come light-weighted."[42]

"The Satan has placed his mouth in the heart of the son of Adam. As he engages in dhikr, the Satan moves away. As soon as he becomes heedless and stops doing dhikr, Satan swallows his heart!"

This hadith symbolically designates that, as one engages in dhikr, the jinn will stay away from him and not incite and blur his thoughts. But when the person stops doing dhikr, the jinn begin to manipulate the person's brain as they like.

"The greatest good Allah gives a servant is the inspiration to do His dhikr."

"No charity is a greater virtue than engaging in the dhikr of Allah."

"The people of Paradise are not grieved by anything more than the time they spend in the world not doing dhikr."[43]

---

[39] Sahih al-Bukhari, Sahih al-Muslim.
[40] Ahmad ibn Hanbal. *Al-Musnad.*
[41] Ahmad ibn Hanbal. *Kitab al-Zuhd.*
[42] Al-Tirmidhi.
[43] Al-Tabarani, al-Bayhaqi.

"He who does not engage in the dhikr of Allah will drift away from faith."

"Man will feel great remorse for every moment he spent not remembering Allah."[44]

"If any group of people gather and depart without remembering Allah, this gathering will cause regret for them on the Day of Resurrection!"[45]

"He who remembers Allah much will be far from hypocrisy!"

These hadith of the Rasul of Allah (saw) and many more are a great warning to us.

---

[44] Al-Bayhaqi.
[45] Abu Dawud.

8

WHY IS DHIKR SO IMPORTANT?

Though I had extensively covered this in *The Mystery of Man*, due to its importance I want to talk about the necessity of dhikr here also.

Let it be known without doubt that religion is a symbolic narration founded completely upon scientific principles.

All laws and regulations in the religion of Islam – the Quran and hadith – have come to provide the necessities of both this life and the afterlife. When man complies with these proposed laws, he will be protected from many things that may harm him in the future. Man's life is structured by way of the brain. Everything that transpires from man is by way of his brain. In fact, even the 'spirit,' which is the body of the afterlife, is uploaded by the brain!

The meanings denoted by the Names of Allah become manifest in the human brain. Man's consciousness may only know and attain certainty (yakeen) of Allah dependent on the capacity of his brain. This being the case, to understand the importance of dhikr, we must first grasp how the brain works and what kind of activity takes place in the brain during the practice of dhikr.

The brain is an organic structure composed of billions of cells that produce bioelectrical energy. It then converts this into radial energy and uploads the meanings that form within itself to the structure we call the spirit, while also emanating it to its surrounding. Generally, the brain works at an efficiency level in the single digits due to the influences it receives at inception. For this reason, most people that we know will have a 'typical' existence.

But this capacity can be increased!

The importance of dhikr was already explained in the world of science ten years before I provided information regarding this topic. The excerpts below prove my point:

From an article titled, 'The West was Late to Discover the Power of Dhikr!' in the 1994 publication of the Turkish Magazine *NOKTA.*[46]

Did you the know the views by John Horgan published in the January 1994 edition of the Scientific American under the article named, 'Fractured Functions' was initially expressed by Ahmed Hulusi in 1986?

It seems we still need time to get over our inferiority complex when it comes to scientific discoveries. Instead of taking heed of the view of Turkey's own thinkers, we wait for the notion to gain credibility in the Western world. And sometimes we encounter surprising coincidences, as with the Ahmed Hulusi example.

In his article 'Fractured Functions', John Horgan explores the answer for the question, 'Does the brain have a supreme integrator?' and presents various theories based on certain experiments conducted in 1993. However, Ahmed Hulusi seems to have already answered this question in 1986 in his books, 'The Mystery of Man – In the Light of Religion and Science' and 'The Power of Prayer – The Art of Channeling Brainwaves through Dhikr'.

In his article John Horgan talks about an experiment where volunteers are given a list of nouns and are asked to read these nouns aloud, proposing a verb for each noun they read. For example, when reading the noun 'dog,' the verb 'bark' may be suggested. This experiment showed increased neural activity in different regions of the brain, but when the task was repeated with

---

[46] *Nokta*, 6 March, 1994, The West was Late to Discover the Power of Dhikr, page 11.

the same list a number of times the neural activity shifted to other regions of the brain. When the volunteers were given a new list of nouns the activity was seen to increase again and shift back to the first areas.

In his book, 'Mystery of Man' written in 1986, under the chapter titled, 'Dhikr: The Most Important Practice in the World', Ahmed Hulusi says the following in regards to this topic:

"Of the human brain, comprised of approximately 14 billion cells, only a very small region becomes activated with the rays it receives during birth. After this, new exterior effects cannot bring about new activations. External effects after birth cannot activate new cell groups in the brain. It can only enhance the capacity determined at birth. But this does not necessarily mean the inactivated regions of the brain are meant to remain inert forever.

When you say the word 'Allah' for example, a flow of bioelectrical energy occurs among the cell groups that correspond to the meaning of this name. Essentially, all functions in the brain are merely bioelectrical activities among various cell groups. Different cell groups are involved in this bioelectrical flow depending on different meanings. Resultantly, innumerous meanings are spawned from the dynamics of this activity... "

In his article 'Fractured Functions' John Horgan refers to the same topic in the following way:

"The experiment suggests that one part of the brain handles the short-term memory requiring verbal invention and another part takes over once the task has become automatic. In other words, memory might be subdivided not only according to its content, but also according to its function."

Ahmed Hulusi's answer to this, again from the Mystery of Man, is as follows:

"When one does dhikr, that is, when one repeats a word whose meaning is known to pertain to Allah, a bioelectrical flow takes place in the brain, which then gets uploaded to one's magnetic body in the form of a type of energy. When one continues to repeat this word and thus the meaning that correlates to it, the bioelectrical

flow is strengthened and begins to spread to other cells nearby, hence increasing one's brain capacity."

As a result, we have two sources of information in regards to the science of dhikr. One shared by Ahmed Hulusi in 1986, and one shared eight years after by John Horgan in an internationally well known science magazine. Before we grip onto what the West has to say about this, I suggest we re-read the works of Ahmed Hulusi.

The following is an excerpt from John Horgan's article 'Fractured Funcions' in the December 1993 edition of *Scientific American*.

Fractured Functions

Does the brain have a supreme integrator?

The brain, as depicted by modern neuroscience, resembles a hospital in which specialization has been carried to absurd lengths. In the language wing of the brain, some neurons are trained to handle only proper nouns, others only verbs with irregular endings. In the visual-cortex pavilion, one set of neurons is dedicated to orange-red colors, another to objects with high-contrast diagonal edges and still another to objects moving rapidly from left to right.

The question is how the fragmentary work of these highly specialized parts is put together again to create the apparent unity of perception and thought that constitutes the mind. This puzzle, known as the binding problem, has loomed ever larger as experiments have revealed increasingly finer subdivisions of the brain.

Some theorists have suggested that the different components of perceptions funnel into "convergent zones," where they become integrated. Among the most obvious candidates for convergent zones are regions of the brain that handle short-term, or "working," memories so that they can be quickly accessed for a variety of tasks. Yet two different sets of experiments done this year—one in which monkeys were monitored by electrodes and the other in which humans were scanned with positron emission tomography (PET)—

show that the parts of the brain that cope with working memory are also highly specialized.

The monkey experiments were performed by Fraser A. W. Wilson, Séamas P. Ó Scalaidhe and Patricia S. Goldman-Rakic of the Yale University School of Medicine. The workers trained the monkeys to accomplish two tasks requiring working memory. In one task, each monkey stared at a fixed point in the middle of a screen while a square flashed into view at another location on the screen. Several seconds after the square disappeared, the monkey would direct its gaze to the spot where the square had been.

The other task required storing information about the content of an image rather than its location. The investigators flashed an image in the center of the screen. Each monkey was trained to wait until the object had disappeared and then turn its eyes left or right, depending on what type of object it had observed. Electrodes monitored the firing of neurons in the monkey's prefrontal cortex, a sheet of tissue that cloaks the top of the brain and has been implicated in mental activities requiring working memory.

In each test, a set of neurons started firing as soon as the image flashed on the screen and remained active until the task had been completed. But the "where" test activated neurons in one region of the prefrontal cortex, whereas the "what" test activated neurons in an adjacent but distinct region. "The prefrontal cortex has always been thought of as a region where information converges and is synthesized for purposes of planning, thinking, comprehension and intention," Goldman-Rakic says. "We've shown that this area is just as compartmentalized as the sensory and motor regions."

Complementary findings described this year by investigators at Washington University have emerged from PET scans of humans. (PET measures neural activity indirectly by tracking changes in blood flow in subjects injected with a short-lived radioactive tracer.) In the experiments, volunteers were provided with a list of nouns. They were required to read the nouns aloud, one by one, and to propose for each noun a related verb. On reading the noun "dog," for example, the volunteer might suggest the related verb "bark."

When the subjects first did this task, several distinct parts of the brain, including parts of the prefrontal and cingulate cortex, displayed increased neural activity. But if the volunteers repeated the task with the same list of nouns several times, the activity shifted to different regions. When the volunteers were given a fresh list of nouns, the neural activity increased and shifted back to the first areas again.

The experiment suggests that one part of the brain handles the short-term memory requiring verbal invention and that another part takes over once the task has become automatic. In other words, memory might be subdivided not only according to its content but also according to its function. "Our results are consistent with Goldman-Rakic's ideas," comments Steven E. Petersen, a member of the Washington University team.

So how do all the specialists of the brain manage to work together so smoothly? Are their activities coordinated by a central once or through some form of distributed network? Petersen favors "a localized region or a small number of localized regions," where perceptions, memories and intentions are integrated. Goldman-Rakic is leaning toward a nonhierarchical model in which "separate but equal partners are interconnected, communicating with each other."

Larry R. Squire, a memory researcher at the University of California at San Diego, thinks the binding problem may take many years to solve. He concedes that "we still don't really have a clue" as to what the binding mechanism is. But he is hopeful that the answer will inevitably emerge, given the rapid advances in techniques for studying the brain—including microelectrodes, noninvasive imaging technologies (such as PET and magnetic resonance imaging) and computers, which can help make coherent models out of empirical data. "We need it all," Squire says. —John Horgan[47]

---

[47] *Scientific American*, December 1993.

Therefore, since only a very small percentage of the brain is employed while a large part of brain capacity remains unused, dhikr allows the activation of this larger percentage.

The bioelectrical energy produced in specific regions in the brain via dhikr spreads to other regions and activates the dormant cells, thereby increasing brain activity. Whatever dhikr is about, the frequency corresponding to that meaning is emanated to the cells and thus brain capacity relevant to that particular meaning is increased.

For example, when one does dhikr with the name Mureed, which is the name that references the will of Allah, the dormant cells in the person's brain become programmed with the vibration of the frequency of this name, and thus in a short time, the person's willpower is strengthened and things that were previously impossible to achieve become possible. Here, I would like to make note of an important point: Each brain has a unique make-up and so, when doing dhikr of the Names of Allah, it is important to obtain information from a learned person. Doing dhikr without such guidance can inadvertently lead to engaging in the kind of dhikr incited by the jinn, hence unconsciously surrendering the self to them. This is why some saints have said, "Satan will be the guide of the one who does not have a guide."

To recap, unprogrammed brain cells can be programmed in accord with the meaning of the word that is repeated during dhikr to reach a desired result and strengthen and increase brain power and capacity.

Some may ask, "If dhikr is such a powerful tool, why hasn't the world of Islam produced an extraordinary brain as yet, why do all advancements stem from the West, from among non-Muslims?"

The answer is quite simple, at least for someone who knows its technique and procedure... Allow me to share the technique of dhikr with you, which was inspired to me as the favor of Allah and with the guidance of the Rasul of Allah (saw)...

9

GENERAL AND SPECIFIC DHIKR

There are a few types of dhikr. Here is a general outline:

1. General dhikr

   a. Spiritual dhikr

   b. Dhikr done for a specific purpose

2. Specific dhikr

   a. Dhikr done to achieve a specific result

   b. Dhikr that are specific to the person

As previously stated, dhikr is the continual repetition of a specific word or phrase.

Whatever the word may be, every dhikr produces a wavelength with a specific frequency in the brain with which inactive cells in the brain become programmed.

If it is a word incited by the jinn or a word like 'om', the popular Budhhist mantra, the brain begins to develop in those specific areas as the person unknowingly gets into resonance with the jinn and begins to receive incitations from them. Consequently, he begins to stray toward certain absurd thoughts and conceives himself as a saint, the Mahdi, an extraterrestrial, a prophet or even Allah.

The general dhikr taught in Islamic sources, on the other hand, assist solely in strengthening the person's spirit-power and allow him to get closer to his Rabb.

Here are some examples of general dhikr:

Subhaana L-Llahi wa bihamdihi

Subhaana L-Llah wa-l hamdulillah wa laa ilaha illa l-Llahu wa Llahu akbar

Laa ilaaha illa Allah wa-h dahu la shareeka lah

Laa ilaha illal Laahul malikil haqqul mubeenu

Subbuhun quddusun Rabb-al-mala'ikati wa-r-ruh

General dhikr done for a specific purpose include things like acquisition of knowledge, confessions of one's mistakes, requests for forgiveness and so on. Here are some examples:

Rabbi zidnee ilma

Laa ilaaha illaa anta subḥaanaka inni kuntu mina l-ẓaalimeen

Rabbi ij`alnee muqeema l-ṣalaati wa min dhurriyyatee

Specific dhikr are done with the intention to develop one's state in a specific area, towards a specific goal. Such dhikr formulas are essentially devised according to the person's brain, qualities, characteristics and personal desires. These formulas are comprised of the divine Names and certain prayers derived from hadith and verses from the Quran, in order to enable rapid personal progress.

Most of the dhikr formulas given in tariqahs are in the scope of general dhikr; hence, development times can take up to 30-40 years.

However, those who have tried these specific dhikr have seen massive progress in their lives in as short a time period as 1-2 years.

Some examples of specific dhikr done to achieve a specific result are:

Allahumma inni as-aluka Hubbaka

Allahumma al-himni rushdi

Quddus'ut Tahiru Min Kulli Sooin

As for specific dhikr that are specific to the person they usually comprise the Names of Allah, such as:

MUREED

QUDDUS

FATTAH

HAKEEM

MU'MIN

RAHMAN

RAHIM

BAASIT

WADUD

JAMI

RAFI

Such names and others are usually formulated according to the person's needs in respect of their brain program and its effects are usually observed in short frames of time.

Let me add an important note here. When the capacity of the brain expands as a result of dhikr, one must immediately utilize this extra potential by turning to knowledge, otherwise the newly expanded capacity will be susceptible to the influences of the jinn, which is not a favorable result.

It is also crucial to read the prayers for protection (included in the beginning of this book) taught in the Quran as protection from the jinn.

Now, let us answer some frequently asked questions.

Due to the practice of dhikr, which increases one's spiritual strength, the Islamic community has given rise to many spiritually elevated people; however, few scientifically advanced minds have emerged! If the brain was reinforced with dhikr to develop in the area of worldly sciences, surely there would have been distinguished brains in that field as well.

However, the world of Islam refrains from striving for, and giving value to worldly affairs, based on the principle, "Protect yourself from the suffering in the future of having to let go of the things you possess today."

Let me share a very simple example with you.

Imagine you were given a box filled with invaluable jewelry and you were told:

"If you can attain the key, you can open this box and everything inside it can be yours."

And you ask, "Ok, but what and where is its key? How can I attain it? How can I open it?"

"The key..." you are told, "Is a special type of iron whose tip has been shaped and formed in a unique way. To attain it you must pay its price."

But you think to yourself, "The box is with me anyway, instead of paying so much to obtain the key I'll just get a bar of iron and chip and file it myself to make a key!"

But, no matter how much you chip and file, you cannot make a key that is exactly the same as the key that opens the jewelry box and hence you can never obtain the precious jewels inside the box, for each lock may only be opened by its own unique key.

Thus, just like in this example, each brain needs its own unique formula to obtain great progress. For this, it is a must to find a learned person to guide you.

Since it is quite challenging and difficult to find such a person in this time and age, I have devised certain formulas in this book to the best of my knowledge, all of which have been experientially confirmed to be very beneficial.

Whoever wants to may try these special formulas on themselves and see if it benefits them, if so they may continue, otherwise they may continue doing their general dhikr for general spiritual development.

10

WILL TOO MUCH DHIKR CAUSE ONE TO LOSE THEIR MIND?

"Don't do too much dhikr or you'll lose the plot!" is an often heard phrase among Muslims… This fear-induced statement is purely based on cultural conditioning driven by ignorance.

While the Quran advises the constant practice of dhikr, while standing, sitting or lying down, it is unfortunate that perspectives spawned by ignorance drive people away from dhikr out of fear.

"They (those who have attained the essence of the reality) **remember Allah while standing or sitting or** (lying) **on their sides and they contemplate the creation of the heavens and the earth** (depending on the day, the universe and its depths, or in terms of the brain, the place of the body and its attributes) **and say, 'Our Rabb, You have not created these things for nothing! You are Subhan** (free from creating meaningless things; you are in a state of creating anew at every instant)**! Protect us from burning** (remorse for not being able to duly evaluate your manifestations).'"[48]

Man is always in one of the following three states… He is either upright on his feet, sitting or lying down. The above verse clearly tells us to do dhikr in all of these states. In other words, we should strive to engage in dhikr at all times and in all states. Wherever we may be, whether we have ablution or not, we should do dhikr to develop our brains and attain certainty (yakeen) of Allah.

---

[48] Quran 3:191

I have advised many drinkers, in fact alcoholics, to practice dhikr, where they start doing dhikr even while in clubs or bars, holding prayer beads in one hand and a drink in the other. Yet, as a result of the profound effects dhikr has in terms of brain development and the increase of insight, they have autonomously stopped drinking and assumed certain spiritual practices, such as praying five times a day and going on pilgrimage (hajj).

I say dhikr is the single unique key for an ultimate future because it is the most effective and powerful tool to increase the capacity of the brain. But how about those who really have lost the plot after doing too much dhikr?

Let me make it absolutely clear that no normal person can ever become mentally impaired from doing dhikr!

The truth is, there are many who have psychopathic and megalomaniac tendencies, but their condition reveals itself only in the later stages of their lives. If it so happens that such a person has done dhikr at some point in their life, after which their condition has become apparent, those with vested interests will try to exploit this by linking this situation to prayer and dhikr and thus drive people away.

Even though tariqahs were banned in Turkey, there is literally a sheikh in every city of Turkey and nearly as many dervishes as half of Turkey's population. That is roughly ten million people who do dhikr in Turkey. What percentage of them or how many of them have lost their sanity due to doing dhikr?

No normal, healthy, sane person will become insane from doing dhikr; this I say with certainty. If one person out of ten million has become ill, I recommend you do a little research on his health background. Perhaps his deformity is related to his genes or birth.

A healthy and sane person with a healthy mind will never be adversely affected by dhikr. In fact, dhikr can even be healing for those with these kinds of conditions; it can bring balance to their extreme tendencies.

11

MUST DHIKR BE DONE IN SECLUSION?

Some people who haven't really grasped the essence of it claim one must be in a state of silence and seclusion to do dhikr. This is absolutely incorrect.

Obviously, dhikr done in seclusion in a contemplative state is very beneficial, this can't be denied. However, this does not mean that one who has no means to attain this state should not do dhikr at all. Dhikr can be silently performed everywhere at all times. Whether we take the verse that says dhikr should be done while 'standing, sitting or lying down' or the hadith that says the dhikr, "la ilaha ila Allah wahdahu la sharika lah, lahu al-mulk wa lahu al-hamdu yuhyi wa yumitu, wa Huwa hayyun la yamutu, bi yadihil-khairu kulluhu, wa Huwa ala kulli shay'in Qadir" brings invaluable benefit even when done in public places, it is evident that dhikr can and should be done in all circumstances.

This is actually a very important topic.

Is it a must to contemplate while doing dhikr?

Will salat, which is another form of prayer and dhikr, be ruined if one's mind drifts off to other thoughts while praying, thus rendering the recited prayers and dhikr ineffective?

Let me say with certainty that thoughts that pop into one's mind while praying or doing dhikr do not cause any harm.

The brain continually fulfills innumerous tasks simultaneously.

It is quite possible to hold a prayer bead and do dhikr while taking a walk and thinking about something and watching the scenery all at the same time. Each of these activities is rendered by different compartments of the brain. You can be reading a book, doing dhikr and hear what people are saying around you while also watching TV all at the same time. This has to do with the brain's ability to multi-task. Those with advanced spirituality may also conduct spiritual connections in addition to all of this.

What matters is the activity that occurs in the brain and the automatic upload of its result to the spirit. Whether you realize this or not, it doesn't change! As I mentioned earlier, someone who started doing dhikr for the first time, and most of the time while in a bar, ended up going on pilgrimage (hajj) only eight months later! Therefore, seclusion is not a requisite to do dhikr.

12

WHY IS DHIKR DONE IN ARABIC?

Usually, the first question that is asked in regards to dhikr is, "Why do we have to say these words in Arabic? Can't we say their English or Turkish translations instead? Does Allah not understand other languages?"

The spoken word is the final stage of the activity! The real phenomenon begins in the brain via an impulse or a micro-wave – a radial effect – from the cosmic dimension or a cosmic being.

As a result of this effect, the bio-magnetic and bio-chemical make-up of the brain is influenced and the resulting data is passed on bio-electrically to stimulate the relevant nervous system and organ. We only perceive the result as the activity that reflects from the organ. But it's not the audio-visual that we perceive outside, but the radial, bioelectrical, bio-chemical system that takes place in the higher levels that matters! That is to say, it is not the letters that comprise the word that is of significance, but the vibration of the frequency that forms the words!

As I previously explained in my audios and videos under *Higher Matter*, the universe and everything in it are quant-based radial beings by origin. And each of these radial energy beings who have specific meanings and who fulfill unique functions in accord with that meaning are called 'angels' (malak) in Islamic literature. The original word 'malak' comes from 'malk', which means 'force and energy'.

Just like every vibration-frequency in the universe carries a meaning, every cosmic ray that reaches the brain also carries a specific meaning and has a place in the universe in accord with that meaning, these structures are called 'angels'.

Man is the most comprehensive manifestation in the world created to know his own essential reality, to know Allah. When man thinks he is only the body, he is described as "the lowest of the low" in the Quran. On the other hand, when he lives in line with his essential ruling, he is described in the Quran as living in the "state of Paradise." Man's single most important duty is to know his essential self!

In religious terms, this is referenced as, "He who knows himself will know his Rabb."

When the brain is freed from thinking this material realm is in fact real, from the limitation of the five-senses and the obstruction caused by this conditioning to realize his essential luminous self, he will autonomously desire to experience his essential self.

This desire will strengthen his relation to his luminous self and enable him to realize that everything that transpires through him is the manifestation of these radial luminous meanings.

That is, the brain transfers these luminous meanings to our 'known' dimension and then loads these concepts to our holographic radial body while at the same time emitting it to its surroundings.

Thus, due to what can only be discerned after the aforementioned is understood, dhikr is something that can only be done by the original form in Arabic.

Every word and letter is a vibration-frequency turned into sound waves in the brain. Since every frequency carries a specific meaning, every word is a collection of frequencies carrying meanings turned into sound waves – this is what forms the words and concepts of dhikr.

That is, the quant meanings are present in the universe as wavelengths and vibrations, when they are converted into sound waves they are called words, and words that best capture these meanings are in Arabic; thus, the words of dhikr are in Arabic.

Therefore, once you change a word, you can never capture the same frequency and thus the meaning carried by that frequency can never be reached.

So, if one wants to attain the secrets explained by the Quran and the Rasul of Allah (saw) and understand the universal realities, one must repeat the words as they came, in their original Arabic format.

It is also important to recite the entire Quran at least once in a lifetime in its original Arabic in order to upload its energy to the spirit – the holographic radial body – to benefit from this source of knowledge in the life after death.

Another reason why these words must be recited in their original Arabic is if you try to translate these Arabic words into another language you'll end up having to write an entire page or more to adequately capture their meanings. Clearly, it is easier to repeat a single word as opposed to a whole page.

13

UNDERSTANDING THE QURAN

The Quran was revealed so that it may be 'understood'. In broad strokes, I would like to go over how the Quran, which is the greatest dhikr of all, should be understood.

The only way one can carry out certain activities is by becoming conditioned or by learning something by heart. This applies to all of creation. Only MAN has the ability to comprehend and contemplate and is thus honored as 'Allah's vicegerent on earth.' Those who discern this truth and live by it are called 'honored Muslims'. Surely, those who imitatively engage in certain activities will also take their share depending on their state of certainty (yakeen) of their essence.

To understand the Quran, one must be 'clean', that is 'pure', for "those who aren't purified should not touch the Quran." Unfortunately, this verse is often very misunderstood. We think by washing with water and taking ablution we are suddenly 'purified'; however, the Quran describes the opposite of 'purity' that is 'impurity' with the following verse:

""**Verily the dualists** (who claim the existence of their ego-identities alongside the Absolute Oneness) **are contaminated** (filth)!"[49]

In other words, being in a state of impurity is being in a state of 'duality' (shirq)!

---

[49] Quran 9:28.

This verse instructs the dualists who have become impure with the filth of duality to not touch the Quran without becoming purified from this impure system of thought, for while in a state of duality, one cannot discern the Oneness of Allah in the Quran.

The Oneness of Allah and the idea of observing the 'many' from the 'one' as opposed to the perspective of a god up in the heavens, spawned from the illusion of thinking we have a separate existence, may not be easy to understand. This is why, if we really want to understand the Quran, we must first cleanse ourselves from the filth of duality.

But what is duality?

In simple terms, the conception of a 'god' or a 'deity' separate from existence is what underlies the dualistic outlook.

In other words, to think there is a god who is far and beyond you, who sees and hears you from a distance, who sometimes intervenes with your activities and sometimes leaves you to your own accord, who casts those who anger Him to Hell and sends those who can manage to please Him to Paradise, who is sometimes benevolent and sometimes enraged, is to be in a state of duality. Such thoughts and concepts of god/godhood constitute the very foundation of dualistic perception.

The Rasul of Allah (saw) has formulated the understanding to free one from the concept of duality as:

"There is no god, only Allah" (La ilaha illa Allah)

What this means in short is: There is no god or godhood. There is only Allah and His system.

"The most virtuous dhikr is 'La ilaha illa Allah.'"[50]

"One who says 'La ilaha illa Allah' will go to Paradise, even if he steals or commits adultery."[51]

Such hadith point to the importance of this formula. That is to say, even if one is to do all of this, if he comprehends the meaning of

---

[50] Al-Tirmidhi.
[51] Kanz al-Ummal 1:208.

the Kalima-I Tawhid (La ilaha illa Allah), at some point he will repent and not make the mistakes that result from the illusion there is a deity-god. He will turn his face to Allah and live accordingly, and this will bring him to a state of Paradise.

Those who would like more detail on this topic can refer to *Muhammad's Allah.*

So, how can one begin to experience Paradise? It is said, "They perceive the scent of Paradise while in the world." What does this mean?

This is the experience that takes place when one begins to be cleansed from the illusion of an external deity-god and recognizes the limitless infinite concept of Allah.

This is, when one will realize that the limitless infinite Allah is present in every iota of existence with His perfection in accord with His Absolute essence (dhat). The One whom for years he thought was far and beyond has now shown His face from himself!

To look for Him everywhere only to find Him within…

There we will grasp the hidden meaning behind the verse **"…So, wherever you turn, there is the face of Allah** (you are face to face with the manifestation of Allah's Names)"[52] and begin to love Him everywhere and in everything. He will no longer feel anger or hold grudges towards anyone. He will not gossip or criticize anyone or force anyone into anything. Rather than wasting his time on temporary pleasures, he will engage in services of permanence and remember his beloved with his actions, words and consciousness. Practicing Islam will become easy for him.

Rather than repeating the word of testimony (la ilaha illa Allah), he will begin to live and experience it.

Praying five times a day will no longer be a chore… We wash our hands and faces once we wake up anyway – if we just wash our feet as well our ablution is complete… Add two minutes for prayer and we're done.

---

[52] Quran 2:115.

And at noon, can we not set aside four minutes for four rakats of prayer? When we are fully immersed in the full materialism of the world around us, what is four minutes to take us back to our essence?

And in the afternoon? Can we not free up four more minutes for the required four rakat to open that window that reaches out to our actual dimension?

When we come home in the evening, three minutes for three rakats of prayer and we leave all our worldly worries behind, the peace of mind that accompanies the eternal.

And last but not least, before going to bed, a final four minutes for four rakat, with the clarity of having left all of our daily troubles behind. So, there it is, that's all that is required of us, clear and simple. If we add it all together seventeen minutes a day! Seventeen minutes out of a day made up of fourteen hundred and forty minutes – that's all!

But if you want to do more, if you have fully comprehended that there is an eternal life awaiting you, and you want to do all that you can, you are free to increase your efforts at will.

Pilgrimage is the next pillar of Islam after salat.

I've explained the importance of pilgrimage (hajj) in detail in the *Mystery of Man*.

The Rasul of Allah (saw) says:

"Hasten to perform pilgrimage (hajj) for one does not know what obstacle he may face in the future!"[53]

And:

Hazrat Abi Umama (ra) reports that Rasulullah (saw) said: "Whoever fails to perform hajj while not being prevented from it by a definite and valid necessity, or by oppression from an unjust ruler, or by severe illness, and then passes away, in such a state has the

---

[53] Abu Dawud.

choice to die as a Jew, if he so wishes, or as Christian if he so wishes."[54]

This is why hajj is a mandatory worship that must be performed in all urgency.

When one completes his pilgrimage, all past mistakes are purged, including transgression of others' rights. One becomes as pure as a newborn. The Rasul of Allah (saw) says to doubt whether your sins have been forgiven after your pilgrimage is the biggest sin of all.

Is it not absurd to miss such an opportunity? Especially when the time of death is unknown, is it not rational to become cleansed and purified from all negative energies and to not pass on to the life after death with such burdens?

As to the spiritual component of pilgrimage, even if for a very short time, you wear a shroud to symbolize being stripped of all worldly and material values and dive into the infinite values of higher matter.[55] To become stripped of the identity and swim without an ego in the ocean of infinite consciousness. To see the face of Allah at the Kaba and converse with the beloved...!

As for fasting and giving alms...

Fasting is a special requisite to enable the experience of one's angelic state. It is a profound blessing. It is to allow you to recognize that you are essentially a being independent of food, drink, sex, ill thoughts and ill speech. Only 29 days in 365 days! It is to help you realize that you are not your body, but a being of consciousness consisting of angelic properties.

Paying alms (zakat), on the other hand, is based on the understanding that it is He who is present in every iota of existence, and thus to share with them at least one-fortieth of your wealth...

Here is the simplest explanation of Islam taught in the Quran by the Rasul of Allah (saw) who says, "Ease and facilitate do not harden, cause to love not hate"...[56]

---

[54] Al-Tirmidhi.
[55] Refer to the chapter 'Higher Matter' in the *Observing One.*
[56] Al-Nasai, Ahmad ibn Hanbal. *Al-Musnad.*

Having outlined what the Quran requests of us, as taught by the Rasul (saw) let us now have a look at the concept of sin and what repentance means.

The sin of the ego has enclosed you like mountains

You seek the forgiver while unaware of your sins

(Niyazi Mısri)

14

REPENTANCE

إِنَّ اللّهَ لاَ يَغْفِرُ أَن يُشْرَكَ بِهِ وَيَغْفِرُ مَا دُونَ ذَلِكَ لِمَن يَشَاء

InnaLlaaha laayaghfiru anyushrakabihi wayaghfiru maadoona dhaalika limanyashaa'[57]

Indeed, Allah does not forgive (apparent or discrete forms of) **shirq** (i.e. directly or indirectly assuming the existence of beings 'other' than Allah, whether external objects [apparent] or our own egos [discrete], thereby fragmenting the non-dual reality), **but He forgives lesser sins other than this** (ma doona – 'lesser sins' here connotes the perception that actions are initiated by the self/ego rather than by Allah), **as He wills...**

---

[57] Quran 4:48.

قُلْ يَا عِبَادِيَ الَّذِينَ أَسْرَفُوا عَلَى أَنفُسِهِمْ لَا تَقْنَطُوا مِن رَّحْمَةِ اللَّهِ
إِنَّ اللَّهَ يَغْفِرُ الذُّنُوبَ جَمِيعًا إِنَّهُ هُوَ الْغَفُورُ الرَّحِيمُ

Qulyaa`ibaadiyalladheena asrafoo `alaaanfusihim laataqnatoo minrahmatiLlaahi innaLlaaha yaghfirul-dhunooba jamee`an innahuhuwal-ghafoorul-raheem[58]

Say, 'O my servants who have transgressed against themselves (who have squandered their lives in pursuit of bodily pleasures rather than duly experiencing their essential reality)! **Do not lose hope from the grace of Allah! Indeed, Allah forgives all mistakes** (of those who repent)**... Indeed, He is the Ghafur, the Rahim.'**

وَهُوَ الَّذِي يَقْبَلُ التَّوْبَةَ عَنْ عِبَادِهِ وَيَعْفُو عَنِ السَّيِّئَاتِ وَيَعْلَمُ مَا
تَفْعَلُونَ وَيَسْتَجِيبُ الَّذِينَ آمَنُوا وَعَمِلُوا لصَّالِحَاتِ وَيَزِيدُهُم مِّن
فَضْلِهِ

Wa huwalladhee yaqbalul-tawbata`an`ibaadihi waya`foo`anil-sayyi'aati waya`allamu maataf`aloona wa yastajeebulladheena aamanoo wa`amilool-saalihaati wayazeeduhum min fadlihi[59]

It is He who accepts repentance from His servants, and pardons misdeeds and the One who knows what you do. And He responds to the believers who fulfill the requisites of faith and increases (His blessings for them) **with His bounty**

---

[58] Quran 39:53.
[59] Quran 42:25-26.

يَا أَيُّهَا الَّذِينَ آمَنُوا تُوبُوا إِلَى اللهِ تَوْبَةً نَصُوحًا عَسَى رَبُّكُمْ أَن يُكَفِّرَ عَنكُمْ سَيِّئَاتِكُمْ وَيُدْخِلَكُمْ جَنَّاتٍ تَجْرِي مِن تَحْتِهَا الْأَنْهَارُ

Yaa ayyuhaalladheena-amanoo tooboo ilaaLlaahi-tawbatan naṣoohan ʿasaa-rabbukum anyukaffiraʿankum sayyiʾaatikum wa yudhkilakum jannaatin tajreemin taḥtihal-anhaaru.[60]

O believers! Repent to Allah with a sincere, genuine repentance. Perhaps your Rabb will cover your bad deeds and admit you to Paradises underneath which rivers flow.

The four verses above elucidate Allah's system of repentance in the Quran. To summarize these verses:

1. Duality (shirq), that is, to believe in a deity-god is unforgivable. For, there is only Allah, there is no 'god'! The concept of godhood has nothing to do with the reality of Allah. This is why we MUST learn what Allah means and shape our lives accordingly. On the contrary, we may easily end up deifying things besides Allah, and this is a big risk to take. More information on this topic may be obtained in *Muhammad's Allah.*

2. Not knowing the reality of ourselves will lead us to do wrong by ourselves and thus become of the transgressors and in great loss. But this shouldn't lead us into hopelessness either, for there is a way to be forgiven for mistakes that have been made. The important thing is to recognize the mistake and stop repeating it.

3. Repentance means to consciously stop making a particular mistake. If you recognize it is wrong and ask to be forgiven

---

[60] Quran 66:8.

with the feeling of regret, then forgiveness definitely awaits you. Let us not postpone repentance thinking we still have time to repent for many have died thinking they had time and now they are living the consequences of the things for which they did not repent.

4. Repentance should be done in a conscious manner, not because someone told you to or just for the sake of doing it. Conscious repentance means to truly recognize the wrong in the committed deed, feel deep regret for committing it and make a conscious decision not to do it again. To apologize for a mistake is asking for forgiveness, not to be confused with genuine repentance.

The word 'Astaghfirullah' (I apologize Allah) is not something that should be said without contemplation lest it gives the impression that the addressee is taken lightly. Certain tariqahs unconsciously and ignorantly recommend the repetition of this word. Even if energy is loaded to the spirit due to this repetition, it definitely doesn't achieve the intended purpose.

To grasp the topic, one must be cognizant of the cause for repentance. The Rasul of Allah (saw) says:

"Sometimes I perceive a veil over my heart and I ask for forgiveness from Allah a hundred times in a day."[61]

As evident, repentance should not be done without an effort to be conscious about it. It should be done after perceiving a blockage or veil in one's heart, impeding them from the observation of the One.

It should be a sincere turn from the distress of not being able to observe the One.

Compare sincerely repenting a hundred times a day as a result of feeling one's inadequacy to unconsciously and imitatively asking for

---

[61] Sahih al-Muslim, Ibn Majah, Abu Dawud.

forgiveness by repeating the word 'Astaghfirullah' over and over again without any conscious thought.

Those who want to attain the truth and live with the dignity of being a human must understand they cannot take a lesson from an imitator and they cannot attain the reality via imitation. Sufism is entirely about authentic knowledge and leaves no room for imitation. Some even claim the imitative practice of sharia is unacceptable.

But of course, one who lacks the strength for authenticity will inevitably resort to imitation.

15

WHY REPENT?

'Repentance' is feeling genuine regret for making a significant mistake. Asking for forgiveness, on the other hand, is related more to our inadequacy in duly living up to our creational purpose during our daily activities.

If man, as vicegerent on earth, lives in contradiction to this potential, asking for forgiveness becomes necessary.

When one asks for forgiveness, they should say, "O Rabb, You've appointed me Your vicegerent on earth; however, I've done things that are not aligned with this state, and I have become aware of this mistake! Please forgive me for this mistake (action or thought) that goes against the perfection of my creation. If You do not forgive me, I will suffocate in the swamp of my primitive evaluations, please be merciful towards me and ease for me a life that is worthy of my creational perfection."

Asking for forgiveness with this kind of approach will reach its purpose.

So, what are some of the things for which we should ask for forgiveness?

Allah, who is ever present everywhere, in every iota of existence, wishes that we observe Him both in our own essence and on the creation as a whole. This is why the Quran prompts us with verses such as "He is present in your being, can you not comprehend?" and "Wherever you turn there is the face of Allah"...[62]

However, this being the reality, we live oblivious to this truth and our vicegerency potential, and thus fail to put forth the actions that are in line with this level of consciousness.

So, all of what transpires as a result of not living according to one's essential reality, actions and judgments that are driven by ego-based thoughts, emotions, conditionings, etc. are all the things for which we should ask for forgiveness.

This is why we should not merely repeat the word 'Astaghfurillah' without conscious thought, but actually become aware of our mistakes and make a conscious decision not to repeat them while asking for forgiveness.

---

[62] Quran 2:115

16

SAYYID AL-ISTIGHFAR

اَللّٰهُمَّ اَنْتَ رَبِّى لَاۤ اِلٰهَ اِلاَّ اَنْتَ خَلَقْتَنِى وَ اَنَا عَبْدُكَ وَ اَنَا عَلٰى عَهْدِكَ وَ وَعْدِكَ مَا اسْتَطَعْتُ اَعُوذُ بِكَ مِنْ شَرِّ مَا صَنَعْتُ اَبُوءُ لَكَ بِنِعْمَتِكَ عَلَىَّ وَ اَبُوءُ بِذَنْبِى فَاغْفِرْلِى ذُنُوبِى فَاِنَّهُ لَاۤ يَغْفِرُ الذُّنُوبَ اِلاَّ اَنْتَ بِرَحْمَتِكَ يَاۤاَرْحَمَ الرَّاحِمِينَ

Allaahumma-antarabbee, laa-ilaaha-illaa antakhalaqtanee-wa ana `abduka wa ana `alaa `ahdika wa wa`dika ma-astaṭa`tu-a`oodhu bika min-sharri maa-ṣana`tu aboo'u-lakabini`matika`alayya wa aboo'u-bi-dhambee faghfirlee- dhunoobee fa'innahu laa yaghfirul-dhunooba illaa-antabiraḥmatika yaa al-rḥama-al-raaḥimeena.

O Allah! You are my Rabb, there is no deity-god. Only You exist, You created me, I am Your servant and I am upon the Word I gave You as much as my strength allows me. (O Allah) I seek refuge in You from the evil of the mistakes I have made. I admit the blessing You have given me to the Uluhiyyah of your Absolute Essence. I confess my mistakes. Please forgive me. For grace and forgiveness belongs to You, o Arhamurrahimeen!

Muhammad (saw) says:

"Whoever reads this sayyid al-istighfar during the day with faith and comprehension awaiting its return only from Allah and dies

58

before the night will go to Paradise... And whoever reads it at night and dies before the morning will also go to Paradise."[63]

Surely, if we choose not to make use of this opportunity, its consequence will only be ours to face...

أَللَّهُمَّ لَكَ الْحَمْدُ لَاإِلَهَ إِلاَّ أَنْتَ رَبِّى وَ أَنَا عَبْدُكَ امَنْتُ بِكَ مُخْلِصًا لَكَ فِى دِينِى إِنِّى اَصْبَحْتُ {اَمْسَيْتُ} عَلَى عَهْدِكَ وَ وَعْدِكَ مَا اسْتَطَعْتُ أَتُوبُ اِلَيْكَ مِنْ سَيِّءِ عَمَلِى وَأَسْتَغْفِرُكَ بِذُنُوبِ الَّتِى لَايَغْفِرُهَا اِلاَّ أَنْتَ

Allaahumma laka l-ḥamdu laa ilaaha illaa anta rabbee wa ana `abduka aamantu bika mukhliṣan laka fee deenee innee aṣbaḥtu `alaa `ahdika wa wa`dika maa staṭa`tu atoobu ilayka min sayy'i `amalee wa astaghfiruka bidhunoobillatee laa yaghfiruhaa illaa anta.

"By Allah and by the qualities of Allah inherent within me (B-illahi), whoever reads this istighfar three times in the morning and night will definitely go to Paradise."

Note that the Rasul of Allah (saw) begins his words 'by Allah,' which is a solemn promise. This is why I shared this straight after the Sayyid al-istighfar. What can we possibly lose by reading this three times in the morning and night as opposed to what we can gain?

رَبِّ إِنِّي ظَلَمْتُ نَفْسِي ظُلْمًا كَبِيرًا وَلَا يَغْفِرُ الذُّنُوبَ إِلَّاأَنْتَ فَاغْفِرْ لِي مَغْفِرَةً مِنْ عِنْدِكَ وَرْحَمْنِي إِنَّكَ أَنْتَ الْ غَفُورُ الرَّحِيمُ

---

[63] Sahih al-Bukhari.

Rabbi innee ẓalamtu nafsee ẓalman katheera-wa laa yaghfirul-dhunooba illaa anta faghfirlee maghfiratan-min `indaka warḥamnee innaka-antal-ghufoorul-raḥeem.[64]

My Rabb, I have done great wrong to myself (I failed to live up to my essential reality) **and there is none other than You who can forgive me. Forgive me with a forgiveness from Your Self** (min indika)**, have mercy on me. Indeed, You are forgiving and Rahim.**

Hadhrat Abu Bakr (ra) asked the Rasul of Allah (saw): "O Rasul of Allah, what shall I read before I end my salat?" The Rasul of Allah (saw) told Abu Bakr as-Siddiq and to read this prayer in his salat before giving salam. What could the subtlety be in this recommendation of the Rasul of Allah (saw) who says, "If Abu Bakr's faith was put into one pan of a scale and the faith of all believers was put into the other pan, Abu Bakr's faith would weigh heavier"?

The key lies in the expression 'from Your Self (min indika)'...

The word 'ind' or 'indAllah' points to the Unity of Existence in Sufism and means 'from Allah; the forces that are revealed through dimensional emergence to consciousness from the Names of Allah that comprise one's essence.'

There is an external aspect, an internal aspect and the ladun... The word ladun is a reference to the potential of the Names comprising one's essence, it points to the power of Allah that manifests from that person's essence... The secret of power manifesting in the system of wisdom!

The 'world' is the abode of wisdom. Everything is formed with a reason, a cause. These rules of wisdom and worldly laws of physics do not apply in the abode of the Hereafter.

The muqarriboon observe the secrets of power with the blessing of 'ladun' given to them as a favor while in the world.

---

[64] Sahih al-Bukhari, Sahih al-Muslim.

To request forgiveness from Allah means to request that the flaws resulting from one's ego are covered and that the nur (light of knowledge) pertaining to the reality is disclosed from one's self.

اَللّٰهُمَّ إِغْفِرْلِى خَطِيئَتِى وَجَهْلِى وَإِسْرَافِى فِى أَمْرِى وَمَا أَنْتَ اَعْلَمُ بِهِ مِنِّى اَللّٰهُمَّ إِغْفِرْلِى هَزْلِى وَجِدِّى وَخَطَئِ وَعَمْدِى وَكُلُّ ذَالِكَ عِنْدِى

Allaahumma-ghfirlee khatee'atee wa jahlee wa israfee fee amree wa maa anta a'lamu bihi minnee Allaahumma ighfirlee hazalee wa jiddee wa khata'i wa `amdee wa kullu dhaalika `indee.[65]

O Allah, forgive my mistakes, my ignorance, my transgressions and all my flaws of which You are best aware. O Allah, forgive me for what I've done consciously, unconsciously, seriously, unknowingly or deliberately. I admit all of these are present within me!

Abu Musa al-Ashari (ra) narrates this is the way the Rasul of Allah (saw) used to ask for forgiveness.

Why did the Rasul of Allah (saw) continually ask for forgiveness when he was told in the Quran (48:2) "That Allah may forgive (cover/conceal) **your past and** (in spite of the conquest – fath) **future misdeeds** (the veils resulting from corporeality) **and complete His favor upon you..."**

Perhaps we should contemplate this...

Let us put the more profound aspects of the matter aside and at least realize that our behavior directly contradicts our vicegerency quality and we are doing wrong to ourselves by not living up to our essential reality. Let us be mindful of the fact we can only attain the

---

[65] Sahih al-Bukhari, Sahih al-Muslim.

infinite beauties of the eternal abode of the Hereafter through the practices we do here in this world.

So, instead of wastefully using our brain on things we are indefinitely going to leave behind and never even remember, let us turn to our essence and become aware of our inadequacies.

اَسْتَغْفِرُ اللهَ الَّذِى لآ إِلهَ اِلاَّ هُوَ الْحَىُّ الْقَيُّومُ وَ اَتُوبُ اِلَيْهِ

AstaghfiruLlaah-alladhee laa ilaaha illaa huwa-al-ḥayyul-qayyoomu wa atoobu ilayhi.[66]

I ask for forgiveness from Allah, there is no deity-god, only the One who is Hayy and Qayyum. My repentance is to Him!

The Rasul of Allah (sa) says: "He who says, 'I ask for forgiveness from Allah, there is no deity-god, only the One who is Hayy and Qayyum. My repentance is to Him!' will be forgiven even if he has fled from battle."

Two important points to consider are, using the Ismi Azam while repenting and that even major mistakes are forgiven with such repentance.

I will cover the wisdom behind using the Ismi Azam when praying in the section titled Ismi Azam. As for forgiving even those who may have fled from battle... Fleeing from battle is one of the seven major sins according to the Rasul of Allah (saw).

He says, "Stay away from the seven things that cause destruction:

Assigning partners to Allah (duality)

Killing someone who Allah has forbidden to kill

---

[66] Abu Dawud, al-Tirmidhi.

Engaging in black magic and usury

Consuming the property of an orphan

Fleeing from battle

Slandering a chaste woman with adultery."[67]

Therefore, forgiveness encompasses the major sins also, and yet to be forgiven one needs not confess to someone as the Christians do; one can directly turn to the Sublimity and Greatness of Allah and confess his mistakes to Him and ask for forgiveness from Him alone.

This being the case, no matter how great our mistakes and sins may be, let us never lose hope, let us turn to Allah and not postpone repenting.

أَللَّهُمَّ إِغْفِرْلِى ذَنْبِى كُلَّهُ وَ دِقَّهُ وَجِلَّهُ وَ اَوَّلَهُ وَ آخِرَهُ وَعَلاَنِيَتَهُ وَ سِرَّهُ

Allaahumma-ghfirleedhanbee kullahu wa diqqahu wa jillahu wa awwalahu wa aakhirahu wa `alaa niyatahu wa sirrahu

O Allah, forgive all of my mistakes, the old ones and the new ones the small ones and the big ones, ones that I have done openly and ones that I thought of.

This is one that the Rasul of Allah (saw) most frequently recited...

Note the scope of his repentance. Like I said before, it is imperative that we not repeat these as a parrot would, but approach things the way the Rasul of Allah (saw) did...

There is also great benefit in reading this istighar before giving salam in salat.

---

[67] Sahih al-Bukhari, Sahih al-Muslim.

17

HIDDEN DUALITY

> اَللّٰهُمَّ اِنّی اَعُوذُ بِكَ اَنْ اُشْرِكَ بِكَ شَیْءًا وَ اَنَا اَعْلَمُ وَ اَسْتَغْفِرُكَ لِمَا لاَ اَعْلَمُ
> اِنَّكَ اَنْتَ الْعَلاَّمُ الْغُیُوبَ

Allaahumma innee a`oodhu bika anushrika bika shay'a wa ana-a`lamu wastaghfiruka limaa laa-a`lamu innaka l-`allaamul-ghuyooba.[68]

O Allah, I seek refuge in You from deliberately assigning partners to You. I ask for forgiveness for what I've done inadvertently. Indeed, You are the due knower of the unknown!

Hidden duality is the biggest danger for man. The reason why it's called 'hidden' duality is because it is not an explicitly observable act of assigning partners to Allah, but rather an implicit thought-based association!

The verse **"Do not turn to** (assume the existence of) **a god** (exterior manifestations of power or your illusory self) **besides**

---

[68] Musnad of Ahmad, al-Tabarani.

Allah..."[69] evidently declares the gravity of associating partners to Allah even at the level of thought...

Islam necessitates that all actions are done genuinely and sincerely for the sake of Allah!

While doing something for the sake of Allah, if one assumes either a material or immaterial return from others, this expectation itself forms 'duality'...

For example, if one stands for salat and rather than saying the takbir (Allahuakbar) genuinely to express the greatness of Allah, says it to imply something to the people around him, this is a hidden form of duality (shirq).

If one writes a book, not purely for the sake of Allah and to obey the Rasul's command 'spread knowledge', but for the sake of making financial gain or to receive praise and compliments, this is also a hidden form of duality...

In short, 'intention' is like the bridge of 'Sirat'; it is thinner than a hair and sharper than a knife!

Our thoughts and intentions should be purely and genuinely for Allah, without expecting anything in return from anyone. Otherwise, whatever we do with the slightest bit of expectation – from whoever it may be – there will inevitably be a hidden form of duality in it.

The saints and friends of Allah have stood by this reality with such sensitivity that they even believed the spiritual pleasure gained from salat should be abandoned.

Thus is the prayer the Rasul of Allah (saw) has taught us for protection against the calamities of hidden duality. I guess I don't need to make further emphasis on the benefits of reading this after our five daily prayers.

---

[69] Quran 28:88.

18

THE MOST POWERFUL DHIKR: THE QURAN

In this section I would like to cover some of the verses of the Quran. The most significant verses of prayer in the Quran are in the opening chapter, al-Fatiha; hence, it is mandatory to recite these verses in every rakah of salat. The Rasul of Allah (saw) says: "Salat cannot be salat without the Fatiha!"[70]

In another hadith he says, "Shall I tell you which chapter in the Quran is the greatest in terms of benefit? It is the chapter that begins with 'Alhamdulillahi Rabbil Alameen...'"[71] Another hadith says, "The chapter al-Fatiha is the key to the Quran."[72] There are many more hadith denoting the importance of the chapter al-Fatiha.

One who recites it 41 times every day will definitely see its benefits in time.

Some of the disciples have narrated reciting this chapter when afflicted with an illness or pain and many have been reported to have tried and confirmed this.

It has also been claimed by many saints that reciting the Fatiha forty thousand times at least once in a lifetime brings much benefit in the afterlife.

Additionally, there are many hadith that mention the importance of saying 'Amen' at the end of reciting each Fatiha.

---

[70] Sahih al-Bukhari, Sahih al-Muslim, Musnad of Ahmad, Bayhaqi.
[71] Sahih al-Bukhari, Musnad of Ahmad, Ibn Hibban, Abu Dawud.
[72] Musnad of Ahmad, Ibn Marduyah.

1. AL-FATIHA

بِسْم اللهِ الرَّحْمن الرَّحِيم {1}
الْحَمْدُ للّهِ رَبِّ الْعَالَمِينَ {2} الرَّحْمنِ الرَّحِيم {3}
مَالِكِ يَوْم الدِّين {4} إِيَّاكَ نَعْبُدُ وإِيَّاكَ نَسْتَعِينُ {5}
اهدِنَــــا الصِّرَاطَ الْمُسْتَقِيمَ {6}
صِرَاطَ الَّذِينَ أنعَمتَ عَلَيهِمْ غَيرِ المَغضُوبِ عَلَيهِمْ
وَلاَ الضَّالِّينَ {7}

A`oodhu biLlaahi minal-shaytaanil-rajeem

1. Bismi Llaahi l-rahmaani l-raheem

2. Al-hamduliLlaahi rabbil-`aalameen

3. Al-rahmaanil-raheem

4. Maalikiyawmil-deen

5. Iyyaakana`budu wa-iyyaakanasta`een

6. Ihdinaal-siraatal-mustaqeem

7. Siraat alladheena-an`amta-`alayhim-ghayril-maghdoobi`alayhim wa lal-daalleen

I seek refuge in the protective forces of the Names of Allah comprising my Essence from impulses generated by the accursed and rejected (rajim) Satan, which, as a result of preconditioning, causes our sense of illusion to perceive the existent as non-existent and the non-existent as existent, thereby making man believe he is an independent being and body outside the Names of Allah, directing man to the idea of an external deity-God in the heavens.

1. By the one who is denoted by the name Allah (who created my being with His Names in accord with the meaning of the letter 'B'), **the Rahman, the Rahim.**

2. Hamd (the evaluation of the corporeal worlds created with His Names, as He wills) **belongs to Allah, the Rabb** (the absolute source of the infinite meanings of the Names) **of the worlds** (the universe created within the brain of every individual)

3. The Rahman (the quality with which He forms the dimension of Names; the Quantum Potential)**, the Rahim** (the quality with which He continually creates the engendered existence with the meanings of the Names)

4. The Maleek (the Sovereign One, who manifests His Names as he wishes and governs them in the world of acts as He pleases. The One who has providence over all things) **or the Maalik** (the Absolute Owner) **of the eternal period governed by the decrees of religion** (sunnatullah).

5. You alone we serve, and from You alone we seek the continual manifestation of your Names (By manifesting the meanings of Your Beautiful Names we, as the whole of creation, are in a state of natural servitude to You, and we seek guidance to attain and maintain this awareness at all times)

6. Enable the realization that leads to our innermost essential reality (sirat al-mustaqeem)

7. The path of those upon whom You have bestowed favor (those who believe in the Names of Allah as comprising their essential self and experience the awareness of their force) **not of those who have evoked Your wrath** (who have failed to the see the reality of their selves and the corporeal worlds and who have become conditioned with their ego-identities) **nor of those who are astray** (from the reality and the understanding of the One denoted by the name Allah, the al-Wahid-ul Ahad-as-Samad, and who thus associate partners with Allah [shirq; duality]).

19

AYAT AL-QURSI

اللّهُ لاَ إِلَـهَ إِلاَّ هُوَ الْحَيُّ الْقَيُّومُ لاَ تَأْخُذُهُ سِنَةٌ وَلاَ نَوْمٌ لَّهُ مَا فِي السَّمَاوَاتِ وَمَا فِي الأَرْضِ مَن ذَا الَّذِي يَشْفَعُ عِنْدَهُ إِلاَّ بِإِذْنِهِ يَعْلَمُ مَا بَيْنَ أَيْدِيهِمْ وَمَا خَلْفَهُمْ وَلاَ يُحِيطُونَ بِشَيْءٍ مِّنْ عِلْمِهِ إِلاَّ بِمَا شَاء وَسِعَ كُرْسِيُّهُ السَّمَاوَاتِ وَالأَرْضَ وَلاَ يَؤُودُهُ حِفْظُهُمَا وَهُوَ الْعَلِيُّ الْعَظِيمُ

Allaahu laailaaha illaa huwa al-ḥayyul-qayyoomu laa-takhudhuhu-sinatun walaa-nawmun lahu maafee-l-samaawaati wamaa fee-l-arḍ man-dhaalladhee yashfa`u `indahu illaa bi'idhnihi ya`lamu maa bayna aydeehim wa maa khalfahum wa laa yuḥeetoona bishay'in min `ilmihi illaa bimaa shaa' wasi`a kursiyyuhu l-samaawaati wal-arḍa wa laa ya'ooduhu ḥifẓuhumaa wa huwal-`aliyyu l-`aẓeemu.[73]

Allah is HU! There is no God (deity)**, only HU! The Hayy and the Qayyum** (the sole source of life and the One who forms all things in His Knowledge with the meanings of His Names – the One with whom everything subsists)**. Neither drowsiness overtakes Him** (separation from the worlds even for a single instance) **nor sleep** (leaving creation to its own accord and withdrawing to His Self)**. To Him belongs everything in the heavens and on earth** (the dimensions of knowledge and acts)**. Who can intercede in His sight except by the permission of the forces that manifest from**

---

[73] Quran 2:255.

the Names in one's essence? He knows the dimension in which they live and the dimension they are unable to perceive... Nothing of His knowledge can be grasped if He does not will (allow via the suitability of the Names in one's essence). **His throne** (sovereignty and administration [Rububiyyah]) **encompasses the heavens and the earth. It is not difficult for Him to preserve them. He is the Aliy** (illimitably supreme) **and the Azim** (possessor of infinite might).

The Rasul of Allah (saw) says: "There is a verse inside the chapter al-Baqarah that is the chief of all the verses in the Quran... If there are devils (negative energies) inside a house and this verse is recited they will definitely leave. This verse is the Ayat al-Qursi."[74]

And:

"Everything has a peak. The peak of the Quran is the chapter al-Baqarah, inside of which there is a verse that is the chief of all verses... The Ayat al-Qursi!"[75]

One day, the Rasul of Allah (saw) asked his companion Abu Munzir who was next to him: "Do you know which of the verses in Allah's book is the greatest?" Abu Munzir answered, "Allahu la ilaha illa huwal hayyul qayyum..." "O Abu Manzur!" said the Rasul of Allah (saw) "Blessed may be for you knowledge!"[76]

There are countless other hadith that talk about the sublimity of the Ayat al-Qursi, most of them advise its recital immediately after salat, that is straight after performing the fardh of the five salats every day.

Many narrations have also been made as to the importance of reciting the Ayat al-Qursi upon entering a house, exiting a house, before commencing an important task and before going to bed.

---

[74] Sahih al-Muslim, al-Tirmidhi.
[75] Al-Tirmidhi.
[76] Sahih al-Muslim, Abu Ubaid.

Reciting it seven times in the morning provides protection against various possible harms that may occur during the day. The most effective way of reading it is to read and blow each one in every six directions around our body, that is, to the right, left, front, back, top and bottom, and then to read the seventh one and breath it in deeply.

Finally, those who are experienced in this field have also reported the amazing benefits of reciting this verse, which significantly increases one's spiritual strength, forty thousand times.

20

AMANA AL-RASULU

آمَنَ الرَّسُولُ بِمَا أُنزِلَ إِلَيْهِ مِن رَّبِّهِ وَالْمُؤْمِنُونَ كُلٌّ آمَنَ بِاللهِ وَمَلآئِكَتِهِ وَكُتُبِهِ وَرُسُلِهِ لاَ نُفَرِّقُ بَيْنَ أَحَدٍ مِّن رُّسُلِهِ وَقَالُواْ سَمِعْنَا وَأَطَعْنَا غُفْرَانَكَ رَبَّنَا وَإِلَيْكَ الْمَصِيرُ لاَ يُكَلِّفُ اللّهُ نَفْسًا إِلاَّ وُسْعَهَا لَهَا مَا كَسَبَتْ وَعَلَيْهَا مَا اكْتَسَبَتْ رَبَّنَا لاَ تُؤَاخِذْنَا إِن نَّسِينَا أَوْ أَخْطَأْنَا رَبَّنَا وَلاَ تَحْمِلْ عَلَيْنَا إِصْرًا كَمَا حَمَلْتَهُ عَلَى الَّذِينَ مِن قَبْلِنَا رَبَّنَا وَلاَ تُحَمِّلْنَا مَا لاَ طَاقَةَ لَنَا بِهِ وَاعْفُ عَنَّا وَاغْفِرْ لَنَا وَارْحَمْنَا أَنتَ مَوْلاَنَا فَانصُرْنَا عَلَى الْقَوْمِ الْكَافِرِينَ

Aaman-al-rasooulu bimaa unzila ilayhi minrabbihi wal-mu'minoona kullun-aamana biLlaahi wa malaa'ikatihi wa kutubihi wa rusoolihi laa nufarriqu bayna aḥadin min rusoolihi wa qaaloo sami`naa wa aṭa`naa ghufraanaka rabbanaa wa ilayka l-maṣeeru

Laa yukallifu Llaahu nafsan illaa wus`ahaa lahaa maa kasabat wa `alayhaa maa-ktasabat Rabbanaa laa too a'khidhnaa in-naseenaa aw akhṭa'naa, Rabbanaa walaatahmil `alaynaa iṣran kamaaḥamaltahu `alaalladheena min qablinaa Rabbanaa wa laa tuḥammilnaa maa laa ṭaaqata lanaa bihi, wa'a`oofu`annaa waghfir-lanaa warḥamnaa anta mawlaanaa faanṣurnaa`alaa-al-qawmil-kaafireena.[77]

---

[77] Quran 2:285-286.

The Rasul (Muhammad saw) **has believed in what was revealed** (knowledge that emerged from the dimensional depths) **to him** (to his consciousness) **from his Rabb** (the qualities of the Names of Allah comprising his essential reality). **And so have the believers! They have all believed** (in line with the meaning denoted by the letter B) **that the Names of Allah comprise their essence, and in the angels** (the forces of the Names constituting their being), **the Books** (all revealed knowledge) **and the Rasuls... They say, 'We make no distinction between** (the ways in which the knowledge of Allah was revealed to) **His Rasuls... We have perceived and obeyed, we ask for Your forgiveness, our Rabb; our return is to You.'**

Allah will never hold anyone responsible for that which they have no capacity. What he earns (as a result of his good deeds) **is for his self, and the consequences of** (his bad deeds) **is also for his self. Our Rabb, do not punish us if we forget or make a mistake. Our Rabb, do not place upon us heavy duties like the ones you placed on those before us. Our Rabb, do not place on us a burden we cannot bear. Pardon us, forgive us, have grace on us. You are our protector. Give us victory over those who cover the reality** (disbelievers) **and deny You.**

Hadhrat Ali (ra) and Hadhrat Omar (ra) have narrated: "It is not possible for a smart person to sleep without reciting these verses."[78]

It is recorded both in Muslim and Tirmidhi that the Rasul of Allah (saw) has said, "Allah has ended the chapter al-Baqarah with two verses to which He granted from His treasures under the Throne (Arsh). Learn these verses, and teach them to your children and women. It is the Quran, it may be recited in salat, and it is also a prayer." There are also some hadith denoting the importance of adding 'Amen' at the end of their recital.

---

[78] Allama Alusi.

Another hadith narrates:

"Whoever recites the last two verses of the chapter al-Baqarah, he will be protected from the calamities of the night and the evil of the devils (negative energies)!"[79]

Reciting the following verses at least once a day will provide profound benefits.

شَهِدَ اللّهُ أَنَّهُ لاَ إِلَـهَ إِلاَّ هُوَ وَالْمَلاَئِكَةُ وَأُوْلُواْ الْعِلْمِ قَآئِمَاً بِالْقِسْطِ لاَ إِلَـهَ إِلاَّ هُوَ الْعَزِيزُ الْحَكِيمُ

ShahidaLlaahu annahu laa-ilaaha illaa-huwal-malaa'ikatahu wa'awlool-`ilmi qaa'iman-bil-qisti laa-ilaaha-illaa huwal-`azeezul-hakeemu.[80]

Allah knows with certainty that none exists other than He. He is HU, there is no other, only HU... And (so do) **the forces (potentials) of His names** (angels; compositions of qualities that manifest through the knowledge of reality) **and those of knowledge** (those who possess this knowledge also know, and thus testify to this reality) **and maintain themselves in accord with this truth... There is no god, only HU, the Aziz, the Hakim.**

---

[79] Sahih al-Bukhari.
[80] Quran 3:18.

قُلِ اللَّهُمَّ مَالِكَ الْمُلْكِ تُؤْتِي الْمُلْكَ مَن تَشَاء وَتَنزِعُ الْمُلْكَ مِمَّن تَشَاء وَتُعِزُّ مَن
تَشَاء وَتُذِلُّ مَن تَشَاء بِيَدِكَ الْخَيْرُ إِنَّكَ عَلَىَ كُلِّ شَيْءٍ قَدِيرٌ تُولِجُ اللَّيْلَ فِي
النَّهَارِ وَتُولِجُ النَّهَارَ فِي اللَّيْلِ وَتُخْرِجُ الْحَيَّ مِنَ الْمَيِّتِ وَتُخْرِجُ الْمَيَّتَ مِنَ
الْحَيِّ وَتَرْزُقُ مَن تَشَاء بِغَيْرِ حِسَابٍ

Quli Allaahumma maalikil-mulki tu'tee-l-mulka mantashaa' wa
tanzi`ul-mulka mimman tashaa' wa-tu`izzu man tashaa' wa tudhillu
man tashaa' biyadikal-khayru innaka `alaa kulli shay'in qadeer.
Tooliju l-layla feel-nahaari wa toolijul-nahaara fee-layli wa
tukhrijul-ḥayya minal-mayyiti wa tukhrijul-mayyita mina-l-ḥayyi
wa-tarzuqu mantashaa' bighayri hisaabin.[81]

**Say, "Allah, the sovereign of all sovereignty... You give
sovereignty to whom You will and You take sovereignty away
from whom You will. You honor whom You will and You abase
whom You will. In Your hand is all good. Certainly, You are
Qadir over all things. You turn the night into day and turn the
day into night. You bring the living out of the dead and the dead
out of the living. You give provision** (life sustenance) **to whom
You will without account."**

Some saints claim, "If one recites al-Fatiha, Ayat al-Qursi, and
the 18th, 26th and 27th verses of Ali Imran after performing their five
daily prayers they can be sure of the following five things:

1. Allah will not lead them astray from the straight path (the
   sirat al-mustaqeem)

2. They will be protected from all forms of accidents, afflictions
   and calamities.

3. They will not die without faith.

4. They will not be short of material or spiritual provisions.

---

[81] Quran 3:26-27.

5. They will be reputable in the community in which they reside.

لَوْ أَنزَلْنَا هَذَا الْقُرْآنَ عَلَى جَبَلٍ لَّرَأَيْتَهُ خَاشِعًا مُّتَصَدِّعًا مِّنْ خَشْيَةِ اللّهِ وَتِلْكَ
الْأَمْثَالُ نَضْرِبُهَا لِلنَّاسِ لَعَلَّهُمْ يَتَفَكَّرُونَ
هُوَ اللّهُ الَّذِي لَا إِلَهَ إِلَّا هُوَ عَالِمُ الْغَيْبِ وَالشَّهَادَةِ هُوَ الرَّحْمَنُ الرَّحِيمُ هُوَ اللّهُ
الَّذِي لَا إِلَهَ إِلَّا هُوَ الْمَلِكُ الْقُدُّوسُ السَّلَامُ الْمُؤْمِنُ الْمُهَيْمِنُ الْعَزِيزُ الْجَبَّارُ
الْمُتَكَبِّرُ سُبْحَانَ اللّهِ عَمَّا يُشْرِكُونَ هُوَ اللّهُ الْخَالِقُ الْبَارِئُ الْمُصَوِّرُ لَهُ الْأَسْمَاء
الْحُسْنَى يُسَبِّحُ لَهُ مَا فِي السَّمَاوَاتِ وَالْأَرْضِ وَهُوَ الْعَزِيزُ الْحَكِيمُ

Law anzalnaa haadhaa l-qur'aana `alaa jabalin lara'aytuhu khaashi`an mutaṣaddi`an min khashiyati-laahi wa tilkal-amthaalu naḍribuhaa lil-naasi-la`allahum yatafakkaroona

Huwa Llaahu lladhee laa ilaaha illaa huwa `aalimul-ghaybi wal-shahaadati huwal-raḥmaanul-raḥeemu

HuwaAllaahulladhee laa-ilaaha illa-huwal-malikul-quddoosul-salaamul-mu'minul-muhayminul-`azeezu l-jabbaaru l-mutakabbiru, subḥaana Allaahi `ammaa yushrikoona

HuwaLlahul-khaaliqul-baari'ul-muṣawwiru lahul-asmaa'ul-ḥusnaa yusabbiḥu lahu maa-feel-samawati wal-arḍi wahuwal-`azeezu l-ḥakeemu.[82]

Had We revealed this Quran (this truth) **upon a mountain** (the ego) **you would have seen it humbled and shattered to pieces in awe of Allah** (the realization of the nothingness of his ego or seeming 'self' in respect to the One denoted by the name Allah). **And these examples** (symbolic language) **We present to mankind so that they will contemplate. HU is Allah, there is no god, only HU** (as HU is the inner essence of the reality of everything that is

---

[82] Quran 59:21-24.

perceived)**! The Knower of the unknown and the witnessed! HU is the Rahman** (the potential of the source of the entire creation; the quantum potential)**, the Rahim** (the One who manifests the infinite qualities denoted by the Names and experiences the world of acts with and through their observation). **HU is Allah; there is no god, only HU!** (as HU is the inner essence of the reality of everything that is perceived)**! HU is the Maleek** (the Sovereign One who manifests His Names as he wishes and governs them in the world of acts as He pleases; the One who has providence over all things)**, the Quddus** (the One who is free and beyond being defined, conditioned and limited by His manifest qualities and concepts)**, the Salam** (the One who enables a state of emancipation from the conditions of nature and bodily life and endows the experience of 'certainty' [yakeen])**, the Mu'min** (the One who enables faith and guides individuals to observe their reality)**, the Muhaymin** (the One who observes and protects the manifestations of His Names with His own system)**, the Aziz** (the One whose will to do as He likes, nothing can oppose)**, the Jabbar** (the One whose will is compelling)**, the Mutakabbir** (the One to whom the word 'I' exclusively belongs; Absolute 'I'ness belongs only to Him)**! Allah is Subhan** (exalted and absolutely pure) **from the concepts of god they attribute to Him! HU is Allah, the Khaliq** (the One Absolute Creator – the One who brings individuals into the existence from nothingness with His Names)**, the Bari** (the One who fashions all of creation [from micro to macro] with unique functions and designs yet all in conformity with the whole)**, the Musawwir** (the fashioner of forms; the One who exhibits 'meanings' as 'forms' and devises the mechanism in the perceiver to perceive them)**; to Him belongs the beautiful Names. Whatever is in the heavens and earth glorify** (tasbih) **Allah** (by manifesting the qualities of the Names comprising their essence, i.e. by actualizing their servitude). **HU is the Aziz** (the One whose will to do as He likes, nothing can oppose)**, the Hakim** (the One whose power of knowledge appears under the guise of 'causes', hence creating causality and leading to the perception of multiplicity).

In regards to the merit of these verses the Rasul of Allah (saw) says:

"If he who reads the end of the chapter al-Hashr during the day or night reaches the end of his term and is to die, if he dies during the day he will go to Paradise for reciting it during the day, and if he does during the night he will go to Paradise for reciting it during the night." (This is the section that begins with 'Huwallahulladhee la ilaha illa Hu...').[83]

Another hadith says:

"Whoever says 'Audhu billahis sami'il alimi minash shaytanrrajeem' three times in the morning and then recites the last three verses of the chapter al-Hashr, Allah will appoint seventy thousand angels for him who will pray for his forgiveness until the night. If that person dies that day he will die a martyr. If he dies at night, again, he will die a martyr."[84]

---

[83] Al-Bayhaqi *Shu`ab al-Iman,* Ibn Marduyah.
[84] Musnad of Ahmad, al-Tirmidhi, al-Bayhaqi *Shu`ab al-Iman.*

21

WAMAN YATAQILLAHA

وَمَن يَتَّقِ اللَّهَ يَجْعَل لَّهُ مَخْرَجًا وَيَرْزُقْهُ مِنْ حَيْثُ لَا يَحْتَسِبُ وَمَن يَتَوَكَّلْ عَلَى اللَّهِ فَهُوَ حَسْبُهُ

Wa man-yattaqiLlaaha yaj`allahu makhrajan wa-yarzuqhu min haythu laa-yaḥtasibu wa man yatawakkal `alaa-Llaahi fahuwa ḥasbuhu[85]

Whoever protects himself from Allah, He will open a way out for him. And He will provide sustenance for him from where he does not expect. He who places his trust in Allah, Allah will be sufficient for him (he who believes in the forces pertaining to the qualities of the Names comprising his essence and complies with their requirements, those forces will be ever sufficient for him). **Indeed, Allah will fulfill His word!...**

Abu Dharr Ghifari (ra) narrates the Rasul of Allah (saw) says:

"Indeed, I know a verse to which if the people held on it would be sufficient for them..."[86]

---

[85] Quran 65:2-3.
[86] Al-Hakim, al-Bayhaqi, Ibn Marduyah.

Ibn Abbas (ra) narrates the Rasul of Allah (saw) says:

"(After reciting the above verse) If the people were to apply this verse in their lives they would be free from all the doubt and distress of the world, the distress of death, and the distress of the Doomsday."[87]

I personally have many experiences in regards to the benefits of this verse.

Whoever is distressed or troubled, suffering from financial hardship or in a troublesome situation should recite this verse at least one thousand times a day, they will be delivered from that situation in no time.

Anyone who is unemployed, in debt or is suffering family-related difficulties, in fact anyone who thinks they may be a victim of black magic, should definitely recite this verse for salvation and healing.

---

[87] Abu Nu'aym, Abu Ya'la.

22

YA-SIN

(36th Chapter)

بِسْمِ اللهِ الرَّحْمنِ الرَّحِيمِ

يس {1} وَالْقُرْآنِ الْحَكِيمِ {2} إِنَّكَ لَمِنَ الْمُرْسَلِينَ {3} عَلَى صِرَاطٍ مُسْتَقِيمٍ
{4} تَنْزِيلَ الْعَزِيزِ الرَّحِيمِ {5} لِتُنْذِرَ قَوْمًا مَا أُنْذِرَ آبَاؤُهُمْ فَهُمْ غَافِلُونَ {6}
لَقَدْ حَقَّ الْقَوْلُ عَلَى أَكْثَرِهِمْ فَهُمْ لَا يُؤْمِنُونَ {7} إِنَّا جَعَلْنَا فِي أَعْنَاقِهِمْ أَغْلَالًا
فَهِيَ إِلَى الْأَذْقَانِ فَهُمْ مُقْمَحُونَ {8} وَجَعَلْنَا مِنْ بَيْنِ أَيْدِيهِمْ سَدًّا وَمِنْ خَلْفِهِمْ
سَدًّا فَأَغْشَيْنَاهُمْ فَهُمْ لَا يُبْصِرُونَ {9} وَسَوَاءٌ عَلَيْهِمْ أَأَنْذَرْتَهُمْ أَمْ لَمْ تُنْذِرْهُمْ لَا
يُؤْمِنُونَ {10} إِنَّمَا تُنْذِرُ مَنِ اتَّبَعَ الذِّكْرَ وَخَشِيَ الرَّحْمنَ بِالْغَيْبِ فَبَشِّرْهُ
بِمَغْفِرَةٍ وَأَجْرٍ كَرِيمٍ {11} إِنَّا نَحْنُ نُحْيِي الْمَوْتَى وَنَكْتُبُ مَا قَدَّمُوا وَآثَارَهُمْ
وَكُلَّ شَيْءٍ أَحْصَيْنَاهُ فِي إِمَامٍ مُبِينٍ {12} وَاضْرِبْ لَهُمْ مَثَلًا أَصْحَابَ الْقَرْيَةِ
إِذْ جَاءَهَا الْمُرْسَلُونَ {13} إِذْ أَرْسَلْنَا إِلَيْهِمُ اثْنَيْنِ فَكَذَّبُوهُمَا فَعَزَّزْنَا بِثَالِثٍ
فَقَالُوا إِنَّا إِلَيْكُمْ مُرْسَلُونَ {14} قَالُوا مَا أَنْتُمْ إِلَّا بَشَرٌ مِثْلُنَا وَمَا أَنْزَلَ الرَّحْمنُ
مِنْ شَيْءٍ إِنْ أَنْتُمْ إِلَّا تَكْذِبُونَ {15} قَالُوا رَبُّنَا يَعْلَمُ إِنَّا إِلَيْكُمْ لَمُرْسَلُونَ {16}
وَمَا عَلَيْنَا إِلَّا الْبَلَاغُ الْمُبِينُ {17} قَالُوا إِنَّا تَطَيَّرْنَا بِكُمْ لَئِنْ لَمْ تَنْتَهُوا لَنَرْجُمَنَّكُمْ
وَلَيَمَسَّنَّكُمْ مِنَّا عَذَابٌ أَلِيمٌ {18} قَالُوا طَائِرُكُمْ مَعَكُمْ أَئِنْ ذُكِّرْتُمْ بَلْ أَنْتُمْ قَوْمٌ
مُسْرِفُونَ {19} وَجَاءَ مِنْ أَقْصَى الْمَدِينَةِ رَجُلٌ يَسْعَى قَالَ يَا قَوْمِ اتَّبِعُوا
الْمُرْسَلِينَ {20} اتَّبِعُوا مَنْ لَا يَسْأَلُكُمْ أَجْرًا وَهُمْ مُهْتَدُونَ {21} وَمَا لِي لَا
أَعْبُدُ الَّذِي فَطَرَنِي وَإِلَيْهِ تُرْجَعُونَ {22} أَأَتَّخِذُ مِنْ دُونِهِ آلِهَةً إِنْ يُرِدْنِ

الرَّحْمَن بِضُرٍّ لاَّ تُغْنِ عَنِّي شَفَاعَتُهُمْ شَيْئًا وَلاَ يُنقِذُونِ {23} إِنِّي إِذًا لَّفِي ضَلاَلٍ مُّبِينٍ {24} إِنِّي آمَنتُ بِرَبِّكُمْ فَاسْمَعُونِ {25} قِيلَ ادْخُلِ الْجَنَّةَ قَالَ يَا لَيْتَ قَوْمِي يَعْلَمُونَ {26} بِمَا غَفَرَ لِي رَبِّي وَجَعَلَنِي مِنَ الْمُكْرَمِينَ {27} وَمَا أَنزَلْنَا عَلَى قَوْمِهِ مِن بَعْدِهِ مِن جُندٍ مِّنَ السَّمَاء وَمَا كُنَّا مُنزِلِينَ {28} إِن كَانَتْ إِلاَّ صَيْحَةً وَاحِدَةً فَإِذَا هُمْ خَامِدُونَ {29} يَا حَسْرَةً عَلَى الْعِبَادِ مَا يَأْتِيهِم مِّن رَّسُولٍ إِلاَّ كَانُوا بِهِ يَسْتَهْزِؤُون {30} أَلَمْ يَرَوْا كَمْ أَهْلَكْنَا قَبْلَهُم مِّنْ الْقُرُونِ أَنَّهُمْ إِلَيْهِمْ لاَ يَرْجِعُونَ {31} وَإِن كُلٌّ لَّمَّا جَمِيعٌ لَّدَيْنَا مُحْضَرُونَ {32} وَآيَةٌ لَّهُمُ الأَرْضُ الْمَيْتَةُ أَحْيَيْنَاهَا وَأَخْرَجْنَا مِنْهَا حَبًّا فَمِنْهُ يَأْكُلُونَ {33} وَجَعَلْنَا فِيهَا جَنَّاتٍ مِن نَّخِيلٍ وَأَعْنَابٍ وَفَجَّرْنَا فِيهَا مِنْ الْعُيُونِ {34} لِيَأْكُلُوا مِن ثَمَرِهِ وَمَا عَمِلَتْهُ أَيْدِيهِمْ أَفَلا يَشْكُرُونَ {35} سُبْحَانَ الَّذِي خَلَقَ الأَزْوَاجَ كُلَّهَا مِمَّا تُنبِتُ الأَرْضُ وَمِنْ أَنفُسِهِمْ وَمِمَّا لاَ يَعْلَمُونَ {36} وَآيَةٌ لَّهُمْ اللَّيْلُ نَسْلَخُ مِنْهُ النَّهَارَ فَإِذَا هُم مُّظْلِمُونَ {37} وَالشَّمْسُ تَجْرِي لِمُسْتَقَرٍّ لَّهَا ذَلِكَ تَقْدِيرُ الْعَزِيزِ الْعَلِيمِ {38} وَالْقَمَرَ قَدَّرْنَاهُ مَنَازِلَ حَتَّى عَادَ كَالْعُرْجُونِ الْقَدِيمِ {39} لاَ الشَّمْسُ يَنبَغِي لَهَا أَن تُدْرِكَ الْقَمَرَ وَلاَ اللَّيْلُ سَابِقُ النَّهَارِ وَكُلٌّ فِي فَلَكٍ يَسْبَحُونَ {40} وَآيَةٌ لَّهُمْ أَنَّا حَمَلْنَا ذُرِّيَّتَهُمْ فِي الْفُلْكِ الْمَشْحُونِ {41} وَخَلَقْنَا لَهُم مِّن مِّثْلِهِ مَا يَرْكَبُونَ {42} وَإِن نَّشَأْ نُغْرِقْهُمْ فَلا صَرِيخَ لَهُمْ وَلا هُمْ يُنقَذُونَ {43} إِلاَّ رَحْمَةً مِّنَّا وَمَتَاعًا إِلَى حِينٍ {44} وَإِذَا قِيلَ لَهُمُ اتَّقُوا مَا بَيْنَ أَيْدِيكُمْ وَمَا خَلْفَكُمْ لَعَلَّكُمْ تُرْحَمُونَ {45} وَمَا تَأْتِيهِم مِّنْ آيَةٍ مِّنْ آيَاتِ رَبِّهِمْ إِلاَّ كَانُوا عَنْهَا مُعْرِضِينَ {46} وَإِذَا قِيلَ لَهُمْ أَنفِقُوا مِمَّا رَزَقَكُمُ اللَّهُ قَالَ الَّذِينَ كَفَرُوا لِلَّذِينَ آمَنُوا أَنُطْعِمُ مَن لَّوْ يَشَاءُ اللَّهُ أَطْعَمَهُ إِنْ أَنتُمْ إِلاَّ فِي ضَلاَلٍ مُّبِينٍ {47} وَيَقُولُونَ مَتَى هَذَا الْوَعْدُ إِن كُنتُمْ صَادِقِينَ {48} مَا يَنظُرُونَ إِلاَّ صَيْحَةً وَاحِدَةً تَأْخُذُهُمْ وَهُمْ يَخِصِّمُونَ {49} فَلا يَسْتَطِيعُونَ تَوْصِيَةً وَلا إِلَى أَهْلِهِمْ يَرْجِعُونَ {50} وَنُفِخَ فِي الصُّورِ فَإِذَا هُم مِّنَ الأَجْدَاثِ إِلَى رَبِّهِمْ يَنسِلُونَ {51} قَالُوا يَا وَيْلَنَا مَن بَعَثَنَا مِن مَّرْقَدِنَا هَذَا مَا وَعَدَ الرَّحْمَنُ وَصَدَقَ الْمُرْسَلُونَ {52} إِن كَانَتْ إِلاَّ صَيْحَةً وَاحِدَةً فَإِذَا هُمْ جَمِيعٌ لَّدَيْنَا مُحْضَرُونَ {53} فَالْيَوْمَ لاَ تُظْلَمُ نَفْسٌ شَيْئًا وَلاَ تُجْزَوْنَ إِلاَّ مَا كُنتُمْ تَعْمَلُونَ {54} إِنَّ أَصْحَابَ الْجَنَّةِ الْيَوْمَ فِي شُغُلٍ فَاكِهُونَ {55} هُمْ وَأَزْوَاجُهُمْ فِي ظِلاَلٍ عَلَى الأَرَائِكِ مُتَّكِؤُونَ {56} لَهُمْ فِيهَا فَاكِهَةٌ وَلَهُم مَّا يَدَّعُونَ {57} سَلاَمٌ قَوْلاً مِن رَّبٍّ رَّحِيمٍ {58} وَامْتَازُوا الْيَوْمَ أَيُّهَا الْمُجْرِمُونَ {59} أَلَمْ أَعْهَدْ إِلَيْكُمْ يَا بَنِي آدَمَ أَن لاَّ تَعْبُدُوا الشَّيْطَانَ إِنَّهُ لَكُمْ عَدُوٌّ مُّبِينٌ {60} وَأَنْ اعْبُدُونِي هَذَا صِرَاطٌ مُّسْتَقِيمٌ {61} وَلَقَدْ أَضَلَّ مِنكُمْ جِبِلاًّ كَثِيراً أَفَلَمْ تَكُونُوا تَعْقِلُونَ {62} هَذِهِ

جَهَنَّمُ الَّتِي كُنتُمْ تُوعَدُونَ {63} اصْلَوْهَا الْيَوْمَ بِمَا كُنتُمْ تَكْفُرُونَ {64} الْيَوْمَ نَخْتِمُ عَلَى أَفْوَاهِهِمْ وَتُكَلِّمُنَا أَيْدِيهِمْ وَتَشْهَدُ أَرْجُلُهُم بِمَا كَانُوا يَكْسِبُونَ {65} وَلَوْ نَشَاء لَطَمَسْنَا عَلَى أَعْيُنِهِمْ فَاسْتَبَقُوا الصِّرَاطَ فَأَنَّى يُبْصِرُونَ {66} وَلَوْ نَشَاء لَمَسَخْنَاهُمْ عَلَى مَكَانَتِهِمْ فَمَا اسْتَطَاعُوا مُضِيًّا وَلَا يَرْجِعُونَ {67} وَمَنْ نُعَمِّرْهُ نُنَكِّسْهُ فِي الْخَلْقِ أَفَلَا يَعْقِلُونَ {68} وَمَا عَلَّمْنَاهُ الشِّعْرَ وَمَا يَنبَغِي لَهُ إِنْ هُوَ إِلَّا ذِكْرٌ وَقُرْآنٌ مُبِينٌ {69} لِيُنذِرَ مَن كَانَ حَيًّا وَيَحِقَّ الْقَوْلُ عَلَى الْكَافِرِينَ {70} أَوَلَمْ يَرَوْا أَنَّا خَلَقْنَا لَهُم مِّمَّا عَمِلَتْ أَيْدِينَا أَنْعَامًا فَهُمْ لَهَا مَالِكُونَ {71} وَذَلَّلْنَاهَا لَهُمْ فَمِنْهَا رَكُوبُهُمْ وَمِنْهَا يَأْكُلُونَ {72} وَلَهُمْ فِيهَا مَنَافِعُ وَمَشَارِبُ أَفَلَا يَشْكُرُونَ {73} وَاتَّخَذُوا مِن دُونِ اللَّهِ آلِهَةً لَعَلَّهُمْ يُنصَرُونَ {74} لَا يَسْتَطِيعُونَ نَصْرَهُمْ وَهُمْ لَهُمْ جُندٌ مُحْضَرُونَ {75} فَلَا يَحْزُنكَ قَوْلُهُمْ إِنَّا نَعْلَمُ مَا يُسِرُّونَ وَمَا يُعْلِنُونَ {76} أَوَلَمْ يَرَ الْإِنسَانُ أَنَّا خَلَقْنَاهُ مِن نُّطْفَةٍ فَإِذَا هُوَ خَصِيمٌ مُّبِينٌ {77} وَضَرَبَ لَنَا مَثَلًا وَنَسِيَ خَلْقَهُ قَالَ مَنْ يُحْيِي الْعِظَامَ وَهِيَ رَمِيمٌ {78} قُلْ يُحْيِيهَا الَّذِي أَنشَأَهَا أَوَّلَ مَرَّةٍ وَهُوَ بِكُلِّ خَلْقٍ عَلِيمٌ {79} الَّذِي جَعَلَ لَكُم مِّنَ الشَّجَرِ الْأَخْضَرِ نَارًا فَإِذَا أَنتُم مِّنْهُ تُوقِدُونَ {80} أَوَلَيْسَ الَّذِي خَلَقَ السَّمَاوَاتِ وَالْأَرْضَ بِقَادِرٍ عَلَى أَنْ يَخْلُقَ مِثْلَهُم بَلَى وَهُوَ الْخَلَّاقُ الْعَلِيمُ {81} إِنَّمَا أَمْرُهُ إِذَا أَرَادَ شَيْئًا أَنْ يَقُولَ لَهُ كُنْ فَيَكُونُ {82} فَسُبْحَانَ الَّذِي بِيَدِهِ مَلَكُوتُ كُلِّ شَيْءٍ وَإِلَيْهِ تُرْجَعُونَ {83}

A`oodhu biLlaahi min al-shayṭaani l-rajeem

Bismi Llaahi l-raḥmaani l-raḥeem

1 Yaa seen 2 wal-qur'aani l-ḥakeem 3 innaka lamina l-mursaleena 4 `alaa ṣiraaṭin mustaqeemin 5 tanzeela l-`azeezi l-raḥeemi 6 litundhira qawman maa undhira aabaa'uhum fahum ghaafiloona 7 laqad ḥaqqa l-qawlu `alaa aktharihim fahum laa yu'minoona 8 innaa ja`alnaa fee a`naqihim aghlaalan fahiya ilaa l-adhqaani fahum muqmaḥoona 9 waja`alnaa min bayni aydeehim saddan wamin khalfihim saddan fa'aghshaynahum fahum laa yubṣiroona 10 wasawaa'un `alayhim a'andhartahum am laa tundhirhum laa yu'minoona 11 innamaa tundhiru mani attaba`a l-dhikra akhshiyaa l-raḥmaana bil-ghaybi fabash-shirhu bimaghfiratin wa ajrin kareemin 12 innaa naḥnu nuḥyee l-mawtaa wa naktunu maa qaddamoo wa athaarahum wa kulla shay'in aḥṣaynaahu fee imaamin mubeenin 13 wa iḍrib lahum mathalan aṣḥaaba l-qaryati idh jaaha l-mursaloona 14 idh arsalnaa

ilayhimu ithnayni fakadh-dhaboohumaa fa`azzaznaa bithaalithin faqaaloo innaa ilaykum mursaloona 15 qaaloo maa antum illaa basharun mithlunaa wamaa anzala l-rahmaanu min shay'in in antum illaa takdhiboona 16 qaaloo rabbunaa ya`lamu innaa ilaykum lamursaloona 17 wa maa `alaynaa illaa l-balaaghu l-mubeenu 18 qaaloo innaa tatayyarnaa bikum la'in lam tantahoo lanarjumannakum walayamassannakum minnaa `adhaabun aleemun 19 qaaloo taa'irukum ma`akum a'in dhukkirtum bal antum qawmun musrifoona 20 wa jaa' min aqsaa l-madeenati rajulun yas`a qaala yaa qawmi ittabi`oo l-mursaleena 21 ittabi`oo man laa yasalukum ajran wahum muhtadoona 22 wa maa lee laa a`budu lladhee fataranee wa ilayhi turja`oona 23 a'attakhidhu min doonihi aalihatan in yuridni l-rahmaanu bidurrin laa tughni `annee shafaa`atuhum shay'an wa laa yunqidhooni 24 innee idhan lafee dalaalin mubeenin 25 innee aamantu birabbikum faa'isma`ooni 26 qeela dkhuli l-jannata qaala ya layta qawmee ya`lamoona 27 bimaa ghafara lee rabbee waja`alnee mina l-mukarabeena 28 wa maa anzalnaa `alaa qawmihi min ba`dihi min jundin mina l-samaa' wa maa kunnaa munzileena 29 in kaanat illaa sayhatan waahidatan fa'idhaa hum khaamidoona 30 yaa hasratan `alaa l-`ibaadi maa ya'teehim min rasoolin illaa kaanoo bihi yastahzi'oona 31 alam yaraa kam ahlaknaa qablahum mina l-qurooni annahum ilayhim laa yarji`oona 32 wa'in killun lammaa jamee`un ladaynaa muhdaroona 33 wa aayatun lahumu l-ardu l-maytatu ahyaynaahaa wa akhrajnaa minhaa habban faminhu ya'kuloona 34 wa ja`alnaa feehaa jannaatin min nakheelin wa a`naabin wa fajjarnaa feehaa mina l-`ayooni 35 liya'kuloo min thamarihi wa maa `amilat-hu aydeehim afalaa yashkuroona 36 subhaana lladhee khalaqa l-awwaaja kullahaa mimmaa tunbitu l-ardu wa min anfusihim wa mimmaa laa ya`lamoona 37 wa aayatun lahumu l-laylu naslakhu minhu l-nahaara fa'idhaa hum muzlimoona 38 wa l-shamsu tajree limustaqarrin lahaa dhaalika taqdeeru l-azeezi l-`aleemi 39 wal-qamara qaddarnaahu manaazila hattaa `aada kaal`urooni l-qadeemi 40 laa l-shamsu yanbaghee lahaa an tudrika al-qamara wa laa l-layli saabiqu l-nahaari wa kullun fee falakin yasbahoona 41 wa aayatun lahum annaa hamalnaa dhurriyyatahum fee l-fulki l-mashhooni 42 wa khalaqnaa lahum main mithlihi maa yarkaboona 43 wa in nashaa; nughriqhum falaa sareekha wa idhaa feela lahum wa laa hum yungadhoona 44 illaa rahmatan minnaa wa mataa`an ilaa heenin 45 wa idhaa qeela lahumu ittaqoo maa bayna

aydeekum wa maa khalfakum la`allakum turḥamoona 46 wa maa
ta'teehim min aayaati rabbihim illaa kaanoo `anhaa mu`riḍeena 47
wa idhaa qeela lahum anfiqoo mimmaa razaqakumu Llaahu qaala
lladheena kafaroo lilladheena aamanoo anuṭa`imu man law yashaa'
Allahu aṭa`amahu in antum illaa fee ḍalaalin mubeenin 48 wa
yaqooloona mataa haadhaa l-wa`du in kuntum ṣaadiqeena 49 maa
yandhuroona illaa ṣayḥatan waaḥidatan ta'khudhuhum wahum
yakhiṣṣimoona 50 falaa yastaṭee`oona tawṣiyatan wa laa ilaa ahlihim
yarji`oona 51 wanufikha fee l-ṣoori fa'idhaa hum mina l-ajdaathi ilaa
rabbihim yansiloona 52 qaaloo yaa waylanaa man ba`athanaa min
marqadina haadhaa maa wa`ada l-raḥmaanu wa ṣadaqa l-mursaloona
53 in kaanat illaa ṣayḥatan waaḥidatan fa'idhaa hum jamee`un
ladaynaa muḥḍaroona 54 faalyawma laa tuṭlamu nafsun shay'an wa
laa tujzawna illaa maa kuntum ta`maloona 55 innaa aṣḥaaba l-jannati
l-yawma fee shughulin faakihoona 56 hum wa'azwaajuhum fee
ḍalaalin `alaa l-araa'iki muttaki'oona 57 lahum feehaa faakihatun wa
lahum maa yadda`oona 58 salaamun qawlan min rabbin raḥeemin 59
wa'imtaazoo l-yawma ayyuhaa l-mujrimoona 60 alam a`had ilaykum
yaa banee aadama an laa ta`badoo l-shayṭaana innahu lakum
`aduwwun mubeenun 61 wa'ani a`budoonee haadhaa ṣiraaṭun
mustaqeemun 62 wa laqad aḍalla minkum jibillan katheeran afalam
takoonoo ta`qiloona 63 haadhihi jahannamu llatee kuntum
too`adoona 64 iṣlawhaa l-yawma bimaa kuntum takfuroona 65
alyawma nakhtimu `alaa afwaahihim watukallimoona aydeehim wa
tashaddu arjuluhum bimaa kaanoo yaksiboona 66 wa law nashaa'u
laṭamasnaa `alaa a`yunihim fa'istabaqoo l-ṣiraaṭa fa'annaa
yubṣiroona 67 wa law nashaa' lamsakhnaahum `alaa makaanatihum
famaa istaṭa`oo muḍiyyan wa laa yarji`oona 68 wa man nu`ammirhu
nunakkishu fee l-khalqi afalaa ya`qiloona 69 wa maa `allamnaahu l-
shi`ara wa maa yanbaghee lahu in huwa illaa dhikrun wa qur'aanun
mubeenun 70 liyundhira man kaana ḥayyan wa yaḥiqqa l-qawlu
`alaa l-kaafireena 71 awalam yaraw annaa khalaqnaa lahum mimmaa
`aamilat aydeena an`aman fahum laha maalikoona 72 wa
dhallalnahaa lahum faminhaa rakoobuhum waminhaa ya'kuloona 73
walahum feehaa manaafi`u wa mashaaribu afalaa yashkuroona 74
wa ittakhadhoo min dooni Llaahi aalihatan la`allahum yunṣaroona
75 laa yastaṭee`oona naṣrahum wahum lahum jundun muḥḍaroona
76 falaa yaḥzunka qawluhum innaa na`lamu maa yusirroona wa maa
yu`linoona 77 awalam yara l-insaanu annaa khalaqnaahu min

nutfatin fa'idhaa huwa khaseemun mubeenun 78 wa daraba lanaa mathalan wa nasiya khalqahu qaala man yuhyee l-`idhama wa hiya rameemun 79 qul yuhyeehaa lladhee anshaaha awwala marratin wa huwa bi kulli khalqin `aleemun 80 alladhee ja`ala lakum mina l-shajari l-akhdari naaran fa'idhaa antum minhu tooqidoona 81 awalaysa lladhee khalaqa l-samawaati wal-arda bi qadarin `alaa an yakhluqa mithlahum balaa wa huwa l-khallaqu l-`aleemu 82 innamaa amruhu idhaa araada shay'an an yaqoola lahu kun fayakoonu 83 fa subhaana lladhee bi yadihi malakootu kulli shay'in wa ilayhi turja`oona

By the one who is denoted by the name Allah (who created my being with His Names in accord with the meaning of the letter 'B'), **the Rahman, the Rahim.**

1. Ya Sin (O Muhammad)!

2. And the Quran full of wisdom (which he disclosed)!

3. You are most definitely of the Rasuls.

4. Upon a straight path.

5. With the comprehensive knowledge disclosed to you by the One who is the Aziz, the Rahim.

6. So that you may warn a people whose forefathers have not been warned and thus who live cocooned (from their reality, the sunnatullah).

7. Indeed, the word ("Hell will be filled with the majority of humans and the jinni") **has come true for most of them! Because of this they do not believe.**

8. Indeed, We have formed shackles (conditionings and judgments) **around their necks up to their chins! Their heads are aloft** (they are unable to see their essential reality; they live driven by their egos)!

9. And We have formed a barrier before them and after them (they can neither see their future nor take lessons from their past) **and thus We covered them... They can no longer see.**

10. Whether you warn them or do not warn them, it is all the same; they will not believe!

11. You can only warn the one who remembers (the reality that is reminded) **and who is in awe of the Rahman, as his unknown.** Give him the good news of forgiveness and an abundant reward.

12. Indeed, it is We, yes only We, who can bring the dead to life! We write their deeds and what they put forth! We record everything (with all its detail) **in a Clear Book** (in their brains and their spirits).

13. Give them the example of the people of that city to which the Rasuls had come.

14. When We sent two Rasuls to them and they denied them both... Upon this We sent a third one and strengthened him, and they (the Rasuls) said, "Indeed, We have been disclosed to you."

15. They responded, "You are not but mere humans like us... And the Rahman has not disclosed anything... You are but liars."

16. (The Rasuls) said, "Our Rabb knows, we have indeed been disclosed to you."

17. "We are only responsible for clear notification."

18. They said, "Indeed, we think you are a bad omen... So, if you do not desist we will definitely stone you to death and a severe suffering will afflict you from us."

19. They said, "Your bad omen is from you... (Is it a bad omen) because you are reminded (of your reality)? No, you are a wasteful people."

20. Then a man came running from the farthest end of the city, saying, "O my people, follow the Rasuls."

21. "Follow those who do not ask you for anything in return, who are upon the reality!"

22. "How can I not serve the One who gave me this disposition? To Him you will be returned."

23. "Shall I take gods besides Him! If the Rahman wills to manifest adversity, their intercession will neither benefit me nor protect me..."

24. "In that case, I would be in clear error!"

25. "I have indeed believed in the Rabb manifest in you, listen to me!"

26. (He was told) "Enter Paradise!" He said, "I wish my people knew my state!"

27. "How my Rabb forgave me and placed me among those who are the receivers of generosity (the Name Karim)."

28. After that We did not disclose upon his people any army from the heavens, nor would We have done so.

29. There was only a single cry, and immediately they were extinguished!

30. What a loss for those servants! Whenever a Rasul came to them, they used to mock and ridicule his message.

31. Did they not see how many generations We destroyed before them, and that none of them will return!

32. And indeed, all of them will be brought present (forcefully).

33. The dead earth is also a sign for them! We brought it to life, and brought forth from it produce of which they eat...

34. And formed therein gardens with date palms and grapevines, and caused springs to gush.

35. So that they eat its fruit and what their hands produce... Are they still not grateful?

36. Subhan is He who created all pairs (DNA helix) **from what the earth** (body) **produces and from themselves** (their consciousness) **and from that which they don't know!**

37. The night is also a sign for them! We pull the day (light) out of it and they are left in darkness.

38. And the Sun runs on its course! This is the determination of the Aziz, the Aleem.

39. As for the Moon, We have appointed stations to it... Until it finally becomes like an old date stalk.

40. Neither will the Sun overtake the Moon nor the night outpace the day! Each floats in its own orbit.

41. And a sign for them are the ships We carried full with their progeny!

42. And that We created for them the like of it in which they can ride!

43. And if We should will, We could drown them, and there will be none to help them, nor will they be saved!

44. Except if We give them a specified life term as grace from Us so that they may benefit.

45. But when they are told, "Protect yourselves from what is before you (the things you will encounter) and what is behind you (the consequences of the things you did in the past) so that you may receive grace" they turn away.

46. And no proof comes to them of the signs of their Rabb from which they do not turn away.

47. And when they are told, "Give unrequitedly from the sustenance with which Allah nourishes you," those who deny the knowledge of the reality say to the believers, "Shall we feed those who, if Allah had willed, He would have fed? You are only in clear error."

48. They say, "If you are true to your word, (tell us) when will this promise (be fulfilled)?"

49. They do not await anything except a single cry (the blowing of the horn [body]), which will seize them while they are disputing.

50. At that time they will neither have the strength to make a bequest nor will they be able to return to their families!

51. And the horn has been blown! At once you will see them leave their graves (bodies) **and hasten towards their Rabb** (to the realization of their essence)!

52. They will say, "Woe to us! Who has delivered us from our sleeping place (the world) **to a new state of existence? This must be the promise of the Rahman; the Rasuls have indeed told the Truth."** (Hadith: Mankind is asleep; with death, they will awaken!)

53. Only a single blow (of Israfil's horn) **took place... At once they are all brought present before Us.**

54. At that time, no soul shall be wronged in any way... You will not be recompensed, except for what you did (you will only live the consequences of your own actions)!"

55. The people of Paradise, at that time, will be occupied with the joy and amusement of the blessings of Paradise.

56. They and their partners shall recline on couches in the shade.

57. They shall have fruits therein... And whatever pleasurable things they shall desire.

58. "Salam," a word from a Rahim Rabb shall reach them (they will experience the manifestation of the Name Salam)!

59. "O guilty ones! Stand apart!"

60. O Children of Adam... Did I not enjoin upon you (inform you)**, that you not serve Satan** (body/bodily and unconscious state of existence deprived of the knowledge of the reality; ego driven existence)**, for indeed, he** (this state of unconsciousness) **is to you a clear enemy?**

61. And that you serve only Me (experience and feel the requisites of the reality)**, as this is the straight path** (sirat al-mustaqim)**?**

62. Indeed, (your belief that you are only the body and that you will become inexistent when you die) **has caused many of you to go astray! Did you not use your intellect?**

63. So, here is the Hell that you have been promised!

64. Experience the results of denying your essential reality now!

65. We will seal their mouths at that time, their hands will speak to Us, and their feet will bear witness about what they have done.

66. And if We willed We could have blinded their eyes and they would have rushed about on the path... But how could they see (this Truth)**?**

67. And if We willed We could have paralyzed them in their places (fixated them upon their current understanding) **and they would not be able to move forward, nor go back to their old states.**

68. And to whom We grant a long life, We weaken in creation. Do they still not use their intellect?

69. We did not teach him poetry! Nor is it befitting for him! It is only a reminder and a clear Quran!

70. To warn the living and justify the word against the deniers of the reality.

71. Do they not see how We created sacrificial animals for them among Our creation... And they are their owners?

72. We tamed them (cattle) **for them... And on some of them they ride, and some of them they eat.**

73. And for them therein are benefits and drinks... Are they still not grateful?

74. They took gods besides Allah, hoping they could be helped!

75. They (the gods) **cannot help them!** (On the contrary) **they are like soldiers** (in service) **to their gods!**

76. So, let not their words grieve you... Indeed, We know what they conceal and what they reveal.

77. Did man not see how We created him from sperm... Despite this, he is now an open enemy!

78. He forgets his own creation and presents for Us an example saying, "Who will give life to the bones when they have rotted away?"

79. Say, "He who brought them to life in the first place will resurrect them and give them life! HU is Aleem of every creation with His Names."

80. It is He who produced fire for you from a green tree, from which you kindle fire!

81. Is He who created the heavens and the earth not able to create their like with His Names? Yes! HU is the Hallaq, the Aleem.

82. Indeed, when He wills a thing, His command is 'Kun – be' (He merely wishes it to be)**, and it is** (formed with ease)**!**

83. Subhan is He in whose hand (governance) **is the Malakut** (the force of the Names) **of all things, and to Him you will be returned** (the illusory self – ego will come to an end and the Absolute Reality will be discerned).

There are many hadith in regards to the benefits of reading the chapter Yaseen. Below are some of them.

"If one, who makes it a habit to read the chapter Yaseen every night before going to bed, passes away during the night, he will die a martyr."[88]

"Read chapter Yaseen frequently because there is prosperity and abundance in it:

1. If a hungry person reads it they will be fed.
2. If a naked person reads it they will be clothed.
3. If a single person reads it they will meet a partner and be wed.

---

[88] Al-Tabarani.

4. If one who is scared reads it they will be safe from their fears.

5. One who is distressed by worldly affairs will be relieved of their distress.

6. The traveler will be freed from the burdens of traveling.

7. One who has lost something will find what they have lost.

8. One who reads it at the time of death will be freed from their troubles.

9. A thirsty one will quench their thirst.

10. A sick person will find healing if it not yet their time of death."[89]

"The chapter Yaseen is the heart of the Quran. If one reads Yaseen longing for Allah and the hereafter, Allah will definitely let Himself be found. Read chapter Yaseen upon our deceased ones."[90]

"Indeed, all things have a heart. The heart of the Quran is the chapter Yaseen. Whoever reads Yaseeen, Allah will give him the reward of having read the whole Quran without the chapter Yaseen – ten times over."[91]

"Just as the chapter Yaseen may be read on a daily basis or once every Friday, one who is distressed may also read it seven times and ask Allah to be freed from his troubles for the sake of this chapter."

One may also read Yaseen forty-one times in times of trouble and need and pray to Allah for the acceptance of one's prayers. Another practice is for a group of people to gather, each one reading Yaseen several times to complete it to forty-one in total, and then pray altogether.

---

[89] Al-Bayhaqi *Shu`ab al-Iman.*
[90] Abu Dawud, Musnad of Ahmad.
[91] Al-Tirmidhi.

23

AL-FATH
(48ᵗʰ Chapter)

بِسْمِ اللهِ الرَّحْمنِ الرَّحِيمِ

إِنَّا فَتَحْنَا لَكَ فَتْحًا مُبِينًا {1} لِيَغْفِرَ لَكَ اللهُ مَا تَقَدَّمَ مِن ذَنبِكَ وَمَا تَأَخَّرَ وَيُتِمَّ نِعْمَتَهُ عَلَيْكَ وَيَهْدِيَكَ صِرَاطًا مُّسْتَقِيمًا {2} وَيَنصُرَكَ اللهُ نَصْرًا عَزِيزًا {3} هُوَ الَّذِي أَنزَلَ السَّكِينَةَ فِي قُلُوبِ الْمُؤْمِنِينَ لِيَزْدَادُوا إِيمَانًا مَّعَ إِيمَانِهِمْ وَلِلّهِ جُنُودُ السَّمَاوَاتِ وَالْأَرْضِ وَكَانَ اللهُ عَلِيمًا حَكِيمًا {4} لِيُدْخِلَ الْمُؤْمِنِينَ وَالْمُؤْمِنَاتِ جَنَّاتٍ تَجْرِي مِن تَحْتِهَا الْأَنْهَارُ خَالِدِينَ فِيهَا وَيُكَفِّرَ عَنْهُمْ سَيِّئَاتِهِمْ وَكَانَ ذَلِكَ عِندَ اللهِ فَوْزًا عَظِيمًا {5} وَيُعَذِّبَ الْمُنَافِقِينَ وَالْمُنَافِقَاتِ وَالْمُشْرِكِينَ وَالْمُشْرِكَاتِ الظَّانِّينَ بِاللهِ ظَنَّ السَّوْءِ عَلَيْهِمْ دَائِرَةُ السَّوْءِ وَغَضِبَ اللهُ عَلَيْهِمْ وَلَعَنَهُمْ وَأَعَدَّ لَهُمْ جَهَنَّمَ وَسَاءتْ مَصِيرًا {6} وَلِلّهِ جُنُودُ السَّمَاوَاتِ وَالْأَرْضِ وَكَانَ اللهُ عَزِيزًا حَكِيمًا {7} إِنَّا أَرْسَلْنَاكَ شَاهِدًا وَمُبَشِّرًا وَنَذِيرًا {8} لِتُؤْمِنُوا بِاللهِ وَرَسُولِهِ وَتُعَزِّرُوهُ وَتُوَقِّرُوهُ وَتُسَبِّحُوهُ بُكْرَةً وَأَصِيلًا {9} إِنَّ الَّذِينَ يُبَايِعُونَكَ إِنَّمَا يُبَايِعُونَ اللهَ يَدُ اللهِ فَوْقَ أَيْدِيهِمْ فَمَن نَّكَثَ فَإِنَّمَا يَنكُثُ عَلَى نَفْسِهِ وَمَنْ أَوْفَى بِمَا عَاهَدَ عَلَيْهُ اللهَ فَسَيُؤْتِيهِ أَجْرًا عَظِيمًا {10} سَيَقُولُ لَكَ الْمُخَلَّفُونَ مِنَ الْأَعْرَابِ شَغَلَتْنَا أَمْوَالُنَا وَأَهْلُونَا فَاسْتَغْفِرْ لَنَا يَقُولُونَ بِأَلْسِنَتِهِم مَّا لَيْسَ فِي قُلُوبِهِمْ قُلْ فَمَن يَمْلِكُ لَكُم مِّنَ اللهِ شَيْئًا إِنْ أَرَادَ بِكُمْ ضَرًّا أَوْ أَرَادَ بِكُمْ نَفْعًا بَلْ كَانَ اللهُ بِمَا تَعْمَلُونَ خَبِيرًا {11} بَلْ ظَنَنتُمْ أَن لَّن يَنقَلِبَ الرَّسُولُ وَالْمُؤْمِنُونَ إِلَى أَهْلِيهِمْ أَبَدًا وَزُيِّنَ ذَلِكَ فِي قُلُوبِكُمْ وَظَنَنتُمْ ظَنَّ السَّوْءِ وَكُنتُمْ قَوْمًا بُورًا {12} وَمَن لَّمْ يُؤْمِن بِاللهِ وَرَسُولِهِ فَإِنَّا أَعْتَدْنَا لِلْكَافِرِينَ سَعِيرًا

{13} وَلِلَّهِ مُلْكُ السَّمَاوَاتِ وَالْأَرْضِ يَغْفِرُ لِمَن يَشَاءُ وَيُعَذِّبُ مَن يَشَاءُ وَكَانَ اللَّهُ غَفُورًا رَّحِيمًا {14} سَيَقُولُ الْمُخَلَّفُونَ إِذَا انطَلَقْتُمْ إِلَى مَغَانِمَ لِتَأْخُذُوهَا ذَرُونَا نَتَّبِعْكُمْ يُرِيدُونَ أَن يُبَدِّلُوا كَلَامَ اللَّهِ قُل لَّن تَتَّبِعُونَا كَذَلِكُمْ قَالَ اللَّهُ مِن قَبْلُ فَسَيَقُولُونَ بَلْ تَحْسُدُونَنَا بَلْ كَانُوا لَا يَفْقَهُونَ إِلَّا قَلِيلًا {15} قُل لِّلْمُخَلَّفِينَ مِنَ الْأَعْرَابِ سَتُدْعَوْنَ إِلَى قَوْمٍ أُولِي بَأْسٍ شَدِيدٍ تُقَاتِلُونَهُمْ أَوْ يُسْلِمُونَ فَإِن تُطِيعُوا يُؤْتِكُمُ اللَّهُ أَجْرًا حَسَنًا وَإِن تَتَوَلَّوْا كَمَا تَوَلَّيْتُم مِّن قَبْلُ يُعَذِّبْكُمْ عَذَابًا أَلِيمًا {16} لَّيْسَ عَلَى الْأَعْمَى حَرَجٌ وَلَا عَلَى الْأَعْرَجِ حَرَجٌ وَلَا عَلَى الْمَرِيضِ حَرَجٌ وَمَن يُطِعِ اللَّهَ وَرَسُولَهُ يُدْخِلْهُ جَنَّاتٍ تَجْرِي مِن تَحْتِهَا الْأَنْهَارُ وَمَن يَتَوَلَّ يُعَذِّبْهُ عَذَابًا أَلِيمًا {17} لَّقَدْ رَضِيَ اللَّهُ عَنِ الْمُؤْمِنِينَ إِذْ يُبَايِعُونَكَ تَحْتَ الشَّجَرَةِ فَعَلِمَ مَا فِي قُلُوبِهِمْ فَأَنزَلَ السَّكِينَةَ عَلَيْهِمْ وَأَثَابَهُمْ فَتْحًا قَرِيبًا {18} وَمَغَانِمَ كَثِيرَةً يَأْخُذُونَهَا وَكَانَ اللَّهُ عَزِيزًا حَكِيمًا {19} وَعَدَكُمُ اللَّهُ مَغَانِمَ كَثِيرَةً تَأْخُذُونَهَا فَعَجَّلَ لَكُمْ هَذِهِ وَكَفَّ أَيْدِيَ النَّاسِ عَنكُمْ وَلِتَكُونَ آيَةً لِّلْمُؤْمِنِينَ وَيَهْدِيَكُمْ صِرَاطًا مُّسْتَقِيمًا {20} وَأُخْرَى لَمْ تَقْدِرُوا عَلَيْهَا قَدْ أَحَاطَ اللَّهُ بِهَا وَكَانَ اللَّهُ عَلَى كُلِّ شَيْءٍ قَدِيرًا {21} وَلَوْ قَاتَلَكُمُ الَّذِينَ كَفَرُوا لَوَلَّوُا الْأَدْبَارَ ثُمَّ لَا يَجِدُونَ وَلِيًّا وَلَا نَصِيرًا {22} سُنَّةَ اللَّهِ الَّتِي قَدْ خَلَتْ مِن قَبْلُ وَلَن تَجِدَ لِسُنَّةِ اللَّهِ تَبْدِيلًا {23} وَهُوَ الَّذِي كَفَّ أَيْدِيَهُمْ عَنكُمْ وَأَيْدِيَكُمْ عَنْهُم بِبَطْنِ مَكَّةَ مِن بَعْدِ أَنْ أَظْفَرَكُمْ عَلَيْهِمْ وَكَانَ اللَّهُ بِمَا تَعْمَلُونَ بَصِيرًا {24} هُمُ الَّذِينَ كَفَرُوا وَصَدُّوكُمْ عَنِ الْمَسْجِدِ الْحَرَامِ وَالْهَدْيَ مَعْكُوفًا أَن يَبْلُغَ مَحِلَّهُ وَلَوْلَا رِجَالٌ مُّؤْمِنُونَ وَنِسَاءٌ مُّؤْمِنَاتٌ لَّمْ تَعْلَمُوهُمْ أَن تَطَئُوهُمْ فَتُصِيبَكُم مِّنْهُم مَّعَرَّةٌ بِغَيْرِ عِلْمٍ لِّيُدْخِلَ اللَّهُ فِي رَحْمَتِهِ مَن يَشَاءُ لَوْ تَزَيَّلُوا لَعَذَّبْنَا الَّذِينَ كَفَرُوا مِنْهُمْ عَذَابًا أَلِيمًا {25} إِذْ جَعَلَ الَّذِينَ كَفَرُوا فِي قُلُوبِهِمُ الْحَمِيَّةَ حَمِيَّةَ الْجَاهِلِيَّةِ فَأَنزَلَ اللَّهُ سَكِينَتَهُ عَلَى رَسُولِهِ وَعَلَى الْمُؤْمِنِينَ وَأَلْزَمَهُمْ كَلِمَةَ التَّقْوَى وَكَانُوا أَحَقَّ بِهَا وَأَهْلَهَا وَكَانَ اللَّهُ بِكُلِّ شَيْءٍ عَلِيمًا {26} لَّقَدْ صَدَقَ اللَّهُ رَسُولَهُ الرُّؤْيَا بِالْحَقِّ لَتَدْخُلُنَّ الْمَسْجِدَ الْحَرَامَ إِن شَاءَ اللَّهُ آمِنِينَ مُحَلِّقِينَ رُؤُوسَكُمْ وَمُقَصِّرِينَ لَا تَخَافُونَ فَعَلِمَ مَا لَمْ تَعْلَمُوا فَجَعَلَ مِن دُونِ ذَلِكَ فَتْحًا قَرِيبًا {27} هُوَ الَّذِي أَرْسَلَ رَسُولَهُ بِالْهُدَى وَدِينِ الْحَقِّ لِيُظْهِرَهُ عَلَى الدِّينِ كُلِّهِ وَكَفَى بِاللَّهِ شَهِيدًا {28} مُّحَمَّدٌ رَّسُولُ اللَّهِ وَالَّذِينَ مَعَهُ أَشِدَّاءُ عَلَى الْكُفَّارِ رُحَمَاءُ بَيْنَهُمْ تَرَاهُمْ رُكَّعًا سُجَّدًا يَبْتَغُونَ فَضْلًا مِّنَ اللَّهِ وَرِضْوَانًا سِيمَاهُمْ فِي وُجُوهِهِم مِّنْ أَثَرِ السُّجُودِ ذَلِكَ مَثَلُهُمْ فِي التَّوْرَاةِ وَمَثَلُهُمْ فِي الْإِنجِيلِ كَزَرْعٍ أَخْرَجَ شَطْأَهُ فَآزَرَهُ فَاسْتَغْلَظَ فَاسْتَوَى عَلَى سُوقِهِ يُعْجِبُ الزُّرَّاعَ لِيَغِيظَ بِهِمُ الْكُفَّارَ وَعَدَ اللَّهُ الَّذِينَ آمَنُوا وَعَمِلُوا الصَّالِحَاتِ مِنْهُم مَّغْفِرَةً وَأَجْرًا عَظِيمًا {29}

A`oodhu biLlaahi min al-shayṭaani l-rajeem

Bismi Llaahi l-raḥmaani l-raḥeem

1 innaa fataḥnaa laka fatḥan mubeenan 2 liyaghfira laka Llaahu maa taqaddam min dhanbika wa maa ta'akh-khara wayutimma ni`matahu `alayka wa yahdiyaka ṣiraaṭan mustaqeeman 3 wa yanṣuraka Llaahu naṣran `azeezan 4 huwa lladhee anzala l-sakeenata fee quloobi l-mu'mineena liyazdadoo eemaanan ma`a eemaanihim wa liLlaahi junoodu l-samawaati wal-arḍi wa kaana Llaahu `aleeman ḥakeeman 5 liyudkhila l-mu'mineena wal-mu'minaati jannatin tajree min taḥtihaa l-anhaaru khaalideena feehaa wa yukaffira `anhum sayyi'aatihim wa kaana dhaalika `inda Llaahi fawzan `aẓeeman 6 wa yu`adh-dhiba l-munaafiqeena wal-munaafiqaati wal-mushrikeena wal-mushrikaati l-ẓaanneena biLlaahi ẓanna l-saw'i `alayhim daa'iratu l-saw'i wa ghaḍiba Llaahu `alayhim wa la`anahum wa `adda lahum jahannama wa saa'at maṣeeran 7 wa liLlaahi junoodu l-samawaati wal-arḍi wa kaana Llaahu `azeezan ḥakeeman 8 innaa arsalnaka shaahidan wa mubash-shiran wa nadheeran 9 litu'minoo biLlaahi wa rasoolihi wa tu`azziroohu wa tuwaqqiroohu wa tusabbiḥoohu bukratan wa aṣeelan 10 inna lladheena yubaayi`oonaka innama yubaayi`oona Llaaha yadu Llaahi fawqa aydeehim faman nakatha fa'innamaa yankuthu `alaa nafsihi waman awfaa bimaa `aahada `alayhu Llaaha fasayu'teehi ajran `aẓeeman 11 sayaqoolu laka l-mukhallafoona mina l-a`raabi shaghalatnaa amwaalunaa wa ahloonaa fa'istaghfir lanaa yaqooloona bil-sinatihim maa laysa fee quloobihim qul faman yamliku lakum mina Llaahi shay'in in araada bikum ḍarran aw araada bikum naf`an bal kaana Llaahu bimaa ta`maloona khabeeran 12 bal ẓanantum an lan yanqaliba l-rasoolu wal-mu'minoona ilaa ahleehim abadan wa zuyyina dhaalika fee quloobikum wa ẓanantum ẓanna l-saw'i wa kuntum qawman booran 13 w man lam yu'min biLlaahi wa rasoolihi fa'inna a`atadnaa lil-kaafireena sa`eeran 14 wa liLlaahi mulku l-samawaati wal-arḍi yaghfiru liman yashaa' wa yu`adh-dhibu man yashaa' wa kaana Llaahu ghafooran raḥeeman 15 sayaqoolu l-mukhallafoona idhaa inṭalaqtum ilaa maghaanima lita`khudhoohaa dharoona nattabi`kum yureedoona an yubaddiloo kalaama Llaahi qul lan tattabi`oonaa kadhaalikum qaala Llaahu min qablu fasayaqooloona bal taḥsudoonaa bal kaanoo laa yafqahoona illaa qaleelan 16 qul lil-mukhallafeena mina l-a`rabi satud`awna ilaa qawmin oolaa ba'sin

shadeedin tuqaatiloonahum aw yuslimoona fa'in tuṭee'oo yu'tikumu Llaahu ajran hasanan wa'in tatawallaw kamaa tawallaytum main qablu yu`adh-dhibkum `adhaaban aleeman 17 laysa `alaa l-a`maa ḥarajun wa laa `alaa l-a`raji ḥarajun wa laa `alaa l-mareeḍi ḥarajun wa man yuṭi`i Llaahi wa rasoolahu yudkhilhu jannaatin tajree min taḥtihaa l-anhaaru wa man yatawalla yu`adh-dhibhu `adhaaban aleeman 18 laqad raḍiya Llaahu `ani l-mu'mineena idh yubaayi`oonaka taḥta l-shajarati fa`alima maa fee quloobihum fa'anzala l-sakeenata `alayhim wa athaabahum fatḥan qareeban 19 wa maghaanima katheeratan ya'khudhoonahaa wa kaana Llaahu `azeezan ḥakeeman 20 wa `adakumu Llaahu maghaanima katheeratan ta'khudhoonaha fa`ajjala lakum haadhihi wakaffa aydiya l-naasi `ankum wa litakoona aayatan lil-mu'mineena wa yahdiyakum ṣiraaṭan mustaqeeman 21 wa ukhraa lam taqdiroo `alayhaa qad aḥaaṭa Llaahu bihaa wa kaana Llaahu `alaa kulli shay'in qadeeran 22 wa law qaatalakumu lladheena kafaroo lawallawoo l-adbaara thumma laa yajidoona wa liyyan wa laa naṣeeran 23 sunnata Llaahi llatee qad khalat min qablu wa lan tajida lisunnati Llaahi tabdeelan 24 wa huwa lladhee kaffa aydiyahum `ankum wa aydiyakum `anhum bibaṭni makkata min ba`di an aẓfarakum `alayhim wa kaana Llaahu bimaa ta`maloona baṣeeran 25 humu lladheena kafaroo wa ṣaddookum `ani l-masjidi l-ḥarami wal-hadya ma`koofan an yablugha maḥillahu wa lawlaa rijaalun mu'minoona wa nisaa'un mu'minaatun lam ta`lamoohum an taṭa'oohum fatuṣeebakum minhum ma`arratun bighayri `ilmin liyudkhila Llaahu fee raḥmatihi man yashaa' law tazayyaloo la`adh-dhabnaa lladheena kafaroo minhum `adhaaban aleeman 26 idh ja`ala ladheena kafaroo quloobihimu l-ḥamiyyata ḥamiyyata l-jaahiliyyati fa'anzala Llaahu sakeenatahu `alaa rasoolihi wa `alaa l-mu'mineena wa alzamahum kalimata l-taqwaa wa kaanoo l-ḥaqqa bihaa wa ahlaha wa kaana Llaahu bi kulli shay'in `aleeman 27 laqad ṣadaqa Llaahu rasoolahu l-ru'yaa bil-ḥaqqi latadkhulunna l-masjida l-ḥaraama in shaa' Alaahu amineena muḥalliqeena ru'oosakum wa muqaṣṣireena laa takhafoona fa`alima maa lam ta`lamoo fa`ala min dooni dhaalika fatḥan qareeban 28 huwa lladhee arsala rasoolahu bil-hudaa wa deeni l-ḥaqqi liyuẓhirahu `alaa l-deeni kullihi wa kafaa bi Llaahi shaheedan 29 Muḥammadun rasoolu Llaahu wa lladheena ma`ahu ashidda' `alaa l-kuffaari ruḥamaa' baynahum taraahum rukka`an sujjadan yabtaghoona faḍlan mina Llaahu wa riḍwaanan seemaahum fee wujoohihim min athari l-sujoodi dhaalika mathaluhum fee l-tawraati wa mathaluhum fee l-injeeli kazar`in akhraja shaṭahu fa'aazarahu fa'istaghlaẓtha fa'istawaa `alaa sooqihi yu`jibu l-zurra`a liyagheeẓa bihimu l-kuffaara wa`ada Llaahu lladheena aamanoo wa`amiloo l-ṣaaliḥaati minhum maghfiratan wa ajran `aẓeeman

By the one who is denoted by the name Allah (who created my being with His Names in accord with the meaning of the letter 'B'), **the Rahman, the Rahim.**

1. Indeed, we have given you the Clear Conquest (fath; the clear observation of the system of the reality)!

2. That Allah may forgive (cover/conceal) **your past and** (in spite of the conquest – fath) **future misdeeds** (the veils resulting from corporeality) **and complete His favor upon you and guide you to the experience of your reality** (essence).

3. Allah will lead you to an unmatched mighty victory!

4. It is HU who sends tranquility (sense of security) **to the hearts of the believers that they would increase in faith! The soldiers of the heavens and the earth belong to Allah! Allah is the Aleem, the Hakim.**

5. And to admit the believing men and women to Paradises, underneath which rivers flow, in which they will abide eternally, in order to remove from them their bad deeds... This is the great attainment in the sight of Allah!

6. And that He may punish the hypocrite men and women and the dualist men and women who misperceive Allah who comprises their essential reality with His Names (as a god)! **May the evil turn of fortune be upon them for their assumptions! Allah's wrath and curse is upon them** (distanced them from the experience of the reality due to their denial) **and prepared Hell for them! What a wretched place of return!**

7. The soldiers (forces) **of the heavens and the earth belong to Allah... Allah is the Aziz, the Hakim.**

8. Indeed, we disclosed you as a witness, giver of good news and as a warner!

9. So, believe in Allah – your essential reality with His Names – **and His Rasul; support him, exalt and respect him, and engage in glorifying Him** (tasbih) **by morning and night.**

10. Indeed, (my Rasul) **those who pledge allegiance to you have pledged allegiance to Allah. The hand of Allah is over their hands** (the hand of Allah administers over the hands of those who pledge allegiance)**! So, he who breaks his word has broken it against his own self, and he who keeps his word to Allah will be given a great reward!**

11. Those who remained behind of the Bedouins say, "Our properties and children kept us occupied, so ask forgiveness for us"... But they say with their tongues what they do not actually mean! Say, "Who can go against the will of Allah if He intended to give you harm or if He willed to benefit you?"... No, Allah is aware of what you do (as the creator of your actions).

12. You thought the Rasul and the believers would not return to their families! This seemed pleasing to your consciousness, and thus you assumed a bad assumption and became a people worthy of suffering!

13. Whoever does not believe in Allah and His Rasul, as their essential reality with His Names, let them know that We have prepared a blaze (of fire – waves of radiation) **for those who deny the knowledge of the reality.**

14. The sovereignty of the heavens and the earth is for (the manifestation of the Names of) **Allah! He forgives** (covers the offensive state of) **whom He wills and gives suffering** (the consequence of corporeality) **to whom He wills! Allah is the Ghafur, the Rahim.**

15. Those who remained behind will say when you go to collect the spoils of war, "Let us come with you." They want to change the words of Allah. Say, "You can never follow us; for this is what Allah said (decreed) **before"... Then they will say, "No, you envy us"... On the contrary, they are people devoid of understanding!**

16. Say to the Bedouins who remained behind, "You will be called to battle with a people of great strength and might... Either you fight them or they will submit (to Islam). If you obey, Allah will give you a good reward... But if you turn away as you turned away before, then He will subject you to a great suffering."

17. There is no obligation upon the blind, the cripple and the one who is ill! If he obeys Allah and His Rasul He will admit him to Paradises underneath which rivers flow... But whoever turns away, He will punish him with a severe suffering.

18. Indeed, Allah was pleased with the believers when they pledged allegiance to you under the tree. He knew what was in their hearts, so He gave tranquility (serenity) to their hearts and rewarded them with an imminent conquest (certainty).

19. And He gave them many spoils of war... Allah is the Aziz, the Hakim.

20. Allah has promised many spoils of war to you... And He has hastened this for you and withheld the hands of people from you that this may be a sign for the believers and that He may guide you to a straight path.

21. And He promised other things to them, which you are not capable of, that Allah had already encompassed (internally and externally). Allah is Qadir over all things.

22. If those who deny the knowledge of the reality were to fight with you they would surely have turned their backs in flight... And then they would not have found a friend (protector) or a helper.

23. This is the established sunnatullah! And never will you find in the sunnatullah (the mechanics of Allah's system) any change!

24. It is HU who withheld their hands from you and your hands from them in the center of Mecca after He made you overcome them. Allah is Basir of your actions (as their creator).

25. They are those who deny the knowledge of the reality, obstruct you from the Masjid al-Haram, and prevent the offerings from reaching their places... **If it was not for the believing men and women** (among them), **of whom you are unaware, and thus could inadvertently trample and then be upset by it** (Allah would not have prevented the battle)**... This was so that Allah may admit whom He wills to His grace... If the** (believers and nonbelievers) **had been separate from one another, surely We would have punished those who disbelieved with a severe suffering.** (Suffering does not befall a place where there are righteous people... 8:33, 29:32)

26. **The deniers of the knowledge of the reality had put patriotism** (ethnocentricity, pride out of ignorance) **and narrow-mindedness** (conservatism) **into their hearts... Allah gave tranquility** (serenity) **to those who believed in Allah and His Rasul and secured them upon the Truth: "There is no god, only Allah"** (La ilaha illaAllah)**... They were those who experienced this reality and were deserving of it... Allah is Aleem of all things.**

27. **Indeed, Allah confirmed to His Rasul his vision in Truth... InshaAllah** (with the manifestation of the Names of Allah comprising your essence)**, you will most definitely enter the Masjid al-Haram, in safety, with** (some of) **your heads shaved or shortened, without any fear!** (Allah) **knowing what you do not know, has arranged before this an imminent conquest** (of closeness/certainty).

28. **He disclosed His Rasul as the articulator of the reality and upon the religion of Truth** (the understanding of the reality of sunnatullah, which is the system and order manifesting the Names of Allah) **superior to all understanding of religion! And sufficient is Allah** (with His presence in their being) **as Shahid** (Witness).

29. **Muhammad is the Rasul of Allah! Those with him are stern against the deniers of the reality, but compassionate among themselves... You will see them bowing** (in awe of the observation of Allah's Names as the absolute administrator over existence at all times)**, prostrating** (with the awareness that existence comprises only the Names and thus experiencing their nonexistence with the realization of not having a separate independent being)**, seeking the bounty** (the awareness of the forces of the Names) **and the pleasure**

of Allah (enlightenment to the reality and the ability to actualize its potentials)**... And on their faces** (consciousness) **is the mark of prostration** (the comprehension of their nonexistence)**! This is their metaphoric description in the Torah** (laws in regards to the identity-self)**... And their description** (similitude) **in the Gospel is that of a plant, which produces its offshoots and strengthens them so they grow firm and stand upon their stalks, giving delight to its sowers... Allah does this to enrage the deniers** (coverers) **of the reality with them** (the manifestations of His Names)**! Allah has promised those who believe and fulfill its requisites, forgiveness and a great reward.**

In terms of its literal meaning, chapter Fath explains the Hudaibiya Treaty and the conquering of Mecca. But the scope of its meaning is certainly not limited to this.

The deeper meaning of this chapter pertains to much profound and elevated truths known only to the qualified ones.

It is not possible to disclose these, but I wish not to move on without sharing some insight in regard to the deeper meaning of the first three verses, for they point to a significant truth of Sufism.

Let us re-read these three verses:

1. Indeed, we have given you the Clear Conquest (fath; the clear observation of the system of the reality)!

2. That Allah may forgive (cover/conceal) your past and (in spite of the conquest – fath) future misdeeds (the veils resulting from corporeality) and complete His favor upon you and guide you to the experience of your reality (essence).

3. Allah will lead you to an unmatched mighty victory!

Since the obvious literal meaning of this chapter can be found in every translation and interpretation of the Quran, there is no need for me to repeat it here. As for the hidden inner meaning that Allah has allowed me to understand in line with the clarity and irfan with which He has blessed me...

The word 'fath' means the opening or conquering of something seemingly unattainable. As such, the greatest attainment in the worldly life is to conquer the Intermediary Realm (barzakh), which is a stage of the life after – and the only way for this is to 'die while living,' as the Sufis would say!

There are two types of *conquest* (*fath*): external and internal...

Internal conquest is also of two types:

  a. Self-conquest

  b. Fath-i Mubin

Essentially, there are seven degrees of conquest. One is said to have attained conquest when the first of these degrees is actualized.

Conquest is *not* a state that can reached by personal effort.

It is a state of living in this world with the qualities of the spirit rather than the body. That is to say, while living in this body and this dimension, the person is relinquished from his bodily ties as though he has died and moves on to the life of the spirit. It is the complete experience of the event to which Sufism refers to as "dying before death." As far as we have been taught, the number of people who are able to attain this state, called the fath-i nurani do not exceed forty individuals.

Conquest can be further categorized as:

  1. Fath-i dhulmani

  2. Fath-i nurani

Fath-i dhulmani can become apparent on all people, whether Muslim or not. What appears to be the result of 'enlightenment', especially observable on Hindu and Buddhist sages and monks, is generally this state. In religious terms it is called istidraj, which refers to supernatural states that are driven by ego and jinn-based energies, observable on those who lack the light (nur) of faith.

There are two significant signs of fath-i dhulmani. Firstly, a person in this state does not accept Muhammad (saw) as the Rasul of Allah, and secondly, he is not saved from the illusion of having a separate individual self!

Those who reach the state of fath-i dhulmani may know your past and be present at a few places simultaneously. They may see the states of the deceased and communicate with the jinn, along with other seemingly superatural behaviors.

Those who reach the state of fath-i nurani show similar abilities, but their distinction is, after adapting to this life in a short time, they continue to develop and reach the third station of fath where they meet the Rasul of Allah (saw) and other Nabis and saints to learn of the states of the intermediary realm (barzakh), after which they take their place among the Rijali Ghayb (Men of the Unknown).

When one reaches the state of fath-i mubin, it is essential that they are able to correctly maintain this state. That is, when one experiences fath-i mubin and is freed from the constraints of the body, it is easy to get carried away and completely sever one's bodily ties, leading to death in a literal sense.

So long as physical death does not occur, one who reaches the state of fath-i mubin continues to progress by increasing their strength and brain capacity and elevating their level of knowledge...

No further information regarding this state may be disclosed here, so let us continue to explore the meaning of the above verses:

"Indeed, we have given you the Clear Conquest (fath; the clear observation of the system of the reality)!"[92]

This 'definite and clear conquest' may not be attained through personal effort; it is entirely a favor from Allah. Thus, the person

---

[92] Quran 48:1.

lives in the world as a citizen of the intermediary realm, aware of all the intrinsic meanings and wisdom behind the things of the world, and no misdeed will be produced by them.

Living at this reality then, Allah will 'forgive (cover/conceal) your past and future misdeeds (the veils resulting from corporeality)' that prevent the observation of the Oneness of Allah and complete His favor upon you by giving you fath – the experience of your reality (essence).

Fath-i nurani is the greatest attainment one can ever have in the life of this world; it is almost like living in Paradise while on earth.

And He will 'lead you to an unmatched mighty victory.'

24

AL-WAQI'A

(56ᵗʰ Chapter)

بِسْمِ اللهِ الرَّحْمنِ الرَّحِيمِ

إِذَا وَقَعَتِ الْوَاقِعَةُ {1} لَيْسَ لِوَقْعَتِهَا كَاذِبَةٌ {2} خَافِضَةٌ رَّافِعَةٌ {3} إِذَا رُجَّتِ الْأَرْضُ رَجًّا {4} وَبُسَّتِ الْجِبَالُ بَسًّا {5} فَكَانَتْ هَبَاء مُّنبَثًّا {6} وَكُنتُمْ أَزْوَاجًا ثَلَاثَةً {7} فَأَصْحَابُ الْمَيْمَنَةِ مَا أَصْحَابُ الْمَيْمَنَةِ {8} وَأَصْحَابُ الْمَشْأَمَةِ مَا أَصْحَابُ الْمَشْأَمَةِ {9} وَالسَّابِقُونَ السَّابِقُونَ {10} أُوْلَئِكَ الْمُقَرَّبُونَ {11} فِي جَنَّاتِ النَّعِيمِ {12} ثُلَّةٌ مِّنَ الْأَوَّلِينَ {13} وَقَلِيلٌ مِّنَ الْآخِرِينَ {14} عَلَى سُرُرٍ مَّوْضُونَةٍ {15} مُّتَّكِئِينَ عَلَيْهَا مُتَقَابِلِينَ {16} يَطُوفُ عَلَيْهِمْ وِلْدَانٌ مُّخَلَّدُونَ {17} بِأَكْوَابٍ وَأَبَارِيقَ وَكَأْسٍ مِّن مَّعِينٍ {18} لَا يُصَدَّعُونَ عَنْهَا وَلَا يُنزِفُونَ {19} وَفَاكِهَةٍ مِّمَّا يَتَخَيَّرُونَ {20} وَلَحْمِ طَيْرٍ مِّمَّا يَشْتَهُونَ {21} وَحُورٌ عِينٌ {22} كَأَمْثَالِ اللُّؤْلُؤِ الْمَكْنُونِ {23} جَزَاء بِمَا كَانُوا يَعْمَلُونَ {24} لَا يَسْمَعُونَ فِيهَا لَغْوًا وَلَا تَأْثِيمًا {25} إِلَّا قِيلًا سَلَامًا سَلَامًا {26} وَأَصْحَابُ الْيَمِينِ مَا أَصْحَابُ الْيَمِينِ {27} فِي سِدْرٍ مَّخْضُودٍ {28} وَطَلْحٍ مَّنضُودٍ {29} وَظِلٍّ مَّمْدُودٍ {30} وَمَاء مَّسْكُوبٍ {31} وَفَاكِهَةٍ كَثِيرَةٍ {32} لَّا مَقْطُوعَةٍ وَلَا مَمْنُوعَةٍ {33} وَفُرُشٍ مَّرْفُوعَةٍ {34} إِنَّا أَنشَأْنَاهُنَّ إِنشَاء {35} فَجَعَلْنَاهُنَّ أَبْكَارًا {36} عُرُبًا أَتْرَابًا {37} لِّأَصْحَابِ الْيَمِينِ {38} ثُلَّةٌ مِّنَ الْأَوَّلِينَ {39} وَثُلَّةٌ مِّنَ الْآخِرِينَ {40} وَأَصْحَابُ الشِّمَالِ مَا أَصْحَابُ الشِّمَالِ {41} فِي سَمُومٍ وَحَمِيمٍ {42} وَظِلٍّ

مِّن يَحْمُومٍ {43} لَّا بَارِدٍ وَلَا كَرِيمٍ {44} إِنَّهُمْ كَانُوا قَبْلَ ذَلِكَ مُتْرَفِينَ {45} وَكَانُوا يُصِرُّونَ عَلَى الْحِنثِ الْعَظِيمِ {46} وَكَانُوا يَقُولُونَ أَئِذَا مِتْنَا وَكُنَّا تُرَابًا وَعِظَامًا أَئِنَّا لَمَبْعُوثُونَ {47} أَوَ آبَاؤُنَا الْأَوَّلُونَ {48} قُلْ إِنَّ الْأَوَّلِينَ وَالْآخِرِينَ {49} لَمَجْمُوعُونَ إِلَى مِيقَاتِ يَوْمٍ مَّعْلُومٍ {50} ثُمَّ إِنَّكُمْ أَيُّهَا الضَّالُّونَ الْمُكَذِّبُونَ {51} لَآكِلُونَ مِن شَجَرٍ مِّن زَقُّومٍ {52} فَمَالِئُونَ مِنْهَا الْبُطُونَ {53} فَشَارِبُونَ عَلَيْهِ مِنَ الْحَمِيمِ {54} فَشَارِبُونَ شُرْبَ الْهِيمِ {55} هَذَا نُزُلُهُمْ يَوْمَ الدِّينِ {56} نَحْنُ خَلَقْنَاكُمْ فَلَوْلَا تُصَدِّقُونَ {57} أَفَرَأَيْتُم مَّا تُمْنُونَ {58} أَأَنتُمْ تَخْلُقُونَهُ أَمْ نَحْنُ الْخَالِقُونَ {59} نَحْنُ قَدَّرْنَا بَيْنَكُمُ الْمَوْتَ وَمَا نَحْنُ بِمَسْبُوقِينَ {60} عَلَى أَن نُّبَدِّلَ أَمْثَالَكُمْ وَنُنشِئَكُمْ فِي مَا لَا تَعْلَمُونَ {61} وَلَقَدْ عَلِمْتُمُ النَّشْأَةَ الْأُولَى فَلَوْلَا تَذَكَّرُونَ {62} أَفَرَأَيْتُم مَّا تَحْرُثُونَ {63} أَأَنتُمْ تَزْرَعُونَهُ أَمْ نَحْنُ الزَّارِعُونَ {64} لَوْ نَشَاء لَجَعَلْنَاهُ حُطَامًا فَظَلْتُمْ تَفَكَّهُونَ {65} إِنَّا لَمُغْرَمُونَ {66} بَلْ نَحْنُ مَحْرُومُونَ {67} أَفَرَأَيْتُمُ الْمَاء الَّذِي تَشْرَبُونَ {68} أَأَنتُمْ أَنزَلْتُمُوهُ مِنَ الْمُزْنِ أَمْ نَحْنُ الْمُنزِلُونَ {69} لَوْ نَشَاء جَعَلْنَاهُ أُجَاجًا فَلَوْلَا تَشْكُرُونَ {70} أَفَرَأَيْتُمُ النَّارَ الَّتِي تُورُونَ {71} أَأَنتُمْ أَنشَأْتُمْ شَجَرَتَهَا أَمْ نَحْنُ الْمُنشِئُونَ {72} نَحْنُ جَعَلْنَاهَا تَذْكِرَةً وَمَتَاعًا لِّلْمُقْوِينَ {73} فَسَبِّحْ بِاسْمِ رَبِّكَ الْعَظِيمِ {74} فَلَا أُقْسِمُ بِمَوَاقِعِ النُّجُومِ {75} وَإِنَّهُ لَقَسَمٌ لَّوْ تَعْلَمُونَ عَظِيمٌ {76} إِنَّهُ لَقُرْآنٌ كَرِيمٌ {77} فِي كِتَابٍ مَّكْنُونٍ {78} لَّا يَمَسُّهُ إِلَّا الْمُطَهَّرُونَ {79} تَنزِيلٌ مِّن رَّبِّ الْعَالَمِينَ {80} أَفَبِهَذَا الْحَدِيثِ أَنتُم مُّدْهِنُونَ {81} وَتَجْعَلُونَ رِزْقَكُمْ أَنَّكُمْ تُكَذِّبُونَ {82} فَلَوْلَا إِذَا بَلَغَتِ الْحُلْقُومَ {83} وَأَنتُمْ حِينَئِذٍ تَنظُرُونَ {84} وَنَحْنُ أَقْرَبُ إِلَيْهِ مِنكُمْ وَلَكِن لَّا تُبْصِرُونَ {85} فَلَوْلَا إِن كُنتُمْ غَيْرَ مَدِينِينَ {86} تَرْجِعُونَهَا إِن كُنتُمْ صَادِقِينَ {87} فَأَمَّا إِن كَانَ مِنَ الْمُقَرَّبِينَ {88} فَرَوْحٌ وَرَيْحَانٌ وَجَنَّةُ نَعِيمٍ {89} وَأَمَّا إِن كَانَ مِنَ أَصْحَابِ الْيَمِينِ {90} فَسَلَامٌ لَّكَ مِنْ أَصْحَابِ الْيَمِينِ {91} وَأَمَّا إِن كَانَ مِنَ الْمُكَذِّبِينَ الضَّالِّينَ {92} فَنُزُلٌ مِّنْ حَمِيمٍ {93} وَتَصْلِيَةُ جَحِيمٍ {94} إِنَّ هَذَا لَهُوَ حَقُّ الْيَقِينِ {95} فَسَبِّحْ بِاسْمِ رَبِّكَ الْعَظِيمِ {96}

A`oodhu biLlaahi min al-shayṭaani l-rajeem

Bismi Llaahi l-raḥmaani l-raḥeem

1 Idhaa waqa`ati l-waaqi`atu 2 laysa li-waq`atihaa kaadhibatun 3 khaafiḍatun raafi`atun 4 idhaa rujjati l-arḍu rajjan 5 wa bussati l-jibaalu bassan 6 fakaanat habaa' munbath-thaa 7 wa kuntum azwaajan thalaathatan 8 fa'aṣḥaabu l-maymanati 9 wa'aṣḥaabu l-mashamati maa aṣḥaabu l-mashamati 10 wa l-sabiqoona l-saabiqoona 11 oolaa'ika l-muqarraboona 12 fee jannaati l-na`eemi 13 thullatun mina l-awwaleena 14 wa qaleenun mina l-aakhireena 15 `alaa sururin mawḍoonatin 16 muttaki'eena `alayhaa mutaqaabileena 17 yaṭoofu `alayhim wildaanun mukhalladoona 18 yatakhayyaroona 21 wa laḥmi ṭayrin mimmaa yashtahoona 22 wa ḥoorun `eenun 23 ka'amthaali l-lu'lu'i l-maknooni 24 jazaa' bimaa kaanoo ya`maloona 25 laa yasma`oona feehaa laghwan wa laa ta'theeman 26 illaa qeelan salaaman salaaman 27 wa aṣḥaabu l-yameeni maa aṣḥaabu l-yameeni 28 fee sidrin makhḍoodin 29 wa ṭalḥilin manḍoodin 30 waẓillin mamdoodin 31 wa maa'in maskoobin 32 wa faakihatin katheeratin 33 laa maqṭoo`atin wa laa mamnoo`atin 34 wa furushin marfoo`atin 35 inaa anshaa'naahunna inshaa' 36 faja`alnaahunna abkaaran 37 `uruban atraaban 38 li'aṣḥaabi l-yameeni 39 thullatun mina l-awwaleena 40 wa thullatun mina l-aakhireena 41 wa aṣḥaabu l-shimaali maa aṣḥaabu l-shimaali 42 fee samoomin wa ḥameemin 43 wa ẓillin min yaḥmoomin 44 laa baaridin wa laa kareem 45 innahum kaanoo qabla dhaalika mutrafeena 46 wa kaanoo yuṣirroona `alaa l-ḥinthi l-`aẓeemi 47 wa kaanoo yaqooloona a'idhaa mitnaa wa kunnaa turaaban wa `iẓaaman a'inna lamab`oothoona 48 awa aabaa'unaa l-awwaloona 49 qul inna al-awwaleena wal-aakhireena 50 lamajmoo`oona ilaa meeqaati yawmin ma`loomin 51 thumma innakum ayyuhaa l-ḍaalloona l-mukadh-dhiboona 52 laakiloona min shajarin min zaqqoomin 53 famaali'oona minhaa l-buṭoona 54 fashaariboona `alayhi mina l-ḥameemi 55 fashaariboona shurba l-ḥeemi 56 haadhaa nuzuluhum yawma l-deeni 57 naḥnu khalaqnaakum falawlaa tuṣaddiqoona 58 afaraa'aytum maa tumnoona 59 a'antum takhluqoonahu am naḥnu l-khaaliqoona 60 naḥnu qaddarna baynakumu l-mawta wa maa naḥnu bi masbooqwwna 61 `alaa an nubaddila amthalaakum wa nunshi'akum fee ma laa ta`lamoona 62 wa laqad `alimtumu l-nashaa'ta l-oolaa fa lawlaa tadhakkiroona 63 afara'aytum maa taḥruthoona 64 a'antum

tazra`oonahu am nahnu l-zari`oona 65 law nashaa' laja`alnahu
hutaaman fazalthum tafakkahoona 66 inna lamughramoona 67 bal
nahnu mahroomoona 68 afara'aytumu l-maa lladhee tashraboona 69
a'antum anzaltumoohu mina l-muzni am nahnu l-munziloona 70 law
nashaa' ja`alnahu ujaajan fa lawlaa tashraboona 71 afara'autumu l-
naara llatee tooroona 72 a'antum ansha'tum shajaratahaa am nahnu
l-munshi'oona 73 nahnu ja`alnahaa tadhkiratan wa mataa`an lil-
muqweena 47 fasabbih bismi rabbika l-`aemi 75 fa laa uqsimu
bimawaaqi`i l-nujoomi 76 wa innahu laqasamun law ta`lamoona
`azeemun 77 innahu laqur'aanun kareemun 78 fee kitaabin
maknoonin 79 laa yamassuhu illaa l-mutahharoona 80 tanzeelun min
rabbi l-`alameena 81 afabihadhaa l-hadeethi antum mud-hinoona 82
wataj`aloona rizqakum annakum tukadh-dhiboona 83 fa lawlaa idhaa
balaghati l-hulqooma 84 wa antum heena'idhin tanzuroona 85 wa
nahnu aqrabu ilayhi minkum walakin laa tubsiroona 86 fa lawlaa in
kuntum ghayra madeeneena 87 tarji`oonahaa in kuntum saadiqeena
88 fa'ammaa in kaana mina l-muqarrabeena 89 farawhun wa
rayhaanun wa jannaatu na`eemin 90 wa'amma in kaana min ashaabi
l-yameeni 91 fa salaamun laka min ashaabi l-yameeni 92 wa'amma
in kaana mina l-mukadh-dhibeena l-daaleena 93 fanuzulun min
hameemin 94 wa tasliyatu jaheemin 95 inna haadha lahuwa haqqu l-
yaqeeni 96 fasabbih bismi rabbika l-`azeemi

By the one who is denoted by the name Allah (who created my
being with His Names in accord with the meaning of the letter 'B'),
the Rahman, the Rahim.

1. **When that truth** (of the second life after death) **occurs.**

2. **There will be none to deny its reality!**

3. **It brings down** (some) **and raises** (some) **up!**

4. **When the earth** (the body) **is shaken with intensity,**

5. **And the mountains** (the organs in the body) **are crumbled,**

6. **And become dust dispersing.**

7. **And you become divided into three kinds:**

8. The people of the right (the fortunate-happy ones who have attained the Truth) – **and what people of the right?**

9. The people of the left (the unfortunate-unhappy ones who have lived their live cocooned from the Truth) – **and what people of the left?**

10. And the forerunners are the forerunners (of certainty);

11. They are the ones who have attained (the state of divine) **closeness.**

12. Within Paradises of Bliss.

13. Most of them of the former people.

14. And the minority of them of the later people.

15. On thrones embroidered with jewels. (The verses in regards to Paradise as of this verse should be read in light of the statement "The example [metaphoric representation] of Paradise" mentioned in various verses [13:35, 47:15]. All expressions are symbolic and should not be taken literally.)

16. Seated facing one another.

17. With eternally youthful servants around them...

18. With vessels filled from the source, pitchers and cups...

19. Neither headache nor intoxication caused by them!

20. Whatever fruit they prefer;

21. Whichever meat of fowl they desire;

22. And the houris (partner-bodies with superior and clear vision – unrestricted by the limitations of the biological body – enabling the conscious man to experience his essential qualities. The state of living with multiple forms [bodies] under the administration of a single consciousness).

23. Like hidden pearls (raised in the mother of pearl; formations of the Names of Allah [bodies] and the manifestations of their qualities through the human consciousness).

24. This is the reward (result) **of their deeds!**

25. They will neither hear any empty discourse therein, nor any concept of sin!

26. Only saying, "Salam, salam" (meaning; "may the experience of the quality denoted by this Name be continual").

27. And the people of the right (the believers) – and what people of the right?

28. Among the lote trees with their fruits,

29. And banana trees layered with fruit...

30. In extended (eternal) shade,

31. And flowing waterfalls,

32. Among many (varieties of) fruits,

33. (Fruits that) neither run out nor are forbidden!

34. (They are) upon lounges raised high.

35. Indeed, We designed them (the partners of consciousness; bodies) with a (new) design.

36. And formed them of a kind never used before!

37. In love with their partners (bodies that have never been seen or used before, who enable the peak experience of the qualities of the human consciousness, as opposed to the animalistic body that made man 'descend to the world as enemies,' directing him towards materialistic gains) and who are equal in age (came into existence with consciousness)!

38. (These are) for the people of the right (the fortunate ones).

39. A group of them (the people of the right) are from the former people.

40. And some from later people.

41. And the people of the left (the unfortunate ones who deny the reality and live in their cocoon worlds) – and what people of the left?

42. In samum (poisonous fire, radiation) and hamim (scalding water; unrealistic/baseless data and conditionings),

43. And a shade of black smoke (unable to see and experience the forces in their essence),

44. (That shade) **that is neither cool nor generous** (in what it brings)!

45. Indeed, before this they were rampaging in an abundance of worldly, lustful pleasures!

46. They used to persist in committing that great offence (denying their essential reality and its experience).

47. They used to say, "Will we really continue to live (be resurrected) **with another body once we have died and become dust and bones?"**

48. "Even our forefathers?"

49. Say, "Indeed, the former and the latter,"

50. "They will surely be gathered for the appointment of a known time!"

51. After which, O those astray deniers (of the reality)...

52. Indeed, (you) will be eating from the trees of zaqqum (the fruits/products of thinking you are only the body).

53. Filling your bellies with it.

54. And drinking scalding water on top of it.

55. And you will drink it like the drinking of thirsty camels that are unable to quench their thirsts due to their afflictions.

56. Thus shall be their state (what manifests through them) **on the day of the religion** (the system – the time when the reality of the sunnatullah is realized)!

57. We created you! So, will you not accept?

58. Have you seen the sperm that you emit?

59. Is it you who creates it or are We the creators?

60. We determined death among you and you cannot overpass Us!

61. (We determined death) **so that We may bring** (new bodies of) **your like and that We reconstruct you** (anew) **in a form which you do not know.**

62. Indeed, you have already known the first creation... So, **should you not contemplate?**

63. Did you see what you sowed?

64. Is it you who makes it grow or Us?

65. Had We willed, We could have made it a dry, weak plant, and you would be left in wonder!

66. "Indeed, we are in loss!"

67. "No, we are the deprived."

68. And have you seen the water that you drink?

69. Is it you who discloses that from the white clouds or are We the disclosers?

70. Had We willed, We could have made it bitter (water)... **Should you not be grateful?**

71. And have you seen the fire that you ignite (from the tree)?

72. Did you make that tree or are We the makers?

73. We made it a reminder and provision for the ignorant wayfarer!

74. So, glorify (tasbih) **your Rabb whose name is Azim!**

75. I swear by the universe full of stars (where the Names become manifest)!

76. If only you knew how great an oath this is!

77. Indeed, that (universe) **is the noble Quran** (for those who can 'READ' it).

78. Contained within the knowledge that cannot be seen! (The universal data in the form of an endless ocean of waves and the data within the brain based on the holographic principle.)

79. None but the purified (from the dirt of shirq – duality – animalistic nature) **can touch it** (i.e. become enlightened with the knowledge of the Absolute Reality).

80. A disclosure (detailed explanation) **from the Rabb of the worlds.**

81. Now, you take this lightly and make little of it!

82. But was your denial the means of your livelihood?

83. And when the soul reaches the throat (at the time of death)!

84. You will be left (helpless)!

85. We are closer to it than you are, but you do not see.

86. If you are not to be recompensed for your deeds,

87. And if you are truthful, then turn (death) **away** (if you think there is no sunnatullah)!

88. (Everyone shall taste death) **but if he is of those who have attained divine closeness;**

89. For him there will be a life with the Rahman qualities, the observation of the reflections of the Names and a Paradise of bliss.

90. If he is of the people of the right,

91. (It will be said)**, "Salam to you" by the people of the right.**

92. But if he of is the deniers (of the reality) **who are astray in faith,**

93. Then scalding water will be spilled over him!

94. He will be subject to burning conditions!

95. Indeed, this is the very reality (that will be personally experienced)!

96. So, glorify (tasbih) **your Rabb whose name is Azim!**

The Rasul of Allah (saw) has said the following in regards to this chapter:

"One who reads the chapter Waqi'a every night will never be afflicted with poverty."[93]

In the past, many had made it a habit to read the chapters Yaseen, Fath, Waqi'a, Mulk and Naba every night. There is so much benefit in this, it is not possible for me to explain it.

I can only hope you spare half an hour of your time every night to read these five chapters. Half an hour from twenty-four hours every day is not much considering you will be preparing for your eternal life and strengthening your spirit. May Allah ease this for all of us.

---

[93] Abu Ubaid, al-Bayhaqi *Shu`ab al-Iman.*

25

AL-MULK
(67th Chapter)

بِسْمِ اللهِ الرَّحْمنِ الرَّحِيمِ

تَبَارَكَ الَّذِي بِيَدِهِ الْمُلْكُ وَهُوَ عَلَى كُلِّ شَيْءٍ قَدِيرٌ {1} الَّذِي خَلَقَ الْمَوْتَ وَالْحَيَاةَ لِيَبْلُوَكُمْ أَيُّكُمْ أَحْسَنُ عَمَلًا وَهُوَ الْعَزِيزُ الْغَفُورُ {2} الَّذِي خَلَقَ سَبْعَ سَمَاوَاتٍ طِبَاقًا مَّا تَرَى فِي خَلْقِ الرَّحْمَنِ مِن تَفَاوُتٍ فَارْجِعِ الْبَصَرَ هَلْ تَرَى مِن فُطُورٍ {3} ثُمَّ ارْجِعِ الْبَصَرَ كَرَّتَيْنِ يَنقَلِبْ إِلَيْكَ الْبَصَرُ خَاسِئاً وَهُوَ حَسِيرٌ {4} وَلَقَدْ زَيَّنَّا السَّمَاء الدُّنْيَا بِمَصَابِيحَ وَجَعَلْنَاهَا رُجُومًا لِّلشَّيَاطِينِ وَأَعْتَدْنَا لَهُمْ عَذَابَ السَّعِيرِ {5} وَلِلَّذِينَ كَفَرُوا بِرَبِّهِمْ عَذَابُ جَهَنَّمَ وَبِئْسَ الْمَصِيرُ {6} إِذَا أُلْقُوا فِيهَا سَمِعُوا لَهَا شَهِيقًا وَهِيَ تَفُورُ {7} تَكَادُ تَمَيَّزُ مِنَ الْغَيْظِ كُلَّمَا أُلْقِيَ فِيهَا فَوْجٌ سَأَلَهُمْ خَزَنَتُهَا أَلَمْ يَأْتِكُمْ نَذِيرٌ {8} قَالُوا بَلَى قَدْ جَاءنَا نَذِيرٌ فَكَذَّبْنَا وَقُلْنَا مَا نَزَّلَ اللَّهُ مِن شَيْءٍ إِنْ أَنتُمْ إِلَّا فِي ضَلَالٍ كَبِيرٍ {9} وَقَالُوا لَوْ كُنَّا نَسْمَعُ أَوْ نَعْقِلُ مَا كُنَّا فِي أَصْحَابِ السَّعِيرِ {10} فَاعْتَرَفُوا بِذَنبِهِمْ فَسُحْقًا لِّأَصْحَابِ السَّعِيرِ {11} إِنَّ الَّذِينَ يَخْشَوْنَ رَبَّهُم بِالْغَيْبِ لَهُم مَّغْفِرَةٌ وَأَجْرٌ كَبِيرٌ {12} وَأَسِرُّوا قَوْلَكُمْ أَوِ اجْهَرُوا بِهِ إِنَّهُ عَلِيمٌ بِذَاتِ الصُّدُورِ {13} أَلَا يَعْلَمُ مَنْ خَلَقَ وَهُوَ اللَّطِيفُ الْخَبِيرُ {14} هُوَ الَّذِي جَعَلَ لَكُمُ الْأَرْضَ ذَلُولًا فَامْشُوا فِي مَنَاكِبِهَا وَكُلُوا مِن رِّزْقِهِ وَإِلَيْهِ النُّشُورُ {15} أَأَمِنتُم مَّن فِي السَّمَاء أَن يَخْسِفَ بِكُمُ الْأَرْضَ فَإِذَا هِيَ تَمُورُ {16} أَمْ أَمِنتُم مَّن فِي السَّمَاء أَن يُرْسِلَ عَلَيْكُمْ حَاصِبًا فَسَتَعْلَمُونَ كَيْفَ نَذِيرِ {17} وَلَقَدْ كَذَّبَ الَّذِينَ مِن قَبْلِهِمْ

فَكَيْفَ كَانَ نَكِيرِ {18} أَوَلَمْ يَرَوْا إِلَى الطَّيْرِ فَوْقَهُمْ صَافَّاتٍ وَيَقْبِضْنَ مَا يُمْسِكُهُنَّ إِلَّا الرَّحْمَنُ إِنَّهُ بِكُلِّ شَيْءٍ بَصِيرٌ {19} أَمَّنْ هَذَا الَّذِي هُوَ جُندٌ لَّكُمْ يَنصُرُكُم مِّن دُونِ الرَّحْمَنِ إِنِ الْكَافِرُونَ إِلَّا فِي غُرُورٍ {20} أَمَّنْ هَذَا الَّذِي يَرْزُقُكُمْ إِنْ أَمْسَكَ رِزْقَهُ بَل لَّجُّوا فِي عُتُوٍّ وَنُفُورٍ {21} أَفَمَن يَمْشِي مُكِبًّا عَلَى وَجْهِهِ أَهْدَى أَمَّن يَمْشِي سَوِيًّا عَلَى صِرَاطٍ مُّسْتَقِيمٍ {22} قُلْ هُوَ الَّذِي أَنشَأَكُمْ وَجَعَلَ لَكُمُ السَّمْعَ وَالْأَبْصَارَ وَالْأَفْئِدَةَ قَلِيلًا مَّا تَشْكُرُونَ {23} قُلْ هُوَ الَّذِي ذَرَأَكُمْ فِي الْأَرْضِ وَإِلَيْهِ تُحْشَرُونَ {24} وَيَقُولُونَ مَتَى هَذَا الْوَعْدُ إِن كُنتُمْ صَادِقِينَ {25} قُلْ إِنَّمَا الْعِلْمُ عِندَ اللَّهِ وَإِنَّمَا أَنَا نَذِيرٌ مُّبِينٌ {26} فَلَمَّا رَأَوْهُ زُلْفَةً سِيئَتْ وُجُوهُ الَّذِينَ كَفَرُوا وَقِيلَ هَذَا الَّذِي كُنتُم بِهِ تَدَّعُونَ {27} قُلْ أَرَأَيْتُمْ إِنْ أَهْلَكَنِيَ اللَّهُ وَمَن مَّعِيَ أَوْ رَحِمَنَا فَمَن يُجِيرُ الْكَافِرِينَ مِنْ عَذَابٍ أَلِيمٍ {28} قُلْ هُوَ الرَّحْمَنُ آمَنَّا بِهِ وَعَلَيْهِ تَوَكَّلْنَا فَسَتَعْلَمُونَ مَنْ هُوَ فِي ضَلَالٍ مُّبِينٍ {29} قُلْ أَرَأَيْتُمْ إِنْ أَصْبَحَ مَاؤُكُمْ غَوْرًا فَمَن يَأْتِيكُم بِمَاء مَّعِينٍ {30}

A`oodhu biLlaahi min al-shayṭaani l-rajeem

Bismi Llaahi l-raḥmaani l-raḥeem

1 tabaaraka lladhee biyadihi l-mulku wa huwa `alaa kulli shay'in qadeerun 2 alladhee khalaqa l-mawta wal-ḥayaata liyablookum ayyukum aḥsanu `amalan wa huwa l-`azeezu l-ghafooru 3 alladhee khalaqa sab`a samawaatin ṭibaqan maa taraa fee khalqi l-raḥmaani min tafaawutin fa'irji`i l-baṣara hal taraa min fuṭoorin 4 thumma irji`i l-baṣara karratayni yanqalib ilayka l-baṣaru khaasi'an wa huwa ḥaseerun 5 wa laqad zayyannaa l-samaa' l-dunya bimaṣaabeeḥa waja`alnaha rujooman lil-shayṭaani wa a`tadnaa lahum `adhaaba l-sa`eeri 6 wa lilladheena kafaroo bi rabbihim `adhaabu jahannama wabi'sa l-maṣeeru 7 idhaa ulqoo feehaa sami`oo lahaa shaheeqan wa hiya tafooru 8 takaadu tamayyazu mina l-ghayẓi kullamaa ulqiya feeha fawjun sa'alahum khazanatuhaa alam ya'tikum nadheerun 9 qaaloo balaa qad jaa'naa nadheerun fakadh-dhabnaa wa qulnaa maa nazzala Llaahu min shay'in in antum illaa fee ḍalaalin kabeerin 10 wa qaaloo law kunnaa nasma`u aw na`qilu ma kunnaa fe aṣḥaabi l-sa`eeri 11 fa`tarafoo bidhanbihim fasuḥqan li'aṣḥaabi l-sa`eeri 12 inna lladheen yakhshawna rabbahum bil-ghaybi lahum maghfiratun wa'ajrun kabeerun 13 wa asirroo qawlakum awi ijharoo bihi innahu

'aleemun bidhaati l-ṣudoori 14 alaa ya`lamu man khalaqa wa huwa l-laṭeefu l-khabeeru 15 huwa lladhee ja`ala lakumu l-arḍa dhaloolan fa'imshoo fee manaakibihaa wa kuloo min rizqihi wa ilayhi l-nushooru 16 a'amintum man fee l-samaa'i an yakhsifa bikumu l-arḍa fa'idhaa hiya tamooru 17 am amintum man fee l-samaa'i an yursila `alaykum ḥaaṣiban fasata`alamoona kayfa nadheeri 18 wa laqad kadh-dhaba lladheena min qablihim fakayfa kaana nakeeri 19 awalam yaraw ilaa l-ṭayri fawqahum ṣaaffaatin wayaqbiḍna maa yumsikuhunna illaa l-raḥmaanu innahu bikulli shay'in baṣeerun 20 amman haadhaa lladhee huwa jundun lakum yanṣurukum min dooni l-raḥmaani ini l-kaafiroona illaa fee ghuroorin 21 amman haadhaa lladhee yarzuqukum in amsaka rizqahu bal lajoo fee `uttuwwin wanufoorin 22 afaman yamshee mukibban `ala wajhihi ahdaa amman yamshee sawiyyan `alaa ṣiraaṭin mustaqeemin 23 qul huwa lladhee anshaakum waja`ala lakumu l-sam`a wal-abṣaara wal-afi'data qaleelan maa tashkuroona 24 qul huwa lladhee dhara'akum fee l-arḍi wa'ilayhi tuḥsharoona 25 wa yaqooloona mataa haadha l-wa`du in kuntum ṣaadiqeena 26 qul innama l-`ilmu `inda Llaahi wa'innamaa ana nadheerun mubeenun 27 falammaa ra'awhu zulfatan see'at wujoohu lladheena kafaroo waqeela haadha lladhee kuntum bihi tadda`oona 28 qul ara'aytum in ahlakaaniya Llaahu wa man ma`iya aw raḥimanaa fa man yujeeru l-kaafireena min `adhaabin aleemin 29 qul huwa l-raḥmaanu aamannaa bihi wa `alayhi tawakkalnaa fasta`lamoona man huwa fee ḍalaalin mubeenin 30 qul ara'aytum in aṣḥaba maa'ukum ghawran faman ya'teekum bimaa'in ma`eenin

By the one who is denoted by the name Allah (who created my being with His Names in accord with the meaning of the letter 'B'), **the Rahman, the Rahim.**

1. Supreme is He in whose hand is dominion (the dimension of acts, which He administers as He wills at every instance)! **He is Qadir over all things.**

2. It is HU who created life and death to reveal which of you is best in deed. He is the Aziz, the Ghafur.

3. It is HU who created the heavens as seven dimensions. You cannot see any inconsistency in the creation of the Rahman. So, turn your gaze and have a look! Can you see any conflict or discrepancy?

4. Then turn your gaze twice again and have a look! Your vision will return to you fatigued (unable to find what it was looking for) **and humbled!**

5. Indeed, We have adorned the nearest heaven (of earth – the thought processes) **with illuminants** (the knowledge of the reality). We made them to stone and fend off the devils (satanic ideas). And We have prepared for them the suffering of the blazing Fire.

6. There is the suffering of Hell for those who deny their Rabb who comprises their essence! What a wretched place of return!

7. When they are cast into it, they will hear it rumble as it boils up and gushes!

8. It almost bursts from rage. Every time a group is cast into it, its keepers will ask them, "Did no warner come to you?"

9. And they (the people of Hell) **will say, "Yes, indeed, a warner did come to us, but we denied him in disbelief! We told them, 'Allah did not reveal anything, and you are in gross error.'"**

10. They will say, "If only we had listened to them and used our reason, we would not be among the people of Hell now!"

11. Thus they will confess their mistakes. Let the people of the blazing Fire experience isolation!

12. As for those who are in awe of their Rabb as their unknown, there is forgiveness for them and a great reward.

13. Conceal your thoughts or reveal them! Indeed, He is Aleem of what is in the hearts (consciousness) as the absolute essence therein.

14. Will He not know what He created! He is the Latif, the Habir.

15. He made the earth (body) **obedient** (to your consciousness)! So, walk upon its slopes and eat of its provisions. To Him will be your resurrection!

16. Are you confident that that which is in the heaven will not cause you to be swallowed up by the earth, when suddenly it begins to shake!

17. Or are you confident that that which is in the heaven will not send upon you a cyclone? You will know how true My warning is!

18. Indeed, those before them also denied! And how was My recompense for their denial!

19. Do they not see the birds above them spreading their wings and ascending, then folding them in and descending! They do this with the forces of the Rahman. Indeed, He, as the essence of the all things, is the Basir.

20. Or do you have an army to help you against the Rahman? Those who deny the knowledge of the reality are in nothing but delusion!

21. If He was to cut your provision off, who will nourish you? No, they persist in their escapism, in rage and hatred!

22. Is one who blindly crawls on his face better guided or the one who walks upright upon the straight path?

23. Say, "It is HU who formed you and gave you the ability to **perceive and comprehend** (insight) **and hearts** (heart neurons that reflect the meanings of the Names to the brain). **How little you thank** (evaluate)!"

24. Say, "It is HU who created you on the earth. To Him you will be gathered!"

25. They say, "If you are truthful, when will your warning be fulfilled?"

26. Say, "Its knowledge is with Allah. I am only a clear warner!"

27. When they see it (death) **approaching, the faces of those who deny the knowledge of the reality will darken. And it will said, "This is that which you impatiently wanted to experience!"**

28. Say, "Think! If Allah were to destroy me and those with me or give grace to us, who can save the deniers of the reality from the severe suffering?"

29. Say, "He is the Rahman; we believe He comprises our essence and we have placed our trust in Him. Soon you will know who is in clear error!"

30. Say, "Think! If your water was to recede, who could bring you flowing water (knowledge)?

Muhammad (saw), the Rasul of Allah says in regard to this chapter:

"It is like a barrier. It is a savior. It protects and saves man from the suffering of the grave."[94]

We know that death is not about becoming inexistent or dying and waiting in a state of nonexistence... Death is an experience; hence, we're told we're going to 'taste' it! This body is going to become dysfunctional and obsolete and we're going to be eqipped with a new body in the grave. We're going to be alive and conscious, completely aware of everything around us, with the same mental activity as always.

I covered this topic in detail in *Muhammad's Allah* in the chapter on death. Those who wish to obtain further information about how and why death is an 'experience' can refer to this book or to *Man, Spirit, Jinn*...

The event to which the Quran refers as 'tasting of death' is the conscious experience of being buried and making the transition to the life of the grave and thus the afterlife... Those who are

---

[94] Al-Tirmidhi.

unequipped or ill prepared for this will be subject to enormous suffering.

Hence, the Rasul of Allah (saw) advises us to recite this chapter as a precaution and preparation for the suffering of the grave, and says:

"There is a chapter composed of 30 verses in the Quran that acted as an intercessor for a man and he was forgiven. That is the chapter 'Tabarakalladhee biyadihil Mulk.'"[95]

Abdullah b. Masud (ra) narrates the words of the Rasul of Allah (saw) regarding the life of the grave:

"When a person is buried in his grave, the angels of suffering will approach his feet... Then the angels in charge of the chapter al-Mulk will object and say, 'There is no passage for you through us, for he used to recite the chapter al-Mulk when he was alive.' Then the angels of suffering will approach his breast and stomach, again they will say, 'There is no passage through us for he used to recite the chapter al-Mulk when he was alive.' Then they will try and approach from his head, again they will object with the same strength and reasoning. The chapter al-Mulk is a preventor. It prevents the suffering of the grave. Whoever reads it at night will have accrued great merit and will have done an excellent thing."[96]

---

[95] Al-Tirmidhi.
[96] Al-Dailami.

26

AN-NABA

(78th Chapter)

بِسْمِ اللهِ الرَّحْمنِ الرَّحِيمِ

عَمَّ يَتَسَاءلُونَ {1} عَنِ النَّبَإِ الْعَظِيمِ {2} الَّذِي هُمْ فِيهِ مُخْتَلِفُونَ {3} كَلَّا
سَيَعْلَمُونَ {4} ثُمَّ كَلَّا سَيَعْلَمُونَ {5} أَلَمْ نَجْعَلِ الْأَرْضَ مِهَادًا {6} وَالْجِبَالَ
أَوْتَادًا {7} وَخَلَقْنَاكُمْ أَزْوَاجًا {8} وَجَعَلْنَا نَوْمَكُمْ سُبَاتًا {9} وَجَعَلْنَا اللَّيْلَ لِبَاسًا
{10} وَجَعَلْنَا النَّهَارَ مَعَاشًا {11} وَبَنَيْنَا فَوْقَكُمْ سَبْعًا شِدَادًا {12} وَجَعَلْنَا
سِرَاجًا وَهَّاجًا {13} وَأَنزَلْنَا مِنَ الْمُعْصِرَاتِ مَاء ثَجَّاجًا {14} لِنُخْرِجَ بِهِ
حَبًّا وَنَبَاتًا {15} وَجَنَّاتٍ أَلْفَافًا {16} إِنَّ يَوْمَ الْفَصْلِ كَانَ مِيقَاتًا {17} يَوْمَ
يُنفَخُ فِي الصُّورِ فَتَأْتُونَ أَفْوَاجًا {18} وَفُتِحَتِ السَّمَاء فَكَانَتْ أَبْوَابًا {19}
وَسُيِّرَتِ الْجِبَالُ فَكَانَتْ سَرَابًا {20} إِنَّ جَهَنَّمَ كَانَتْ مِرْصَادًا {21} لِلْطَّاغِينَ
مَآبًا {22} لَابِثِينَ فِيهَا أَحْقَابًا {23} لَا يَذُوقُونَ فِيهَا بَرْدًا وَلَا شَرَابًا {24}
إِلَّا حَمِيمًا وَغَسَّاقًا {25} جَزَاء وِفَاقًا {26} إِنَّهُمْ كَانُوا لَا يَرْجُونَ حِسَابًا
{27} وَكَذَّبُوا بِآيَاتِنَا كِذَّابًا {28} وَكُلَّ شَيْءٍ أَحْصَيْنَاهُ كِتَابًا {29} فَذُوقُوا
فَلَن نَّزِيدَكُمْ إِلَّا عَذَابًا {30} إِنَّ لِلْمُتَّقِينَ مَفَازًا {31} حَدَائِقَ وَأَعْنَابًا {32}
وَكَوَاعِبَ أَتْرَابًا {33} وَكَأْسًا دِهَاقًا {34} لَا يَسْمَعُونَ فِيهَا لَغْوًا وَلَا كِذَّابًا
{35} جَزَاء مِّن رَّبِّكَ عَطَاء حِسَابًا {36} رَبِّ السَّمَاوَاتِ وَالْأَرْضِ وَمَا
بَيْنَهُمَا الرحْمَن لَا يَمْلِكُونَ مِنْهُ خِطَابًا {37} يَوْمَ يَقُومُ الرُّوحُ وَالْمَلَائِكَةُ صَفًّا
لَا يَتَكَلَّمُونَ إِلَّا مَنْ أَذِنَ لَهُ الرحْمَنُ وَقَالَ صَوَابًا {38} ذَلِكَ الْيَوْمُ الْحَقُّ فَمَن

شَاءَ اتَّخَذَ إِلَى رَبِّهِ مَآبًا {39} إِنَّا أَنذَرْنَاكُمْ عَذَابًا قَرِيبًا يَوْمَ يَنظُرُ الْمَرْءُ مَا قَدَّمَتْ يَدَاهُ وَيَقُولُ الْكَافِرُ يَا لَيْتَنِي كُنتُ تُرَابًا {40}

A`oodhu biLlaahi min al-shaytaani l-rajeem

Bismi Llaahi l-rahmaani l-raheem

1 `amma yatasaaloona 2 `ani l-nabaa'i l-`azeemi 3 alladhee hum feehi mukhtalifoona 4 kallaa saya`lamoona 5 thumma kalla saya`lamoona 6 alam naj`ali l-arda mihaadan 7 wal-jibaala awtaadan 8 wa khalaqnaakum azwaajan 9 waja`alnaa nawmakum subaatan 10 waja`alnaa l-layla libaasan 11 wa ja`alnaa l-nahaara ma`aashan 12 wa banaynaa fawqakum sab`an shidaadan 13 waja`alnaa siraajan wahhaajan 14 wa anzalnaa mina l-mu`siraati maa' thajaajan 15 linukhrija bihi jabban wa nabaatan 16 wa jannaatin alfaafan 17 inna yawma l-fasli kaana meeqaatan 18 yawma yunfakhu fee l-soori fata'toona afwaajan 19 wafutihati l-samaa' fakaanat abwaaban 20 wa suyyirati l-jibaalu fakaanat saraaban 21 inna jahannama kaanat mirsaadan 22 lil-taagheena maaban 23 laabitheena feehaa ahqaaban 24 laa yadhooqoona feehaa bardan wa laa sharaaban 25 illa hameeman wa ghassaaqan 26 jazaa' wifaaqan 27 innahumkaanoo laa yarjoona hisaaban 28 wa kadh-dhaboo bi aayaatinaa kidh-dhaaban 29 wa kulla shay'in ahsaynaahu kitaaban 30 fadhooqoo falan nazeedakum illaa `adhaaban 31 inna lil-muttaqeena mafaazan 32 hadaa'iqa wa a`naaban 33 wa kawaa`iba atraaban 34 wa ka'san dihaaqan 35 laa yasma`oona feeha laghwan wa laa kidh-dhaaban 36 jazaa min rabbika `ataa' hizaaban 37 rabbi l-samawaati wal-ardi wa maa baynahumaa l-rahmaani laa yamlikoona minhu khitaaban 38 yawma yaqoomu l-roohu wal-malaa'ikatu saffan laa yatakallamoona illaa man adhina lahu l-rahmaanu waqaala sawaaban 39 dhaalika l-yawmu l-haqqu fa man shaa' ittakhadha ilaa rabbihi maaban 40 inna andharnaakum `adhaaban qareeban yawman yanzuru l-mar'u maa qaddamat yadaahu wa yaqoolu l-kaafiru yaa laytanee kuntu turaaban

By the one who is denoted by the name Allah (who created my being with His Names in accord with the meaning of the letter 'B'), **the Rahman, the Rahim.**

1. What are they questioning?

2. The mighty news (regarding life after death)?

3. Over this, they are in disagreement.

4. But no! Soon (when they die) **they will know** (that it is not like what they think)!

5. Again, no! Soon they will know (it is not like what they think)!

6. Did We not make the earth (the body) **a cradle** (a temporary place in which you can grow and develop yourselves)?

7. And the mountains (the organs in the body) **as stakes.**

8. And created you as partners (consciousness – body).

9. And made sleep a means for rest.

10. And the night a blanket.

11. And made the day for livelihood.

12. And constructed seven strong (heavens) **above you** (the system with seven orbits – the dimension of consciousness).

13. And a luminous lamp (Sun – intellect).

14. And disclosed pouring water from the rain clouds.

15. So that We may produce therein grain and vegetation.

16. Gardens within gardens!

17. Indeed, that time (of sorting and separating) **is an appointed time.**

18. The Horn will be blown at that time and you will come forth in groups.

19. The heaven will open and become gateways (consciousness will be opened to perception without the bodily senses).

20. And mountains will be made to vanish as if they were a mirage (the limitations of the organs are removed).

21. Indeed, Hell has become a place of passage (everyone will pass from it).

22. A place of settlement for the transgressors (the wrongdoers who failed to protect themselves according to the sunnatullah).

23. To remain therein for a very long time!

24. They will not taste therein any coolness or a delightful drink!

25. Only boiling water and pus!

26. As the direct result of their deeds!

27. Indeed, they did not expect (to be called to) **account** (for their lives)!

28. They persistently denied Our signs within their beings!

29. But We have recorded everything in detail!

30. So taste it, never We will increase you in anything except suffering!

31. Indeed, there is an attainment for the protected ones.

32. Gardens and grapevines... (Remember that all descriptions pertaining to Paradise are metaphoric expressions.)

33. Magnificent partners of equal age! (Magnificently capacitated bodies bearing the qualities of that dimension of existence, without the concept of gender, formed to manifest the qualities of the Names emanating from the essence of the individual consciousness... Note again, without any differentiation of gender! Allah knows best.)

34. And cups that are full!

35. They will hear neither baseless speech therein nor any falsehood.

36. As respite from your Rabb, an endowment for their deeds!

37. He is the Rabb of the heavens, the earth and everything in between; He is the Rahman! The One of whom no one has the authority to speak.

38. At that time the Spirit (the single reality of the Names that manifests in the consciousness of all humans) **and the angels will stand in rows. None will be able to speak, except for whom the**

Rahman has given permission (allowed his natural disposition). **And he will speak the truth.**

39. This is the time of the Truth! Then, whoever wills may take a way to his Rabb!

40. Indeed, we have warned you of a close suffering (caused by the realization of the Truth through the experience of death)! **On that day, man will observe what his hands have put forth, and those who denied the knowledge of the reality will say "Oh, how I wish I was made of dust!"**

27

AL-ALAQ
(96th Chapter 1-5 verses)

بِسْمِ اللهِ الرَّحْمنِ الرَّحِيمِ
اقْرَأْ بِاسْمِ رَبِّكَ الَّذِي خَلَقَ {1} خَلَقَ الْإِنسَانَ مِنْ عَلَقٍ {2} اقْرَأْ وَرَبُّكَ الْأَكْرَمُ {3} الَّذِي عَلَّمَ بِالْقَلَمِ {4} عَلَّمَ الْإِنسَانَ مَا لَمْ يَعْلَمْ {5}

A`oodhu biLlaahi min al-shayṭaani l-rajeem

Bismi Llaahi l-raḥmaani l-raḥeem

1 `iqra bismi rabbika lladhee khalaqa 2 khalaqa l-insaana min `alaqin 3 iqra wa rabbuka l-akramu 4 alladhee `allama bil-qalami 5 `allama l-insaana ma lam ya`lam

By the one who is denoted by the name Allah (who created my being with His Names in accord with the meaning of the letter 'B'), **the Rahman, the Rahim.**

1. READ with the Name of your Rabb (with the knowledge that comprises your being)**, who created.**

2. Created man from alaq (a clot of blood; genetic composition).

3. READ! For your Rabb is Akram (most generous).

128

4. Who taught (programmed the genes and the essential qualities) **by the Pen.**

5. Taught man that which he knew not.

I advise those who want to reach the hidden secrets in the depths of the truths of religion to recite these verses 313 times a day!

What does 'READ' mean? What is to be read? How can it be read? If it's not about reading and writing in the literal sense, then what does Muhammad (saw) being 'illiterate' (ummi) mean? I've tried to answer all of these in *What did Muhammad Read?* But let us know with certainty that this is not about reading a physical object, such as a book.

Again, those who want to READ the truths in the sight of their Rabb should make it a habit to recite these verses 313 times on a daily basis.

28

ASH-SHARH
(94ᵗʰ Chapter)

بِسْمِ اللهِ الرَّحْمنِ الرَّحِيمِ

أَلَمْ نَشْرَحْ لَكَ صَدْرَكَ {1} وَوَضَعْنَا عَنكَ وِزْرَكَ {2} الَّذِي أَنقَضَ ظَهْرَكَ {3} وَرَفَعْنَا لَكَ ذِكْرَكَ {4} فَإِنَّ مَعَ الْعُسْرِ يُسْرًا {5} إِنَّ مَعَ الْعُسْرِ يُسْرًا {6} فَإِذَا فَرَغْتَ فَانصَبْ {7} وَإِلَى رَبِّكَ فَارْغَبْ {8}

A`oodhu biLlaahi min al-shayṭaani l-rajeem

Bismi Llaahi l-raḥmaani l-raḥeem

1 alam rashraḥ laka ṣadraka 2 wa waḍa`ana `anka wizraka 3 alladhee anqaḍa ẓahrak 4 wa rafa`ana laka ẓikraka 5 fa'inna ma`a l-`usri yusran 6 inna ma`a l-`usri yusran 7 fa'idhaa faraghta fa'inṣab 8 wa ilaa rabbika faarghab

By the one who is denoted by the name Allah (who created my being with His Names in accord with the meaning of the letter 'B'), **the Rahman, the Rahim.**

1. Did We not expand your breast (broaden your capabilities)?

130

2. Did We not remove your burden (of your identity) **from you** (by revealing the reality to you)?

3. Which had weighed (heavy) **upon your back** (overburdened you)!

4. Did We not exalt your remembrance (by reminding you of, and making you live by the reality)?

5. So surely with every hardship there is ease.

6. Yes, surely with every hardship, there is ease.

7. So when you are free (of your duties) **labor** (for your actual duty)!

8. And evaluate your Rabb!

Those who want to:

- Progress spiritually

- Fathom with ease the knowledge, observations and discoveries they encounter

- Be free from distress, hardship or depression

Should recite these verses 70 times a day. They will definitely reach the outcome they desire.

29

REGARDING THE MERITS OF SOME SHORT CHAPTERS

The Rasul of Allah (saw) says:

"Idhaa zulzilat is equivalent to half of the Quran! Kul huwallahu ahad is equivalent to a third of the Quran. Kul ya ayyuhal kafiroom' is equivalent to a quarter of the Quran."[97]

According to my understanding, this hadith means the Quran is based upon two primary themes:

1. There is no deity-god; we are here to realize the Unity and Oneness of Allah and to fulfill its requirement as best we can.

2. The necessity of engaging in certain practices to prepare for the life after death and the truth that the individual will face the consequences of every action transpired from them, whether good or bad, even an iota's weight.

So, since chapter Zalzala mentioned above is the perfect summary of the second point above, it is equivalent to half of the Quran.

---

[97] Al-Tirmidhi.

30

AL-ZALZALA

(99th chapter)

بِسْمِ اللهِ الرَّحْمنِ الرَّحِيمِ

إِذَا زُلْزِلَتِ الْأَرْضُ زِلْزَالَهَا {1} وَأَخْرَجَتِ الْأَرْضُ أَثْقَالَهَا {2} وَقَالَ الْإِنسَانُ مَا لَهَا {3} يَوْمَئِذٍ تُحَدِّثُ أَخْبَارَهَا {4} بِأَنَّ رَبَّكَ أَوْحَى لَهَا {5} يَوْمَئِذٍ يَصْدُرُ النَّاسُ أَشْتَاتًا لِّيُرَوْا أَعْمَالَهُمْ {6} فَمَن يَعْمَلْ مِثْقَالَ ذَرَّةٍ خَيْرًا يَرَهُ {7} وَمَن يَعْمَلْ مِثْقَالَ ذَرَّةٍ شَرًّا يَرَهُ {8}

A`oodhu biLlaahi min al-shayṭaani l-rajeem

Bismi Llaahi l-raḥmaani l-raḥeem

1 idhaa zulzilati l-arḍu zilzaalahaa 2 wa akhrajati l-ardu athqaalahaa 3 waqaala l-insaanu maa lahaa 4 yawma'idhin tuḥaddithu akhbaarahaa 5 bi'anna rabbaka awḥaa lahaa 6 yawma'idhin yaṣduru l-naasu ashtaatan liyuraa a`maalahum 7 faman ya`mal mithqaala dharratin khayran yaraahu 8 waman ya`mal mithqaala dharratin sharran yaraahu

By the one who is denoted by the name Allah (who created my being with His Names in accord with the meaning of the letter 'B'), **the Rahman, the Rahim.**

1. When the earth (the body) **is shaken with an intense quake;**

2. And the earth discharges its burdens,

3. And man (consciousness panics and) **asks, "What is wrong with it** (the body)**?"**

4. That is the time it will report its news.

5. With a revelation from your Rabb.

6. That day the people will go forth in groups to see the results of their deeds!

7. Whoever does an iota's weight of good will see it,

8. And whoever does an iota's weight of evil will see it.

The external meaning of chapter Zalzala is what I have mentioned above. However, to confine the meaning of this chapter to this much is like seeing the one-seventh observable part of an iceberg on the water and assuming it to be only that much!

In hope of presenting an example, I have decided to talk more about the inner meaning of this chapter...

The word earth is usually interpreted as the body in the Sufi tradition. So, if we try to discern this chapter in this light, we may instantly recognize the difference between the external meaning presented above...

Based on the truth 'When a person dies, his Doomsday will have taken place,'[98] this chapter, which talks about the state of Doomsday, can be construed as talking about the individual's Doomsday, i.e. the death of the body...

---

[98] Al-Dailami.

1.   When the body is shaken with an intense quake due to the termination of the bioelectrical power in the nervous system and thus begins to near its end

2.   And the body discharges its hidden point of burden, the Spirit, i.e. the holographic radial body

3.   And man, feeling no difference in his consciousness, becomes aware of the change that's occurring in the body, begins to identify with the spirit body, and asks in great shock and panic, "What is wrong with it (the body)?"

4-5. With a revelation from its Rabb, the body begins to disclose all of its properties, its system, state and consequence, what the person could have done with it and now that it is disconnected from it, what it is deprived of achieving without it, and how much of a blessing the bodily life was to the person in the past, etc…

6.   So, those who experience death, disconnection from their bodies, will live their Doomsday through death and then be resurrected into new bodies so they may see the results of their deeds…

7.   Whoever does an iota's weight of good, that is, a good that results from a thought or action that is seemingly insignificant, will find it inscribed in their book and see their products…

8.   And whoever does an iota's weight of bad thought or action, they will also find it in their book and before them, formed by the waves of their very brain!

This construal was in light of the person's physiological-biological make-up and its Doomsday.

The following construal is in regards to the experience referred to as 'dying before death':

1.   When existence is shaken with an intense quake and begins to lose its meaning in your sight… When you realize the essence and origin of existence is the Names of Allah and the seeming external world is shattered in your view…

2. When the meanings of the Names of Allah comprising the essence of existence become apparent and the secrets therein begin to reveal themselves...

3. When man sees what he thought existed disappear like a mirage and realize that in the sight of Allah everything is an illusion, he will say in great shock and panic, "What is happening to these things? Why is everything disappearing and only that which pertains to Allah is eternal..."

4. Existence will begin to explain everything to the person whose insight will now be active and open... They will inform him of which unit manifests which name of Allah... And man will understand that everything he thought was other than Allah was actually the manifestation of His Names!

5. All of this will occur with the revelation of the Rabb, the judgments of the dimension of Rububiyyah will become disclosed though existence, and man will become aware of this!

6. These people who have died before death will now see clearly what and why they have done things in the past, and become aware of the secrets pertaining to them.

7. Whoever does an iota's weight of good shall see its results

8. Whoever does an iota's weight of bad shall also see it.

Surely there are deeper meanings than this, but this isn't the place to extrapolate them. I pray that Allah enables us all to go further than the surface meanings and observe the inner and deeper aspects of all of the verses...

It is inadequate for us to merely recite the Quran in Arabic without knowing at least the general outline of what the verses are saying. So, in any case, we must take advantage of a translation to at least grasp the main theme.

There is a verse in the Quran stating it has been revealed 'so that it may be understood'... Surely, not everyone may be able to acquire the deeper meanings, but it is more appropriate for those who claim they believe in the Quran to know at least the general meaning of what they claim to be believing in, for clearly it goes against logic to claim one believes in something they have no idea about.

As for why 'Kul huwallahu ahad' is equivalent to one-third of the Quran... If we were to divide the Quran into three general categories, it would be: the Oneness of Allah, life after death and the practices that are recommended in preparation for life after death. In this case, chapter al-Ikhlas correlates to the first of these.

There is actually a lot that can be said about this short chapter, but here I would like to share as much as the scope of this book allows...

I have tried to comprehensively explain the meaning of the chapter al-Ikhlas in *Muhammad's Allah* so I shall not repeat it here, I shall only share a memory of mine regarding this little chapter.

One Friday, when I was around seventeen years old, I had gone to the Carrahpasha Mosque opposite our house in Carrahpasha, Istanbul. I was newly taking up interest in such topics... Somebody tapped my shoulder and said "The master is calling you." This was a man whom I heard was 104 years old and was generally referred to as the Friday Sheikh... I later found out he was a sheikh of the Naqshibandi order. I don't know how he saw me from such a distance that day, given he had very poor sight. Anyway, I went next to him and kissed his hands. He asked me, "If I were to give you a task, will you do it?" Full of the vigor and enthusiasm of my age, I aptly responded, "Yes, of course!" But I had no idea about anything at that time. Then he said, "Recite the chapter al-Ikhlas 100 thousand times, however long it may take you, and then come back to me."

Unfortunately, he passed away a week after this incident. But I kept my word and finished the recital of 100 thousand al-Ikhlas in twenty days. I pray and hope that Allah will forgive me and enable me to reach the secrets of this chapter for the sake of these recitals.

This is why I recommend all my believing brethren to recite this chapter as much as they can. May Allah ease it!

The Rasul of Allah (saw) told his companions:

"Gather you all, I'm going to recite to you one-third of the Quran." So all the companions gathered. Then the Rasul of Allah (saw) came to his house, recited the chapter al-Ikhlas and then went back inside. The companions all looked at each other and said, "He must have received a revelation to have gone back inside;" they thought was receiving a new revelation... Then the Rasul of Allah (saw) came out again and said, "I told you I was going to recite one-third of the Quran to you and I did... The chapter al-Ikhlas is equivalent to one-third of the Quran!"[99]

Abu Hurairah (ra) narrates:

"We came somewhere with the Rasul of Allah (saw) and saw a man reciting Kul huwallahu ahad allahus samad lam yalid wa lam yulad walam yakun lahu kufuwan ahad... The Rasul of Allah (saw) said, 'It has become a requisite.' So, I asked, 'What has become requisite, O Rasul of Allah?' And he said, 'Paradise!' I wanted to run and give the good news to the man, but I feared losing the honorable chance of eating with the Rasul of Allah... I went later, but unfortunately the man had gone."[100]

Abu Darda (ra) narrates:

"The Rasul of Allah (saw) said, 'Can any of you be lacking ability to read one-third of the Quran at night?' Upon which his companions asked, 'How can we read one-third of the Quran?' and the Rasul of Allah (saw) said, 'Allah has divided the Quran into three sections. Kulhuwallahu ahad is one of these!'"[101]

In another hadith, the Rasul of Allah (saw) says in regards to the chapter al-Ihklas:

"Whoever recites one thousand Ikhlas and blows it to his spirit, Allah will emancipate him from Hell."[102]

Thus, if we make it a habit to recite a thousand Ihklas on special nights or for our kin who have passed away, both them and us will benefit immensely.

---

[99] Al-Tirmidhi.
[100] Al-Tirmidhi.
[101] Al-Tirmidhi.
[102] Ibrahim ibn Muhammad *al-Fawaid.*

31

AL-FALAQ and AN-NAS
(113rd and 114th Chapters)

113. AL-FALAQ

بِسْمِ اللهِ الرَّحْمنِ الرَّحِيمِ

قُلْ أَعُوذُ بِرَبِّ الْفَلَقِ {1} مِن شَرِّ مَا خَلَقَ {2} وَمِن شَرِّ غَاسِقٍ إِذَا وَقَبَ {3} وَمِن شَرِّ النَّفَّاثَاتِ فِي الْعُقَدِ {4} وَمِن شَرِّ حَاسِدٍ إِذَا حَسَدَ {5}

A`oodhu biLlaahi min al-shayṭaani l-rajeem

Bismi Llaahi l-raḥmaani l-raḥeem

1 qul a`oodhu birabbi l-falaqi 2 min sharri maa khalaqa 3 wamin sharri ghaasiqin idhaa waqaba 4 wamin sharri naffaathaati fee l-`uqadi 5 wamin sharri ḥaasidin idhaa ḥasada

By the one who is denoted by the name Allah (who created my being with His Names in accord with the meaning of the letter 'B'), **the Rahman, the Rahim.**

1. Say (recognize, realize, comprehend, experience): **"I seek refuge in the Rabb** (the reality of the Names comprising my essence) **of the Falaq** (the light that prevails over the darkness and brings enlightenment to me)."

2. "From the evil of His creation"

3. "From the evil of the darkness that settles in my mind preventing me from perceiving and comprehending..."

4. "From the evil of the women who blow on knots (those who manipulate brain waves to make black magic)"

5. "And from the evil eye of the envier when he envies!"

114. AN-NAS

بِسْمِ اللهِ الرَّحْمنِ الرَّحِيمِ

قُلْ أَعُوذُ بِرَبِّ النَّاسِ {1} مَلِكِ النَّاسِ {2} إِلَهِ النَّاسِ {3} مِن شَرِّ الْوَسْوَاسِ الْخَنَّاسِ {4} الَّذِي يُوَسْوِسُ فِي صُدُورِ النَّاسِ {5} مِنَ الْجِنَّةِ وَ النَّاسِ {6}

A`oodhu biLlaahi min al-shaytaani l-rajeem

Bismi Llaahi l-rahmaani l-raheem

1 qul a`oodhu birabbi l-naasi 2 maliki l-naasi 3 ilaahi 'naasi 4 min sharri l-waswaasi l-khannaas 5 alladhee yuwaswisu fee sudoori l-naasi 6 mina l-jinnati wa l-naas

By the one who is denoted by the name Allah (who created my being with His Names in accord with the meaning of the letter 'B'), **the Rahman, the Rahim.**

1. Say (recognize, realize, comprehend, experience)**: "I seek refuge in the Rabb** (the reality of the Names comprising the essence) **of the Nas** (mankind)**."**

2. "The Sovereign of man," (The Malik, the One whose sovereignty and administration is absolute over Nas, mankind)

3. "The God of man," (The reality of Uluhiyya that resides within the essence of every human, with which he subsists his existence, and mistakenly thinks this state pertains to a god outside of himself!)

4. "From the evil of the whisperer that covertly pervades then retreats, and reduces man to corporeality."

5. "That which whispers illusory thoughts into man's consciousness about man's essential reality."

6. "From among the jinni (invisible forces) **and man!"**

These two chapters are the biggest weapons against black magic, hypnotism and any other external force that impedes one's will and ability.

Both these chapters were revealed by Allah when black magic was done to the Rasul of Allah (saw).

Reciting them 41 times a day or seven times after every salat has profound benefits.

Uqba b. Amr (ra) narrates the Rasul of Allah (saw) says:

"Do you know the verses that were revealed tonight, whose likes have not yet been seen? They are the short chapters Falaq and Nas."[103]

"Shall I teach you the best two chapters that can be recited; they are the Qul a`oodhu bi rabbi l-falaq and qul a`oodhu bi rabbi l-nas."[104]

We were traveling with the Rasul of Allah (saw) between Juhfa and Abwa when suddenly a fierce storm and darkness overtook us. The Rasul of Allah (saw) started reciting Qul Audhu bi rabbil falaq and qul audhu bi rabbinnas for protection and said, 'O Uqba, protect yourself with these two chapters! No one who has sought protection has been protected as well as these two chapters protect!"[105]

"Nothing that is recited is more acceptable in the sight of Allah than these two chapters. Continue to recite them during your salat as often as possible!"[106]

The Rasul of Allah (saw) usually recited the chapters Ikhlas, Falaq and Nas after performing salat, blew it into his hands and then rubbed his hands over his whole body, and he repeated this three times.

It is said whoever recites the chapters Ikhlas, Falaq and Nas seven times after performing the Friday salat without engaging in any worldly speech and then rubs his body with it will be safe from all harm until the following Friday.

We have also been informed via various sources that reciting these chapters 41 times along with the Ayat al-Qursi, blowing it into a jug of water and then drinking this water is proven to be very beneficial, especially for those who may be under the influence of the jinn or victims of black magic.

---

[103] Al-Tirmidhi.
[104] Al-Hakim, Ibn Marduyah.
[105] Al-Hakim, Ibn Marduyah, Bayhaqi *Shu`ab al-Iman.*
[106] Ibn Marduyah.

32

EXAMPLE PRAYERS FROM THE QURAN

In this section I would like to share some example prayers from the Quran and talk a little about their benefits...

رَبَّنَا آتِنَا فِي الدُّنْيَا حَسَنَةً وَفِي الآخِرَةِ حَسَنَةً وَقِنَا عَذَابَالنَّارِ

Rabbana atina feed-dunya hasanatan wa feel akhirati hasanatan wa qina 'athaban-nari[107]

Our Rabb, give us bounties (the experience of the beauties of the Names) **in the world, and bounties** (the beauties of the Names in our essence) **in the eternal life to come; protect us from the fire** (of falling into separation).

Anas (ra) narrates that the Rasul of Allah (saw) used this verse in many of his prayers. This prayer teaches us to wish for all the good that we may or may not be aware of, and seek protection from things that lead to the suffering of fire.

---

[107] Quran 2:201.

رَبَّنَا لاَ تُزِغْ قُلُوبَنَا بَعْدَ إِذْ هَدَيْتَنَا وَهَبْ لَنَا مِن لَّدُنكَ رَحْمَةً إِنَّكَ أَنتَ الْوَهَّابُ

Rabbana la tuzigh quloobana ba`da idh hadaytana wahab lana min ladunka rahmatan innaka anta alwahhabu[108]

Our Rabb, after giving us guidance (enabling us to recognize and discern the reality) **do not turn our consciousness** (back to the illusory identity – ego based existence), **and bestow your grace upon us. Most certainly you are the Wahhab.**

As denoted by the hadith 'The heart of the believer is between the two fingers of Rahman';[109] our hearts, that is our consciousness, are ever subject to divine power. No matter how much we may have attained the truth, we are always in danger of deviating from it. This prayer is to seek divine protection against such deviation.

Continuing to make this prayer may also prepare one for a graceful death since a prayer that is done persistently is always responded to. Their recital is recommended after the salawats (provided below) before giving salam in salat.

رَبَّنَا مَا خَلَقْتَ هَذا بَاطِلاً سُبْحَانَكَ فَقِنَا عَذَابَ النَّارِ   رَبَّنَا إِنَّكَ مَن تُدْخِلِ النَّارَ فَقَدْ أَخْزَيْتَهُ وَمَا لِلظَّالِمِينَ مِنْ أَنصَارٍ رَبَّنَا إِنَّنَا سَمِعْنَا مُنَادِيًا يُنَادِي لِلإِيمَانِ أَنْ آمِنُواْ بِرَبِّكُمْ فَآمَنَّا رَبَّنَا فَاغْفِرْ لَنَا ذُنُوبَنَا وَكَفِّرْ عَنَّا سَيِّئَاتِنَا وَتَوَفَّنَا مَعَ الأَبْرَارِ رَبَّنَا وَآتِنَا مَا وَعَدتَّنَا عَلَى رُسُلِكَ وَلاَ تُخْزِنَا يَوْمَ الْقِيَامَةِ إِنَّكَ لاَ تُخْلِفُ الْمِيعَادَ

---

[108] Quran 3:8.
[109] Kashf-ul Asrar.

Rabbanaa maa khalaqta haadha baaṭilan subḥaanaka faqinaa
'adhaaban naari, Rabbanaa innaka man tudkhili l-naara faqad
akhzaytahu wa maa lil-ẓaalimeena min anṣaarin, Rabbanaa innanaa
sami'naa munaadiyan yunaadee lil-eemaani an aaminoo bi rabbikum
fa'aamannaa Rabbanaa fa'ighfir lanaa dhunoobanaa wa kaffir 'annaa
sayyi'atinaa wa tawaffanaa ma'a l-abraari, Rabbanaa wa aatinaa maa
wa'adtanaa 'alaa rusulika wa laa tukhzinaa yawma l-qiyaamati
innaka laa tukhlifu l-mee'aada[110]

**Our Rabb, You have not created these things for nothing!
You are Subhan** (free from creating meaningless things; you are in
a state of creating anew at every instant)! **Protect us from burning**
(remorse for not being able to duly evaluate your manifestations).
**Our Rabb, whoever You admit into fire, You have abased. No
one can help** (save) **those who do wrong to themselves! Our
Rabb, we have indeed heard the one who said, 'Believe in your
Rabb who has formed your essence with His Names' and we
have believed him instantly. Our Rabb, forgive us our faults,
erase our mistakes, let us come to You with Your servants who
have united with You. Our Rabb, give us what You have pledged
to Your Rasuls and do not humiliate us during the Doomsday
period. Certainly, You never fail to fulfill Your oath.**

Here Allah is teaching us the most valuable ways of praying. The
verse after this is a confirmation that prayers that are done in this
manner are definitely responded to.

If we aren't even capable of making a prayer to which Allah has
promised to respond, surely all is lost.

---

[110] Quran 3:191-194.

رَبَّنَا ظَلَمْنَا أَنفُسَنَا وَإِن لَّمْ تَغْفِرْ لَنَا وَتَرْحَمْنَا لَنَكُونَنَّ مِنَ الْخَاسِرِينَ

Rabbanaa ẓalamnaa anfusanaa wa'in lam taghfir lanaa wa tarḥmanaa lanakoonanna mina l-khasireena[111]

Our Rabb! We have wronged ourselves... If You do not forgive us and grace us, we will surely be among the losers.

When Adam and Eve made the notorious mistake while living the life of Paradise, out of their grief and sadness, they asked for forgiveness with the above verse. Their prayer was accepted and after living the life of the world for some time, they were returned to the life of Paradise once again.

This prayer teaches us what to do in case of doing wrong to ourselves. Given we wrong ourselves by not giving the due of the infinite perfection in our essence, what better option do we have but recite this prayer.

حَسْبِيَ اللّهُ لا إِلَهَ إِلاَّ هُوَ عَلَيْهِ تَوَكَّلْتُ وَهُوَ رَبُّ الْعَرْشِ الْعَظِيمِ

Hasbiya Llaahu laa ilaaha illaa huwa `alayhi tawakkaltu wa huwa rabbu l-arshi l-`adheemi[112]

Sufficient for me is Allah! There is no god, only HU! I have placed my trust in Him... HU is the Rabb of the Great Throne!

---

[111] Quran 7:23.
[112] Quran 9:129

If you've been unjustly afflicted with a situation, recite this prayer 500 or 1,000 times a day; inshaAllah, you will be delivered from that situation in no time.

Abraham (as) was the first to make this prayer. When he was captured by the Pharaoh and cast into the fire, the angel Gabriel came to him while he was still in the air and asked him, "O Abraham, what can I do for you?" Abraham responded, "I've placed my trust in Allah; He is sufficient for me. There is no god, only HU, I've left my affairs to Him, He is the Rabb of the great Throne…" At this point a miracle occurred and he fell into the fire ever so softly, yet the fire did not burn him… For, as the Quran states, the fire cooled down with the command of Allah and became a place of proximity to Abraham's essential reality (where the name Salam became manifest). This is the kind of miracle effect this verse has.

Regarding this prayer, the Rasul of Allah (saw) says:

"Whoever says, 'Sufficient for me is Allah! There is no god, only HU! I have placed my trust in Him… HU is the Rabb of the Great Throne!' in the morning and at night, whether they mean it or not, upon saying it seven times, Allah will be sufficient for them…"[113]

Take heed! This hadith is pointing to the system of Allah, the system referenced by the verse, 'You will never find an alteration in the sunnatullah (system of Allah)!'

When you engage in certain prayers and dhikrs, whether you believe in them or not, that practice activates the relevant mechanism and inevitably produces an outcome. This hadith proves this point. So, even if you do not believe in this system, pursue its practice for some time and you will definitely see results.

May Allah enable us to attain the meaning of this prayer and allow us to make this prayer.

---

[113] Abu Dawud.

رَبِّ إِنِّي أَعُوذُ بِكَ أَنْ أَسْأَلَكَ مَا لَيْسَ لِي بِهِ عِلْمٌ وَإِلاَّ تَغْفِرْ لِي وَتَرْحَمْنِي أَكُن مِّنَ الْخَاسِرِينَ

Rabbe innee a`oodhu bika an asaalaka maa laysa lee bihi `ilmun wa'illaa taghfir lee watarḥamnee akun mina l-khaasireena[114]

My Rabb! I seek refuge in You from asking for things about which I have no knowledge (into its true meaning)**! If You do not forgive me and bestow Your grace upon me I will be among the losers.**

Noah (as) had warned his people, but they refused to listen to him. So, he built an ark upon the command he received and invited his close ones and a pair of each type of animal on board. His son, however, was not of the believers and refused to join them. When the storm began and Noah saw his son drowning amid the waves he persistently prayed to Allah that his son may be saved, but alas, his prayers were not being responded to…

"O Noah! Indeed, he is not of your family! Indeed, (your persistence about your son against My decree) is an act not required by your faith! So do not ask of Me things about which you have no knowledge! Indeed, I advise you not to be among the ignorant."[115]

After this warning, Noah asked for forgiveness with the prayer above…

There is a great lesson in this for us! Our relatives and close ones may not necessarily believe in the reality, they may stubbornly resist the truth and choose to persist in their erroneous ways. In this case, even though we may be related to them by blood, we need to accept that we are not related to them in terms of the afterlife and hence need not insist or enforce them into believing. All we can do is pray

---

[114] Quran 11:47.
[115] Quran 11:46.

for their guidance and place our trust in Allah. Indeed, what Allah ordains shall be...

رَبَّنَا هَبْ لَنَا مِنْ أَزْوَاجِنَا وَذُرِّيَّاتِنَا قُرَّةَ أَعْيُنٍ وَاجْعَلْنَا لِلْمُتَّقِينَ إِمَامًا

Rabbanaa hab lanaa min azwaajina wa dhurriyyatinaa qurrata `ayunin wa ij`alnaa lil-muttaqeena imaaman[116]

Our Rabb... Grant us partners (or bodies) **and children** (the fruits of our bodily endeavors) **who will cause us joy** (Paradise life) **and make us leaders worthy of being followed for those who want to be protected."**

This prayer is for those who want to have children. If one becomes a parent, while continuing to make this prayer after their salat, it is hoped their lineage will be among the virtuous.

رَبِّ اجْعَلْنِي مُقِيمَ الصَّلَاةِ وَمِن ذُرِّيَّتِي رَبَّنَا وَتَقَبَّلْ دُعَاءِ
رَبَّنَا اغْفِرْ لِي وَلِوَالِدَيَّ وَلِلْمُؤْمِنِينَ يَوْمَ يَقُومُ الْحِسَابُ

Rabbi ij`alnee muqeema l-salaati wa min dhurriyyatee Rabbanaa wa taqannal du`aa'i Rabbanaa ighfir lee wa liwalidayya wa lil-mu'mineena yawma yaqoomu l-hisaabu[117]

---

[116] Quran 25:74
[117] Quran 14:40-41.

My Rabb, allow me to establish salat (experience the return of introspectively turning to the reality of the Names) **and also of my descendants** (allow them to establish salat)**! Our Rabb, fulfill my prayer.** (Note: An individual such as Abraham is requesting the establishment and experience of salat; it is worth contemplating on the importance of this means.) **Our Rabb, in that time when life accounts are openly displayed, forgive me, my parents and the faithful!**

This prayer, made by Abraham (as), is the only prayer in the Quran in regards to salat. It is especially recommended for those who want to reach the essence of salat and perform it duly. Some salats are merely done for the sake of being done, yet some are continuous, they are experienced not just five times a day, but constantly...

May Allah enable us all to experience the reality of salat, which is said to be the "Pole of religion"...

Again, those who want to experience the reality of salat should read this verse during prostration...

رَبَّهُ أَنِّي مَسَّنِيَ الشَّيْطَانُ بِنُصْبٍ وَعَذَابٍ
رَبِّ أَعُوذُ بِكَ مِنْ هَمَزَاتِ الشَّيَاطِينِ وَأَعُوذُ بِكَ رَبِّ أَن
يَحْضُرُونِ وَحِفْظًا مِّن كُلِّ شَيْطَانٍ مَّارِدٍ

Rabbi annee massani ash-shaytaanu binusubin wa `adhaabin rabbi a`oodhu bika min hamazaati ash-shaytaani wa a`oodhu bika rabbi an yahdurooni wa hifzan min kulli shaytaanin maaridin[118]

---

[118] Based on verses Quran 38:41, 23:97-98, 37:7.

My Rabb (The reality of the Names comprising my essence)! **Satan** (the internal mechanism (ego) that promotes the illusory existence of the inexistent and veils the Absolute Reality) **is distressing and tormenting me. My Rabb, I seek refuge in You from the incitements of Satan, and I seek refuge in You from the presence of Satanic influences around me. And You have provided protection from all rejected Satans.**

This prayer is especially recommended as protection against satanic and jinni influences. When these two verses are read together they provide an ultimate protection against the harmful influences of the jinn. The 41st verse of chapter Sad was recited by Job (as) and the 97th and 98th verses of chapter al-Muminun were taught by Allah to Muhammad (saw).

The 7th verse of chapter as-Saffat is claimed to provide protection against jinn-related provocations. Anyone who may be prone to such negative influences should definitely recite these verses to be protected against them.

Psychics, and those who claim they are in contact with spirits, aliens or who think they are saints, sheiks or the Mahdi, should definitely recite these verses for some time; they will probably see that their abovementioned beliefs and assumptions will dissolve in a short time.

There are a few ways for this prayer to be effective...

1. The subject should read this prayer 200 or 300 times every morning and night until such effects are dissolved. It is also highly recommended that the person keeps a jug of water nearby while reciting, then blows into the water once the prayer is complete and drinks the water throughout the day.

2. A few trustworthy people should come together and recite this prayer 300 times each. They should also keep a jug of water and blow the prayer both onto the person and the water, and make the person drink the water. It is advisable for the person to also read these verses.

3. The person should read chapters Falaq and Nas 41 times every morning and night.

If all of these are done at the same time, the effect will be greater and results will be reached quicker.

Let me add, however, both the Ayat al-Qursi and the chapters Falaq and Nas are for passive protection. They are formulas that strengthen the person's brainpower and spirit, and form a protective magnetic field around the person.

The verses I provided above, on the other hand, are active formulas. When the person continues reciting them, their brain emanates such powerful frequencies that, like a laser gun, the jinn are disturbed by it and feel they must stay away.

Though I have provided detailed information about this topic in *Spirit, Man, Jinn*, I would like to share the following information here also:

When those who are under the influence of the jinn begin to recite these verses, they will at first feel great discomfort, in fact, they will be disturbed even if they don't read it themselves, but people around them read it. This is due to the jinn that have possessed them without their conscious choice, who are greatly discomforted by the waves produced by these verses, and their need to distance themselves and hence take the person with them.

Fever, hot flashes or sweaty hands may follow this feeling of discomfort. This is all due to the adrenalin secretion into the blood because of the jinn.

If the person can keep strong and resist all of this and continue to recite the verses, in only a few days time the majority of such effects will greatly diminish and he will begin to feel comforted. It's all up to the person's strength of will and ability to remain strong and fearless.

In my view, there is no need to incur unnecessary expenses by going to sheikhs or hodjas! The person himself or a group of his friends whom he trusts can easily apply this formula and cure themselves.

May Allah increase our awareness in this field and protect us from becoming subjects of the jinn.

> لَّا إِلَهَ إِلَّا أَنتَ سُبْحَانَكَ إِنِّي كُنتُ مِنَ الظَّالِمِينَ

Laa ilaaha illaa anta subḥaanaka innee kuntu mina l-ẓaalimeen[119]

There is no deity-god (there is no 'me') **only You** (the Names comprising my essential reality)**! I glorify You** (through my function that manifests Your Names)**! Indeed, I have been of the wrongdoers.**

The Rasul of Allah (saw) says:

"When Jonah (as) was in the belly of the fish he prayed, 'LAA ILAAHA ILLAA ANTA SUBHAANAKA INNEE KUNTU MINA L-ZAALIMEEN'. There is no Muslim who makes this prayer in regards to a situation and Allah does not accept his prayer."[120]

As mentioned in the Quran, in the 87th verse of chapter al-Anbiya, Jonah (as) was forgiven for a mistake he had made after continually making this prayer. Then he reached a state where he guided a community of over 100 thousand people to the right path.

Anyone who feels like Jonah, entrapped in the belly of this world, should read this prayer for relief and deliverance.

Reciting this prayer 300 times a day, which is a part of the formula I will provide in the following chapters, yields enormous benefits. Definitely continue doing so!

---

[119] Quran 21:87
[120] Al-Tirmidhi.

رَبِّ اشْرَحْ لِي صَدْرِي وَيَسِّرْ لِي أَمْرِي

Rabbi ishraḥ lee ṣadree wa yassir lee amree[121]

My Rabb, expand my consciousness (so that I may digest these and apply their requisites). **Ease my task for me.**

This is a part of Moses' (as) prayer. It has been seen that repeating it 300 times a day lifts grief away, enables assimilation and facilitates things to run smoothly in one's life.

When 300 repetitions of the verse 'Alam nashrah laka sadrak' is also added to this the effect is amplified and results are seen quicker.

Anyone who complains of inner distress, introversiveness, restlessness or depression should also add 1,800 repetitions of the name Basit.

وَإِن يَمْسَسْكَ اللّهُ بِضُرٍّ فَلاَ كَاشِفَ لَهُ إِلاَّ هُوَ وَإِن يُرِدْكَ بِخَيْرٍ فَلاَ رَآدَّ لِفَضْلِهِ يُصَيبُ بِهِ مَن يَشَاء مِنْ عِبَادِهِ وَهُوَ الْغَفُورُ الرَّحِيمُ

Wa'in yamsaska Llaahu biḍurrin falaa kaashifa lahu illaa huwa wa'in yuridka bi khayrin falaa raada lifaḍlihi yuṣeebu bihi yashaa' min `ibaadihi wa huwa l-ghafooru l-raḥeemu[122]

And if Allah should afflict you with an adversity, none can lift it other than Him! If He wills a good for you, none can repel His

---

[121] Quran 20:25-26.
[122] Quran 10:107.

bounty either! He causes His bounty to reach whom He wills of His servants... He is the Ghafur, the Rahim.

This prayer is recommended for those who are suffering from distress, depression or who have been afflicted by an unfavorable situation. Repeating it 100 times a day is proven to bring great benefit. Allah will lead the person out of that state into a state of well-being.

For whomever this kind of turning has been eased by Allah, surely deliverance is near!

رَّبِّ ارْحَمْهُمَا كَمَا رَبَّيَانِي صَغِيرًا

Rabbi irhamhumaa kamaa rabbayanee ṣagheeran[123]

My Rabb... Be merciful to them, as they tamed me when I was young.

The biggest responsibility one has is his responsibility to his parents. It is very difficult for us to pay the due of our parents, the means by which we come to life. But this verse teaches us a prayer we can make for them, simple to utter yet very deep in meaning. If we feel any responsibility at all in our conscience to even partly pay them back for everything they have done for us, we should most definitely include these words in our prayers.

---

[123] Quran 17:24.

رَبِّ أَوْزِعْنِي أَنْ أَشْكُرَ نِعْمَتَكَ الَّتِي أَنْعَمْتَ عَلَيَّ وَعَلَى وَالِدَيَّ وَأَنْ أَعْمَلَ صَالِحًا تَرْضَاهُ وَأَصْلِحْ لِي فِي ذُرِّيَّتِي إِنِّي تُبْتُ إِلَيْكَ وَإِنِّي مِنَ الْمُسْلِمِينَ

Rabbi awzi`anee an ashkura ni`mataka llatee an`amta `alayya wa `alaa waalidayya wa an a`maala ṣaalihan tarḍaahu wa aṣlih lee fee dhurriyyatee innaa tubtu ilayka wa'innee mina l-muslimeena[124]

My Rabb... Enable me and my parents to be grateful for the blessings You have bestowed upon us from Your favor, and to engage in deeds that will please You... And make righteous my offspring. I have repented to You and indeed I am of the Muslims (those who are aware of their submission)**!**

Abu Bakir as-Siddiq (ra) was the cause for the revelation of the above verse. His prayer regarding the guidance of his family was accepted by Allah and confirmed with this verse.

We could do an enormous good for our family and lineage if we also make this prayer on a continual basis. It is especially recommended to include this prayer after salat.

إِنَّ رَبِّي يَبْسُطُ الرِّزْقَ لِمَن يَشَاء وَيَقْدِرُ لَهُ وَأَنتَ خَيْرُ الرَّازِقِين

Inna rabbi yabsutur rizqa liman yashao wa yaqdiroo lah wa anta khayrur raziqeena

---

[124] Quran 46:15.

My Rabb, indeed You expand the provision of whom You will and constrain it for whom You will. You are the best of providers.

If this prayer is made together with the 26-27th verses of chapter Ali-Imran, those who are suffering from scarcity (both spiritual and material) will find great relief. The recommended reading of this prayer is 300 times a day.

رَّبِّ أَدْخِلْنِي مُدْخَلَ صِدْقٍ وَأَخْرِجْنِي مُخْرَجَ صِدْقٍ وَاجْعَل لِّي مِن لَّدُنكَ سُلْطَانًا نَّصِيرًا

Rabbi adkhilnee mudkhala ṣidqin wa akhrijnee mukhraja ṣidqin waaji`al lee min ladunka sulṭaanan naṣeeran[125]

My Rabb, wherever I enter make me enter in Truth and from wherever I exit make me exit in Truth, and form from Yourself (Your ladun; manifestation of a special angelic force from your grace) **victorious power!**

This is one of the most important prayers in the Quran. Here, Allah teaches us to enter something in truthfulness, to complete it upon truthfulness and to be equipped with divine power for its completion.

The word 'truthfulness' (sidq) encapsulates righteousness, submission, good intention and trustworthiness.

The reason why Abu Bakr (ra) is known as the 'siddiq' is because he carries all of these qualities. To initiate an affair or enter a place

---

[125] Quran 17:80.

157

equipped with all of these qualities is obviously the first step toward success. The second step is to have divine support; of course, the qualified ones will know the importance of this...

May Allah support us with a power from His Self, for as long as we work on His path...

رَبَّنَا آتِنَا مِن لَّدُنكَ رَحْمَةً وَهَيِّئْ لَنَا مِنْ أَمْرِنَا رَشَدًا

Rabbanaa aatinaa min ladunka rahmatan wahayy'i lanaa min amrinaa rashadan[126]

Our Rabb (the Name composition comprising our essential reality)**, grant us a grace** (a blessing with Your favor) **from Yourself** (with a special force manifesting from the absolute station of the Names, Your essence) **and form within us a state of perfection in this matter.**

Here, Allah is teaching us to pray to reach success in our affairs. He is also alerting us to seek success from His Self ('Ind'; the forces that are revealed through dimensional emergence to consciousness from the Names of Allah that comprise one's essence)... Thus, whenever we are praying for something regarding His essential qualities, such as Knowledge, Rahmah and Power, we should ask from His 'Ind'.

---

[126] Quran 18:10.

رَبِّ لَا تَذَرْنِي فَرْدًا وَأَنتَ خَيْرُ الْوَارِثِينَ

Rabbi la tadharnee fardan wa anta khayru l-waaritheena[127]

My Rabb... Do not leave me on my own in life (grant me an heir)**! You are the best of heirs.**

Zachariah (as) had grown old, but still did not have any children... So he prayed to his Rabb with the verse above and his prayer was accepted; he was bestowed with a son whom he called John.

This was the John who gave the good news of the coming of Jesus (as)...

Those who want to have children should recite this verse. The most effective way to do so is by performing the salat called 'Hajat' after midnight, and then repeating this prayer 1,000 times for a number of successive nights.

---

[127] Quran 21:89.

33

SALAWAT TO THE RASUL OF ALLAH

إِنَّ اللَّهَ وَمَلَائِكَتَهُ يُصَلُّونَ عَلَى النَّبِيِّ يَا أَيُّهَا الَّذِينَ آمَنُوا صَلُّوا عَلَيْهِ وَسَلِّمُوا تَسْلِيمًا

Inna Allaha wa malaa'ikatihu yasalloona `alaa nabee yaa ayyuhaalladheena-amanoo salloo `alayhi wa sallimoo tasleeman[128]

Indeed, Allah and His angels bestow blessings upon the Nabi... O believers, send blessings (turn to) **him and greet him in submission!**

This verse makes it compulsory for us to send blessings (give salawat) to our master, the Rasul, the light of insight, Allah's beloved... Why is this so? The Rasul of Allah (saw) says:

"One who does not show gratitude to others is incapable of showing gratitude to Allah."[129]

---

[128] Quran 33:56.
[129] Abu Dawud, al-Tirmidhi.

This presents to us one of the deepest truths of Sufism... If we have eradicated at least some of the veils covering the perception of our heart we may see this...

If we can understand the sublimity of the verse "Allah gives to the givers" we will know without doubt that whoever the apparent giver may be, it is always Allah who is giving! And to thank Allah is by thanking the apparent cause through which He has chosen to give! Otherwise, we won't be thanking the real giver, but a god of our own creation!

Since Allah gave to us through the Rasul of Allah (saw) and showed and enabled us to realize the truth through him, then surely to thank the Rasul of Allah (saw) is to thank Allah.

This is why Allah, through the Quran, orders us to thank the Rasul (saw). It is also based on this truth that the Rasul (saw) has asked that we send blessings to him:

"May he be defaced who hears my name yet does not send blessings to me!"[130]

"The stingiest of the stingiest is he near whom my name is mentioned, yet he does not send blessings to me"[131]

"Prayers are too weak to rise to the heavens, but when I am sent blessings they gain strength and rise (they become worthy of response)..."[132]

"Whoever sends one blessing to me, Allah will grant him ten blessings, erase his mistakes and raise him by ten degrees."[133]

"The closest ones to me among mankind are those who send the most blessings to me."[134]

---

[130] Al-Tirmidhi.
[131] Al-Tirmidhi.
[132] Al-Tirmidhi, al-Tabarani.
[133] Al-Nasai.
[134] Al-Tirmidhi.

"Whoever forgets to send blessings to me, he will be made to forget the path to Paradise."[135]

"Whoever sends blessings to me near my grave, I will hear his voice. Whoever sends blessings to me from afar, it will reach me..."[136]

"As long as one who makes a prayer fails to send blessings to the Nabis and Rasuls, his prayer is veiled."[137]

"Allah has angels who travel throughout the earth and inform me of those who send blessings to me."[138]

"Allah enlightens the path on the Bridge of Sirat of those who send blessings to me... If one is of the enlightened, he won't be of the people of fire..."[139]

"If a group of people come together and leave the gathering without remembering Allah or sending blessings to me they will be veiled from Allah!"[140]

"If any of you want to ask for something from Allah, they should first offer hamd to Him in a way that He deserves, then send blessings to His Rasul, and then make his prayer. This is more effective in reaching his goal..."[141]

"Increase your blessings to me on Fridays, for that is the day your blessings are offered to me."[142]

---

[135] Ibn Majah.
[136] Al-Bayhaqi.
[137] Al-Tabarani.
[138] Al-Nasai.
[139] Al-Mustadrak.
[140] Al-Tirmidhi, Abu Dawud.
[141] Al-Tirmidhi.
[142] Al-Nasai.

"Whoever wants to be close to me in Paradise should send blessings to me to that extent."[143]

"I met with Gabriel, he told me, 'I have good news: Allah said whoever sends blessings to you He will give blessings to them, whoever gives blessings to you He will give blessings to them'…"[144]

One of the companions of the Rasul of Allah (saw) asked:

"O Rasul of Allah, I send a lot of blessings to you. How much of my time shall I set aside for this?"

The Rasul of Allah replied, "As much as you want."

"How about a quarter?" the man asked again.

"Do as much as you will… If you increase it, it will be better for you!" said the Rasul of Allah (saw).

"How about a third?" the man continued…

"Do as much as you will… If you increase it, it will be better for you!" the Rasul replied.

"How about a half?" he asked.

"Do as much as you will… If you increase it, it will be better for you!" repeated the Rasul.

"How about all of my time?" the man insisted…

"Then it will be enough, all of your sins will be forgiven" said the Rasul (saw).[145]

I hope these hadith have given an idea on the importance of salawat. Let everyone ponder the importance of this topic and evaluate it according to their understanding.

---

[143] Al-Tirmidhi.
[144] Al-Bayhaqi, al-Hakim.
[145] Al-Tirmidhi.

Here are some recommended salawats.

جَزَىَ اللهُ عَنَّا سَيِّدَنَا مُحَمَّدًا مَا هُوَ اَهْلُهُ

Jazaa Allahu `anaa Sayeedinaa Muhammadan maa huwa ahluhu

O Allah, give blessings to our master Muhammad (saw) as he deserves. We are impotent from duly evaluating him...

The Rasul of Allah (saw) has taught us this salawat himself and said, "Whoever says it like this, 70 angels will write merits for him for a thousand mornings."[146]

اَللّهُمَّ صَلِّ عَلَى مَنْ رُوحُهُ مِحْرَابُ الاَرْوَاحِ وَالْمَلائِكَةِ وَالْكَوْنِ اَللّهُمَّ صَلِّ عَلَى مَنْ هُوَ اِمَامُ الاَنْبِيَاءِ وَالْمُرْسَلِينَ اَللّهُمَّ صَلِّ عَلَى مَنْ هُوَ اِمَامُ اَهْلِ الْجَنَّةِ عِبَادِ اللهِ الْمُؤْمِنِينَ

Allahumma salli `alaa man roohuhu mihraabool arwaahi wa malaa'ikatihi wa kawni. Allahumma salli `alaa man huwa imaamool anbiyaa wa mursaleena. Allahumma salli `alaa man huwa imaam ahli l'jannati abaadi-l Allahi l'muumeena

O Allah! May You give blessings to the One who is the Spirit of the summit (mihrab) of all the spirits, the angels and

---

[146] Al-Tabarani.

164

everything that has come into existence, and grant Your blessings to the imam of all the Nabis and the Rasuls! O Allah, grant Your blessings to the imam of Your believing servants, the people of Paradise.

The Pillar (Ghawth) of the time 300 years ago, Sayyid Abdulaziz ad-Dabbagh, used to attend all the Gatherings of the Diwan, due to his position. In one of these meetings he narrated the following incident between himself and the daughter of the Rasul of Allah (saw), Fatima (ra):

"We were in one of the Gatherings of the Diwan. I was sitting to the right of the Rasul of Allah (saw) with the rest of our friends. Opposite us were some female saints and other spiritual guides. Then Fatima (ra) came and sat in front of them and with the language of Paradise she uttered this salawat... In the language of Paradise every sentence or word is expressed as a letter... The letters preceding some of the chapters of the Quran, such as alif, lam, mim, ra, ta, ha and so on, also pertain to this language. After listening to this salawat, I went next to Fatima (ra) and asked her, 'What is the merit of this salawat, O Fatima?' She replied, 'If all of the trees, leaves, rocks and rubble on earth became jewels they could not pay the due of the person who continues to give this salawat!' I could not believe the scope of its merit, so I went next to the Rasul of Allah (saw) and asked him. He said, 'Fatima told you, what else do you want? It is exactly as she has told you!' The first thing I did upon this was to translate it to Arabic."

Such is the significance of the salawat I provided above... Evaluate it as you like, but I believe we should read it at least 100 times a day.

أَللّٰهُمَّ صَلِّ عَلَى سَيِّدِنَا مُحَمَّدٍ وَ عَلَى أَلِ سَيِّدِنَا مُحَمَّدٍ قَدْ ضَاقَتْ حِيلَتِى اَدْرِكْنِى يَا رَسُولَ اللهِ

Allahumma salli `alaa sayyeedinaa Muhammadin `alaa aali Sayeedinaa Muhammad, qad daaqat heelatee adhriknee yaa Rasool Allah

O Allah... Grant Your blessings to our master Muhammad and his family... I am very distressed and troubled (I feel helpless), **help me** (hold my hand, help me), **O Rasul of Allah!**

Many have read this salawat 125 times after their five prescribed salats and were delivered from their hardships. It is indeed a beautiful thing to ask for help from the spirit of the Rasul of Allah (saw). Even though we may feel unworthy who but Him can we seek refuge in and seek intercession from in this world and the hereafter!

أَللّٰهُمَّ صَلِّ وَسَلِّمْ وَبَارِكْ عَلَى سَيِّدِنَا مُحَمَّدٍ عَدَدَ خَلْقِكَ وَرِضَآءَ نَفْسِكَ وَزِنَةَ عَرْشِكَ وَمِدَادَ كَلِمَاتِكَ

Allahumma salli wa sallim wa baarik `alaa sayeedinaa Muhammadin `adada khalqika wa ridaa nafsika wa zeenata `arsheeka wa midaada kalimaatiq

O Allah... Grant Your praise and blessings and prosperity upon our master Muhammad (saw), to the number of Your creation, until You are pleased, to the weight of Your Throne, to the number of Your words (ink).

The Rasul of Allah taught this salawat to his wife... Nobody can estimate the reward of this salawat when done with the exact same words. If only we can read it at least 100 times a day!

اَللّٰهُمَّ صَلِّ عَلَى سَيِّدِنَا وَمَوْلَانَا مُحَمَّدٍ شَجَرَةِ الْأَصْلِ النُّورَانِيَّةِ وَلَمْعَةِ الْقَبْضَةِ الرَّحْمَانِيَّةِ وَأَفْضَلِ الْخَلِيقَةِ الْإِنْسَانِيَّةِ وَأَشْرَفِ الصُّوَرِ الْجِسْمَانِيَّةِ وَمَنْبَعِ الْأَسْرَارِ الْإِلٰهِيَّةِ وَخَزَائِنِ الْعُلُومِ الْإِصْطِفَائِيَّةِ صَاحِبِ الْقَبْضَةِ الْأَصْلِيَّةِ وَالرُّتْبَةِ الْعَلِيَّةِ وَالْبَهْجَةِ السَّنِيَّةِ مَنْ اِنْدَرَجَتِ النَّبِيُّونَ تَحْتَ لِوَائِهِ فَهُمْ مِنْهُ وَاِلَيْهِ وَصَلِّ وَسَلِّمْ عَلَيْهِ وَعَلَى آلِهِ وَصَحْبِهِ عَدَدَ مَا خَلَقْتَ وَرَزَقْتَ وَأَمَتَّ وَأَحْيَيْتَ اِلَى يَوْمِ تَبْعَثُ مَنْ أَفْنَيْتَ وَصَلِّ وَسَلِّمْ عَلَيْهِ وَعَلَيْهِمْ تَسْلِيمًا كَثِيرًا

Allahumma salli `ala sayeedinaa Muhammadin wa mawlaanaa Muhammadin shajarati 'l-asli 'n-nooraaneeati wa lam`atil qabdati 'r-rahmaaneeati wa afdali 'l-khaleeqati 'l-insaaneeati wa ashrafi l'suwari l'jismaaneeati wa manb` l-asraari l-ilaheeati wa jazaa'ani l-`ulumi l-istifaaiyyati saahibi l'-qabdati l-asleeati wa r-rutbati l'aalitati wa l-bahjati s-saniyaati man indarajati 'n-nabiyyoona tahta liwaa'ihifahum minhu wa ilayhi wa salli wa sallim `alayhi wa `alaa alihi wa sahbihi `adada maa khalaqta wa razaqta wa amata wa ahyayta ilaa yawmi tab`athu man afnayta wa salli wa sallim `alayhi wa `aleehim tasleeman katheeran

O Allah! Grant Your blessings upon our master and Protector Muhammad, the ancestry of the essence of knowledge (Nur), the spark of the handle of the Rahman, the best of human creation, the most honored among all forms, the source of divine secrets, the treasury of the chosen (purified) **knowledge, the possessor of the essential handle, high rank and sublime beauty... All Nabis have been granted their degrees under his banner, they are from him and for him... And grant him, his family and companions blessings** (salat and salam) **to the number of those whom You have created and for whom You have provided, those**

whom You have caused to die and those whom You brought to life, until the day You resurrect those whom You have caused to die... And make Your blessings perpetual upon him and the others.

This salawat was compiled by the leading saints of his time. Sayyid Ahmad al-Badawi has the following story:

This eminent person read the 'Dalail-i Hayrat', a collection composed of salawats to the Rasul of Allah (saw), fourteen times in one day and then peacefully fell asleep... In his dream he saw the Rasul of Allah (saw) who told him, "If instead of reading the Dalaili Hayrat fourteen times you had read this salawat only once, it would have been sufficient."

The Dalail-i Hayrat is an invaluable collection comprising hundreds of salawats! Yet reading the salawat above just once is considered more valuable than reading the entire collection fourteen times over! If only we can read it at least once a day!

اَللّٰهُمَّ صَلِّ عَلَى سَيِّدِنَا مُحَمَّدٍ بَحْرِ اَنْوَارِكَ وَمَعْدَنِ اَسْرَارِكَ وَلِسَانِ حُجَّتِكَ وَعَرُوسِ مَمْلَكَتِكَ وَاِمَامِ حَضْرَتِكَ وَطِرَازِ مُلْكِكَ وَخَزَائِنِ رَحْمَتِكَ وَطَرِيقِ شَرِيعَتِكَ الْمُتَلَذِّذِ بِتَوْحِيدِكَ اِنْسَانِ عَيْنِ الْوُجُودِ وَالسَّبَبِ فِى كُلِّ مَوْجُودٍ عَيْنِ اَعْيَانِ خَلْقِكَ الْمُتَقَدِّمِ مِنْ نُورِ ضِيَائِكَ صَلَاةً تَدُومُ بِدَوَامِكَ وَتَبْقَى بِبَقَائِكَ لاَ مُنْتَهَى لَهَا دُونَ عِلْمِكَ صَلَاةً تُرْضِيكَ وَتُرْضِيهِ وَتَرْضَى بِهَا عَنَّا يَا رَبَّ الْعَالَمِينَ

Allahumma salli `alaa sayyeedinaa Muhammadin bahri anwaarika wa maa`dani asraarika wa lisaani hujjatika wa aroosi mamlakatika wa imaami hadratika wa tiraazi mulkika wa jazaa'ini rahmatika wa tareeqi sharee'aatika l'mutaladhadhi bi-tawhdika insaani 'ayni-l wujoodi wa s'sababi fee kulli mawjoodin 'ayni a'ayaani khalqika l'mutaqaddimi min noori diyaa'ika salatan tadum wa tabqaa bibaqaa'ika la muntahaa lahaa doona 'ilmika salatan turdeeka wa turdeehi wa turdaa bihaa 'aanaa ya Rabba l'alameen

O Allah! Grant Your blessings to our master Muhammad, the ocean of Your Nur, the source of Your secrets, the tongue of Your proof, the bridegroom of Your kingdoms, the leader of Your presence, the embroidery of Your dominion, the vault of Your grace, the way of Your law, the delight of Your Oneness, the pupil of the eye of existence, the cause of all existence. Let these blessings be lasting for as long as You last and be remaining as long as You remain, blessings which are limitless in Your knowledge, blessings that please You, that please him and by which You are pleased with us, O Rabb of the Worlds.

This salawat is recommended especially for those who want to advance spiritually. This is the salawat that Hadhrat Ali (ra), the sultan of the inner world, read and claimed its value was equivalent to 70 thousand salawats. Can one ever comprehend the value of this salawat recommended by the gate of knowledge and wisdom, I do not know...

أَللّٰهُمَّ صَلِّ صَلاَةً كَامِلَةً وَسَلِّمْ سَلاَمًا تَامًّ عَلَى سَيِّدِنَا مُحَمَّدٍ الَّذِى تَنْحَلُّ بِهِ الْعُقُدُ وَتَنْفَرِجُ بِهِ الْكُرَبُ وَتُقْضَى بِهِ الْحَوَآئِجُ وَتُنَالُ بِهِ الرَّغَآئِبُ وَحُسْنُ الْخَوَاتِمِ وَيُسْتَسْقَى الْغَمَامُ بِوَجْهِهِ الْكَرِيمِ وَعَلَى آلِهِ وَصَحْبِهِ فِى كُلِّ لَمْحَةٍ وَنَفَسٍ بِعَدَدِ كُلِّ مَعْلُومٍ لَكَ

Allahumma salli salatan kaamilatan wa sallim salaamaan taamman
`alaa sayydeedinaa Muhammadin l'illadhee tanhallu bihi l-uqadu wa
tanfariju bihi l-kurabu wa tuqdaa bihi l-hawaaij wa tunaalu bihi r-
raghaaibu wa husnu l-khawaatimi wa yustasqaa l-ghamaamu
biwaj'hihi l-kareemi wa `alaa alihi wa sahbihi fee kulli lamhatin wa
nafsin bi `adadi kulli m`aaloomin laka

**O Allah, grant Your blessings to our master Muhammad, the
person via whom all knots are undone, all distress and sadness is
removed, all needs are met, all desires and beauties are reached,
for the sake of whose noble face rain is dispersed from the
clouds, and his family and companions, at all times and
continually, with perfect and consummate praise and blessing.**

I've included this well known salawat here for those who may not
be aware of it. Time and time again, it has been experienced that
favorable results are quickly reached when those in difficulty
assemble and read this salawat 4,444 times in total, with the
intention of finding relief from a particular difficulty.

أللّٰهُمَّ رَبَّ هَاذِهِ الدَّعْوَةِ التَّامَّةِ وَالصَّلاَةِ الْقَائِمَةِ آتِ مُحَمَّدًا الْوَسِيلَةَ وَالْفَضِيلَةَ
وَالدَّرَجَةَ الرَّفِيعَةَ وَابْعَثْهُ مَقَامًا مَحْمُودًا الَّذِى وَعَدْتَهُ إِنَّكَ لاَ تُخْلِفُ الْمِيعَادَ

Allahumma rabba haadhihi-d d`aawati t-taamati wa salati l-qaaimati
aati Muhammadan al-waseelata wa l-fadeelata wa-d darajata wa
rafee`ata wab `ath-hu maqaamaa Mahmudan l-illadhee wa `adtahu
innaka la tuklefu l-mee`aad

O Allah, the Rabb of this perfect call and of this prayer to be performed, bestow upon Muhammad al waseelah (a station in Paradise) **and al fadeelah** (a rank above the rest of creation) **and send him upon a raised platform which You have promised him. Verily, You never fail in Your Promise.**

The Rasul of Allah (saw) says:

"Whoever listens to the adhan without speaking and repeats its words and then reads this prayer, my intercession will be compulsory upon him in the afterlife."[147]

Indeed, all believers, especially those who have committed major mistakes, are going to be in serious need of the Rasul of Allah.

أَللّهُمَّ صَلِّ عَلَى مُحَمَّدٍ وَآدَمَ وَنُوحٍ وَاِبْرَهِيمَ وَمُوسَى وَعِيسَى وَمَا بَيْنَهُمْ مِنَ النَّبِيِّينَ وَالْمُرْسَلِينَ صَلَوَاتُ اللهِ وَ سَلَامُهُ عَلَيْهِمْ اَجْمَعِينَ

Allahumma salli `alaa Sayyeedina Muhammadin wa Aadam wa Noohin wa Ibraheem wa Moosa wa `Isaa wa maa baynahum mina n-nabiyyeena wa l-mursaleena salawaatu l-lillahi wa salaamuhu alayhim ajma`een

O Allah! Grant Your blessings upon Muhammad, Adam, Noah, Abraham, Moses, Jesus, and all the Nabis and Rasuls that have come in between them... May the praise and blessings of Allah be upon them all.

---

[147] Sahih al-Bukhari.

This salawat, taught by the Rasul of Allah (saw), was narrated by Hadhrat Aisha (ra):

"Whoever reads this salawat before going to bed, all of the Nabis and Rasuls that have come to earth will intercede for him in the afterlife."

What better than the intercession of all the Nabis and Rasuls? Let us then read this salawat at least once before going to bed every night...

34

THREE EXPLANATIONS FROM THE RASUL OF ALLAH (SAW)

I would like to highlight three important explanations of the Rasul. The first is about patience.

Muaz bin Jabal (ra) narrates:

When the Rasul of Allah (saw) heard a man praying, "O Allah, please grant me patience!" he said, "You just asked for trouble! Ask for welfare!"

This is important advice. The truth pointed out here by the Rasul of Allah (saw) is that when one asks for patience, one is indirectly asking for trouble, so they may be patient in the face of it! It's almost like saying, "Give me hardship so that I can be patient"! Thus, the Rasul forbids us to ask for patience and advises that we ask for welfare instead![148]

As for the second advice… Again, the Rasul (saw) heard a man praying in which he mentioned the name "O Dhu'l Jalali wal ikram…" Upon this, the Rasul (saw) said, "You have been answered, ask for whatever you want." Here we're given a tip on the

---

[148] Al-Tirmidhi.

powerful effect of mentioning in our prayers the name 'Dhul jalai wal ikram'.[149]

The third explanation: The Rasul of Allah (saw) heard a man praying, "O Allah, I ask from You a comprehensive blessing." They asked him "What is a comprehensive blessing?" He answered, "I made a prayer and I await good tidings as a result (how can a blessing be comprehensive?). Upon this, the Rasul (saw) said, "The comprehensive blessing is to be saved from Hell and to enter Paradise!"[150]

---

[149] Al-Tirmidhi.
[150] Al-Tirmidhi.

35

TASBIH

There is nothing that does not exalt (tasbih) **Him with hamd** (evaluation of the corporeal worlds created with His Names, as He wills)**! But you do not perceive their functions! Indeed, He is the Halim, the Ghafur.**[151]

Everything in the heavens and the earth glorifies (tasbih) **Allah** (through fulfilling their functions)**. HU is the Aziz, the Hakim.**[152]

All perceivable and unperceivable things in the universe have been created to engage in the exaltation through the observation (tasbih) of Allah. Whether good or bad, beautiful or ugly, perfect or imperfect!

So, let us try and understand the verses above in this light:

The limitless infinite beings under the scope of what is denoted by 'Throne' (Arsh) are all compositions of the Names of Allah manifesting divine meanings.

---

[151] Quran 17:44.
[152] Quran 57:1.

'Rahman establishing His sovereignty on the Arsh' points to the reality that existence is a product of the materialization of the qualities denoted by the Names of Allah, i.e. it has come about to manifest the meanings of the divine names... All forms are instances of the Grace of Allah.

Thus, every 'thing', in respect of being the cause of disclosure for Allah's names, is constantly and at every moment rotating around the divine meaning that composes it. This is what 'tasbih' essentially means!

In other words, all things, by way of manifesting the meaning of the name it's comprised of, is inevitably in servitude to Allah, and this servitude is its tasbih.

This type of tasbih is referred to as *non-arbitrary*, it is the first way. The second way is *arbitrary*. Arbitrary tasbih can be carried out in two ways, either by imitation or by enquiry. Tasbih by imitation is when one applies the recommended formulas by repeating certain words without really being conscious of their meaning. Doing this will strengthen the person's spirit and provide much benefit in the various stages of their afterlife, such as the dimension of the grave, the place of resurrection, when crossing the bridge of Sirat and in Paradise!

As for tasbih by enquiry, this is when the person has made the necessary enquiry and consciously acquired the meanings of what is uttered. As a result, not only is the person strengthened in spirit, but also, through the meanings of the words he utters, he inspirationally and insightfully begins to understand Allah within his essence in much greater depth.

During all of these practices, however, one should always be mindful of the fact that contemplating Allah's Absolute Essence (dhat) is not possible as He is ever beyond anything that is perceivable or thinkable.

Now, I would like to provide some recommended tasbihs...

سُبْحَانَ اللهِ وَبِحَمْدِهِ

Subhaana L-Llahi wa bihamdihi

Allah is Subhan with his Hamd (I exalt Allah and exempt Allah through observation, knowing that evaluating His universal perfection (hamd) belongs only to Him! As there is no other, Allah is the evaluator of Himself.)

There are two hadith regarding this tasbih. The Rasul of Allah (saw) says:

"Whoever says 'Subhaana L-Llahi wa bihamdihi' a hundred times a day their sins and mistakes, even if as much as the foam of the oceans, will be cleansed and forgiven."[153]

One day the Rasul (saw) asked his companions:

"Shall I tell you the word Allah loves most?"

"Please tell us, O Rasul of Allah" they said.

"The word that is dearest to Allah is 'Subhaana L-Llahi wa bihamdihi'."[154]

---

[153] Sahih al-Bukhari, al-Tirmidhi.
[154] Sahih al-Muslim, al-Tirmidhi, Musnad of Ahmad ibn Hanbal.

سُبْحَانَ اللهِ وَبِحَمْدِهِ عَدَدَ خَلْقِهِ وَرِضَاءَ نَفْسِهِ وَزِنَةَ عَرْشِهِ وَمِدَادَ كَلِمَاتِهِ

Subhaana L-Llahi wa bihamdihi `adada khalqihi wa ridaa'a nafsihi
wa zinata arshihi wa midaada kalimaatihi

I exalt (through HIS observation) **and exempt** (tanzih) **Allah**
(from my limited understanding) **with His evaluation, to the
quantity of His creations, to the fullness of His pleasure, to the
weight of His Throne and the ink of His words.**

One day, after completing the fajr salat, the Rasul of Allah (saw)
left Juwayriyya (ra) and went away. When he came back mid-
morning he found Juwayriyya (ra) in the same spot still engaged in
tasbih. He asked, "Have you been doing tasbih since I left you until
now?" Juwayriyya answered, "Yes". Upon this, the Rasul said,
"After I left you I repeated four short sentences three times, if they
were out on a scale they would weigh heavier than the tasbih you've
been doing. These four sentences are: **Subhaana L-Llahi wa
bihamdihi `adada khalqihi wa ridaa'a nafsihi wa zinata arshihi
wa midaada kalimaatihi.**[155]

سُبْحَانَ اللهِ وَالْحَمْدُ لِلهِ وَلاَ إِلَهَ إِلاَّ اللهُ وَاللهُ أَكْبَرُ وَلاَ حَوْلَ وَلاَ قُوَّةَ إِلاَّ بِاللهِ
الْعَلِيِّ الْعَظِيمِ

Subhaana L-Llah wa-l hamdulillah wa laa ilaha illa l-Llahu wa Llahu
akbar wa la hawla wa la quwatta iilla bi-l Llahil `aliyyil Adheem[156]

---

[155] Al-Tirmidhi, Musnad of Ahmad ibn Hanbal, Abu Dawud, Sahih al-Muslim.
[156] Musnad of Ahmad ibn Hanbal, al-Nasai, al-Tirmidhi, Sahih al-Muslim.

Subhanallah: Allah is Subhan (beyond being conditioned by existence and anything other than…)

Alhamdulillah: Hamd (absolute evaluation) **is one that is in the scope of the name Allah, thus it pertains to the One denoted by the name Allah…**

La ilaha illa Allah: Nothing exists other than the One denoted by the name Allah!

Allahu akbar: Allah is great! He can never be perceived or evaluated by a being other than Himself and He can never be conditioned or limited by any evaluation, attribute, quality, etc.

Wa la hawla wa la quwwata illa billahil aliyyil Adheem: All strength (motion, action, transformation and state of tasbih) **and power** (with which this is carried out) **is with Allah, the Aliy** (the unsurpassable sublime, the One who destroys the assumption of an 'other' from whom He wills) **the Azim** (the One whose Might none can surpass)**!**

The Rasul of Allah (saw) explains the merit of this tasbih with the following hadith:

"Reciting this dhikr is more beloved than everything upon which the sun rises, the whole world and everything that is in it."

This tasbih is also done in salat and is called 'Salat-i Tasbih'.

لَاَاِلَهَ اِلَّاَاللهُوَحْدَهُ لاَ شَرِيكَ لَهُ، لَهُ الْمُلْكُ وَ لَهُ الْحَمْدُ وَ هُوَ عَلَى كُلِّ شَيْءٍ قَدِيرٌ

Laa ilaaha illa Allah wa-h dahu la shareeka lah lahu l-mulku wa lahu l-hamd wa huwa `alaa kulli shayin qadeer[157]

---

[157] Sahih al-Bukhari, Sahih al-Muslim, al-Tirmidhi.

There is no deity-god (being or existence other than Allah)**, there is only the One denoted by the name Allah, who has no partners. To Him belongs the Sovereignty, to Him belongs evaluation. HU is Qadir over all things.**

Abu Ayyash adh-Dhuraki (ra) narrates:

The Rasul of Allah (saw) says, "Whoever says, 'Laa ilaaha illa Allah wa-h dahu la shareeka lah lahu l-mulku wa lahu l-hamd wa huwa `alaa kulli shayin qadeer' in the morning, he will gain as much merit as though he has freed a slave from the children of Ishmael (as), ten of his mistakes will be erased, he will be raised by ten degrees, and he will be protected from the devil until the end of that day. If he reads it at night, he will earn the same merits and the equivalent will apply until the next morning."

لَاآلَهَ اِلَّااللّٰهُوَحْدَهُ لَا شَرِيكَ لَهُ، لَهُ الْمُلْكُ وَ لَهُ الْحَمْدُ يُحْي وَ يُمِيتُ وَ هُوَ حَيٌّ لَا يَمُوتُ اَبَدًا بِيَدِهِ الْخَيْرُ وَ هُوَ عَلَى كُلِّ شَيْءٍ قَدِيرٌ

Laa ilaaha illa Allahu wa-h dahu la shareeka lahu l-mulku wa lahu l-hamd yuhyee wa yumeetu wa huwa hayyun la yamootu abadan bi yadhihi l-khayru wa huwa `alaa kulli shayin qadeer[158]

There is no deity-god (being or existence other than Allah) **there is only the One denoted by the name Allah. To Him belongs all sovereignty. To Him belongs all evaluation. He brings to life** (with knowledge) **and enables the experience of death; He is the everliving Hayy... All good is eternally in the hands** (power) **of HU... HU is Qadir over all things."**

---

[158] Al-Tirmidhi.

The Rasul of Allah (saw) says:

"Whoever does this tasbih because this is really what he believes about Allah, Allah will put him into Paradises of Bliss."

While other hadith talk about gaining merits or deletion of sins, this hadith is about a direct entrance to Paradise... Thus, it is imperative we understand its meaning. Here it is again:

There is no deity-god, Allah is One, He has no partners, sovereignty and evaluation belong to him, He gives life and takes life, the concept of death does not apply to Him, He is the eternally everliving One, all good is eternally in His power and He is powerful over all things.

سُبْحَانَ اللهِ وَبِحَمْدِهِ سُبْحَانَ اللهِ الْعَظِيمِ اَسْتَغْفِرُ اللهَ وَ اَتُوبُ اِلَيْهِ

Subhaana Allahi wa Bi hamdihi Subhaana Allahi l-`aliyyil adheem asgahfiroo Allaha wa atoobu ilayhi[159]

Allah is Subhan with His hamd (I tasbih and tanzih Allah with His hamd). **Allah, the Azim is Subhan** (I tasbih and tanzih Allah the possessor of might). **I ask for forgiveness from Allah** (I ask that my 'personhood' or ego-based identity is covered). **My repentance** (return) **is to HU.**

Ibn Abbas narrates that the Rasul of Allah (saw) says:

"Whoever says 'Subha-nal-lahi-wa-biham-dihi, Subha-nal-lahil Adeem, astaghfirullaaha wa atubu ilayhe,' this will be recorded in their book of deeds and sent to the Throne. Until the person enters the presence of Allah on the Day of Resurrection this prayer will

---

[159] Sahih al-Bukhari, Sahih al-Muslim.

remain sealed. No mistake or sin he does can erase the merits of this prayer."

As known, mistakes erase merits, but this tasbih is not erased by any sin or mistake. Perhaps we should ponder this...

لَكَ الْحَمْدُ كَمَا يَنْبَغِى لِجَلَالِ وَجْهِكَ وَلِعَظِيمِ سُلْطَانِكَ

Laka l-hamdu kamaa yanbaghee lijalaali wajhika wa li `atheemi sultaanika[160]

Evaluation belongs to You, as the Glory of Your countenance and the might of Your sultanate deserves.

Omar (ra) narrates from the Rasul of Allah (saw):

A servant of Allah said, 'O Rabb, Hamd belongs to You, as the jalal of Your countenance and the might of Your sultanate deserves'. The inscriber angels did not know how to record the merits of this tasbih so they ascended to the heavens and asked, 'O Rabb, Your servant said something we dont know what to write'. Allah, even though He knew, asked, 'What did My servant say?' They answered, 'O Rabb, Your servant said 'Hamd belongs to You, as the jalal of Your countenance and the might of Your sultanate deserves,' whereupon Allah said, 'Write it as it is until My servant meets Me, I will grant the merits of this Myself.'

We know from other hadith that the Rasul (saw) used to say this tasbih in his salat when he arose from the ruku position before prostrating.

---

[160] Ibn Majah *al-Zawa'id.*

This is a practice that I've incorporated into my life for many years and one that I recommend to others.

لآاِلَهَ اِلاَّاللهُوَحْدَهُ لاَ شَرِيكَ لَهُ، لَهُ الْمُلْكُ وَ لَهُ الْحَمْدُ وَ هُوَ عَلَى كُلِّ شَيْءٍ
قَدِيرٌ * اَلْحَمْدُ لِلهِ وَ سُبْحَانَ اللهِ وَ لاَ اِلَهَ اِلاَّاللهُ وَاللهُ اَكْبَرُ وَ لاَ حَوْلَ وَ لاَ قُوَّةَ اِلاَّ
بِااللهِ الْعَلِىِّ الْعَظِيمِ

Laa ilaaha illa Allah wa-h dahu la shareeka lah lahu l-mulku wa lahu l-hamd wa huwa `alaa kulli shayin qadeer. Al-hamdulillahi wa subhaana Allahi wa laa ilaha illa l-Llahu wa Llahu akbar wa la hawla wa la quwatta iilla bi-l Llahil `aliyyil Adheem[161]

There is no deity-god (being or existence other than Allah) **there is only the One denoted by the name Allah. To Him belongs all sovereignty. To Him belongs evaluation. HU is Qadir over all things. Hamd** (absolute evaluation) **is in the scope of the name Allah, it belongs to the One denoted by the name Allah. Allah is Subhan** (beyond being limited or conditioned by existence or anything besides it). **There is no existence besides Allah. Allah is great! He can never be perceived or evaluated by a being other than Himself and He can never be conditioned or limited by any evaluation, attribute, quality, etc. All strength** (motion, action, transformation and state of tasbih) **and power** (with which this is carried out) **is with Allah, the Aliy** (the unsurpassable sublime, the One who destroys the assumption of an 'other' from whom He wills) **the Azim** (the One whose Might none can surpass)**!**

---

[161] Ibn Majah.

The Rasul of Allah (saw) says:

"Whoever wakes up in the middle of the night and while turning from one side to the other remembers to make his prayer and then repents will be forgiven, his prayers will be answered. If he gets up takes ablution and performs two rakats of salat, his salat will be accepted..."

Many have tried this and found it to be very effective. It is especially recommended for those who may be going through a difficult time or who may be afflicted with an adverse situation.

Other than the tasbih I have provided above via various hadith, I would also like to share some other special tasbihs. I believe these too should be read at least 100 times a day.

Subhana dhil Mulki wal Malakuti: Beyond being conditioned is the possessor of sovereighty and the angelic dimension.

Subhanal Malikil hayyil ladhi, la yamūtu: Beyond being conditioned is the Everliving Sovereign One.

Subhana dhil `Izzati wal jabaroot: Beyond being conditioned is the owner of Majesty and Omnipotence.

Subhanal-malikil-quddus, Rabb-al-mala'ikati wa-r-ruh: Beyond being conditioned is the Sublime King , the owner of the angels and the Spirit.

Subhana khaliq-an nur wa bi ham-di-hi: Beyond being conditioned is the creator of the light of knowledge by His own evaluation.

Subhana rabbi kulli shayin: Beyond being conditioned is the Rabb of all things (no 'thing' is besides or other than Him, but no thing can be named Allah either; everything is in a state of tasbih with His hamd!).

36

THE SUPREME NAME

This has been one of the most obscure topics among the acquainted…

The Supreme Name (Ismi Azam) is a concept introduced to us by the Rasul of Allah (saw):

"Allah has such a name if one prays with it his prayers will definitely be accepted."[162]

However, he does not provide detailed information, only gives certain hints…

These hints and signs are linked to some verses in the Quran. We are told, for example, that this name is contained in such and such a verse, etc.

For centuries the learned have come together and worked on these verses in attempt to decipher this sublime name of Allah…

Another such hadith, narrated by Burayda (ra), is:

"O Allah, I ask with Your name that is Ahad and Samad, who begets not, nor was begotten, and to whom nothing is equivalent…"

Upon this, the Rasul of Allah (saw) said, "Indeed, this man has prayed with Allah's Supreme Name, the name with which when one

---

[162] Ibn Majah.

makes a request from Allah, He gives it and when one calls upon Him with it He responds..."[163]

Man, with his infinite wants and endless impotence, surely needs to seek refuge in Allah and ask from Him...

Based on many studies, the names that are found to have the highest probability of being the Ismi Azam are:

1. Allah
2. La ilaha illa Allah
3. Ar-Rahman'ur-Rahim
4. Al hayyul qayyum
5. Allahu rahman'ur Rahim
6. Allahu la ilaha illa hu al hayyul qayyum
7. La ilaha illa hu al hayyul qayyum
8. Rabb
9. Allahu la ilaha illa hu al ahad'us samad'ulladhee lam yalid walam yulad wa lam yakun lahu kufuwan ahad
10. Al hannan'ul mannanu badi'us samawati wal'ardhi dhul jalali wal ikram

There are also strong signs as to the possibility of the following two prayers being the Isim Azam.

اَللَّهُمَّ اِنِّى اَسْأَلُكَ بِاَ نِّى اَشْهَدُ اَنَّكَ اَنْتَ االلهُ الَّذِى لاَاَلَهَ اِلاَّ اَنْتَ الْوَاحِدُ الْأَحَدُ الصَّمَدُ الَّذِى لَمْ يَلِدْ وَلَمْ يُولَدْ وَلَمْ يَكُنْ لَهُ كُفُوًا اَحَدٌ

Allahumma innee as-aluka bi anni ashhadu innaka anta l-Llahulladhee la ilaha illa anta l-waahadu l-ahadu s-samadu l-ladhee lam ya lid wa lam yulad wa lam yakun lahu kufuwwan ahad

---

[163] Ibn Majah.

لَاإِلَهَ إِلاَّ أَنْتَ يَا حَنَّانُ يَا مَنَّانُ يَا بَدِيعَ السَّمَوَاتِ وَالأَرْضِ يَا ذَا الْجَلاَلِ وَالإِكْرَامِ

La ilaha illa anta yaa hanaanu yaa manaanu yaa badee`a s-samawaati wa l-ardi yaa dhaa l-jalali wa l-ikram

These two prayers also meet the criteria set by the Rasul of Allah (saw) in regards to the Supreme Name. We're told if one recites these during prayer, the chances of it being accepted are higher.

On examining all of these signs, if we take the common elements, two names attract attention:

1. **ALLAH**

2. **HU**

In essence, these names aren't separate, many saints and intimates of the reality consider these names as one...

Abdulqadir al-Jilani, a pinnacle in the area of divine Oneness and Unity and the author of *The Perfect Man* says:

"The letter H at the end of the name ALLAH points to the Absolute Essence, which is also known as the name HU and is referenced as the name HU."

Our master, Hadhrat Ali (ra), also makes a lot of reference to the name HU and mentions this name especially in the form:

"Ya HU ya man HU la ilaha illa HU"

To understand and believe the Supreme Name is the name HU one must be allowed by Allah to observe certain deeper realities.

One day the Rasul of Allah (saw) is asked:

"Where was our Rabb before he created the heavens and the earth?"

He answered:

"In the nothingness over and under which there is no air!"[164]

This hadith points to the Absolute Essence (dhat) of Allah...

The name Allah is an encompassing name; it embodies both the Absolute Essence (dhat) and all His infinite qualities and attributes...

Real belief in Allah begins after recognizing the Oneness of Allah and certainty (yakeen) takes place, for this is the end of imitation and the beginning of the reality... Otherwise, one will only be believing in the 'name' Allah and this is the station of the imitators... As for those who have reached the reality, they are referred to as 'mufarridoon' or the 'muqarriboon'; they are those who have annihilated themselves not in the name Allah, but in the Oneness of Allah; the meaning of 'Allah is Baqi' has become an experiential reality for them...

They are those who have reached the secret of the Supreme Name; they live with the consciousness of the One who says 'HU' with every breath...

When they make a prayer and say, "O Allah... O Hu..." as per the Hadith Qudsi, "It will be me who talks through their tongue" it will be He who requests through their tongue, and thus His request will not be left unanswered.

As for us, in light of what the Rasul (saw) says, we say: He who wants a response to his prayers should perform two rakats of salat and recite the chapter Ikhlas 21 times in each rakat after the Fatiha and read the following prayer during the final prostration and repeat this seven times, as Allah loves those who persevere.

---

[164] Ibn Majah.

AstaghfirulLah ya rabbu l-arshi l-`Adheem... AstaghfirulLah ya rabbu l-arshi l-Kareem... AstaghfirulLah ya Rabba-l-'alameen. Allahumma Salli Ala sayyidina Muhammadin biadede ilmika...

Yaa HU yaa man HU, la ilaha illa HU antal Hayyul Qayyum wa la sharika lah, Lahul-mulku wa lahul hamd, wa innaka 'ala Kul-li shayin Qadeer.

Yaa hanaanu yaa manaanu yaa badee`a s-samawaati wa l-ardi yaa dhaa l-jalali wa l-ikram, ashadu an la ilaha illa allahul Ahadu s-Samadu alladhee lam ya lid wa lam yulad wa lam yakun lahu kufuwwan ahad

O Allah, I confess in Your presence that I am infinitely impotent, weak and that I have wronged myself, and I seek from Your Might and Grandeur, unparallelled sublimity, infinite forgiveness and generosity...

O Allah, I ask for the sake of Your Supreme Name, and Your beloved Muhammad (saw) and the great name of which You have not yet informed anyone...

***

You can continue this prayer asking to be among those who Allah has chosen for Himself, those who are most beloved to Him, those who are most valuable in His sight, to engage in activities that are on His path and in line with His Rasul with ease and whatever else you would like to request... and then I recommend you complete your prayer with the following supplication.

Allahumma salli wa sallim wa baarik `ala Sayyidina Muhammadin Wa 'alaa aalihi wa sahbihee wa sallim Amin Amin Amin yaa rabbi l-`arshi l-`Adheem.

I know with certainty that You have heard my prayers and that You are Wahhab, the One who responds to prayers... I ask that You respond to my prayers for the sake of Your Absolute

Essence (dhat) and the meaning denoted by the great name in Your presence... Amen, amen, amen

***

I'm sure the acquainted will know the value of this prayer that has been taught to me and evaluate it accordingly... If those who have imitatively entered the way of Allah continue this prayer with sincerity, I believe they will certainly get a response.

I share this knowledge with you based on the advice 'share from what you have been given', may the blessing of Allah be upon us all.

37

THE NAMES OF ALLAH AND THEIR MEANINGS

What is known as the Beautiful Names of Allah are significant keys for us. We can enter the gate of knowing Allah by using these keys.

Man is the vicegerent of Allah on earth because he manifests the meanings of these sublime names... To put it another way, 'man' exists and subsists with the Names of Allah. In fact, the entire existence is none other than what is perceived as the manifestations of the meanings of the Names of Allah! Thus, if we want to know Allah and gain gnosis of Him, we must learn these names and understand their meanings.

I had covered the universe being a manifestation of the Names of Allah in the *Mystery of Man*; those who wish to acquire more detail on the topic may resort to it. Here, I would like to share a section from *Decoding the Quran*, a comprehensive explanation on the Names of Allah.

38

THE EXALTED, MAGNIFICENT AND PERFECT QUALITIES OF THE NAMES OF ALLAH (*AL-ASMA UL-HUSNA*)

B'ismi-Allah ar-Rahman ar-Rahim... Allah, who created me with His Names (exalted, magnificent, and perfect qualities), is *Rahman* and *Rahim*!

Let us heed the fact that a **'name'** is only used as a **reference** to an object or quality. A name does not explain what it references in totality, but merely alludes to an identity, or an attribute of an identity. Sometimes, a name is used only to channel the attention to multiple qualities, without revealing anything about the identity.

In the case of the **Names of Allah**, let us contemplate the following: Are the Names of Allah *a collection of fancy titles of a God beyond*? Or, are they references made to the creational properties of Allah (which the senses and conditionings externalize!) with which the entire known cosmos and everything in it becomes manifest from **nothingness** into a shadow **existence**?

Once this reality is fully conceived and comprehended we may move on to the Names of Allah.

The Quran, which has been conveyed as a *Dhikr*, i.e. 'the remembrance of man's essential reality', is actually a disclosure of the Names to expound '*Uluhiyyah*'. It is the **Totality of the Names** (all of the Names that have been imparted to us and that comprise our existence) that man has been endowed with and is invited to

remember! Some of these have been disclosed in the Quran and some were revealed by the Rasul of Allah. One can never say that the names that refer to Allah are limited to only 99. Let us give an example... There are many names, such as **Rabb**, **Mawla**, **Kareeb** and **Hallaq**, that are mentioned in the Quran but are not included as part of the 99 Names. The name **Mureed**, which alludes to the attribute of **'will'** (i.e. He does as He wishes) mentioned in the verse '*yaf'alu ma yureed*', is also not included among the 99 Names. Contrarily, the names **Jalil**, **Wajid** and **Majid** are all included in the 99 Names but are not mentioned in the Quran. Thus, it would be a mistake to confine the Names of Allah to only 99, when the **Dimension of the Names** designates the infinite quantum potential, which involves the act of **observing in Allah's Knowledge**. Man is provided with these Names as a reminder of their own true essence. Perhaps once one remembers and lives accordingly to their essential reality, many more Names will be disclosed to them. Also, we may say **heaven** alludes to this truth too, while we may not even be aware of the Names that pertain to and compose the universes within universes of infinite existence!

The enlightened ones (*Ulul Albab*) have used the phrase **'the shadow existence'** to mean 'the things we perceive do not exist in and by themselves but they are compositions of Names that manifest **according to the perceiver'**.

In fact, even the phrase 'Name compositions' is metaphorical; it is only to adapt the dual view to the One reality. Absolute reality is the observing of the **'multidimensional single frame'** by the One who **'manifests Himself every moment in yet another wondrous way'**. (Quran 55:29) What we refer to as 'Name compositions' is only like one stroke of the paintbrush on this magnificent picture.

Due to having a **name** all perceivable things seemingly have a separate individual existence, whereas, because there is no God beyond, **what is really perceived as an existent object is essentially none other than the materialized Names (qualities) of Allah.**

This being said, the One denoted by the Names cannot be divided or fragmented into pieces, it is not composed of parts, it is even beyond concepts such as being 'absolute One', 'illimitable', 'infinite' and so on. It is '*Ahad-us-Samad*' (the Absolute Self-Sufficient One) and only mentioned this way in the Quran once! **Allah, HU, other than whom nothing exists**! This knowledge cannot be comprehended by the human mind unless it is revealed or divinely inspired and observed in one's consciousness! The mind, logic and judgment cannot survive here. He who attempts to intellectualize this reality will only be misguided. This reality is not open for debate! Any urge to do so will only reveal ignorance! This is the reality that pertains to Gabriel's words: **"If I take one more step I will burn"**!

It must be realized that the Names of Allah point to the quality of His knowledge, not His *mind*, as this is inconceivable. The **mind** is a function of the brain designed to create the world of multiplicity. Essentially, even the phrases 'the Universal Intellect' (*Aql-i kull*) and 'the First Intellect' (*Aql-i awwal*) are relative concepts and are used metaphorically to denote the system by which the attribute of **knowledge** is disclosed.

The Universal Intellect refers to the dimension of knowledge that is present within the depths of all beings, within one's essence. This is also the source of revelation.

The First Intellect, on the other hand, is a tailored phrase for the novice mind, to describe the dimension of knowledge present in the manifestation (*sh'an*) of the Names.

'The dimension of Acts' (*af'al*) is nothing but the disclosure of the Dimension of Names which 'manifests itself every moment in yet another wondrous way'! The material world as we know it is this quantal plane, though differences of perception have led to the assumption that it is a **different** dimension.

The observing One, the one being observed, the observation, are all ONE! 'The wine of paradise' alludes to this experience. One who is caught up in the perception of **multiplicity** has no chance but to engage in the chatter of this knowledge, without any experience of its reality.

As for the **Acts**, activities, multiplicity and what we perceive as the corporeal world... Existence belongs only to that which is denoted as the Dimension of Names.

'**Observing knowledge in knowledge with knowledge**' designates that the very disclosure of the Names is the act of **observing**. In this respect, all **forms** are created and observed in knowledge. Hence it has been said '**the worlds (or creation) have not even smelled the scent of existence yet**'. Here, the **part** is the observer, and the **whole** is the observed one!

The force (*kuwwa*) pertaining to the Names is referred to as **angels**, which, in essence, constitute the **reality of mankind**. One who becomes aware of their reality is said to have '**united with their Rabb**'! Once this state is reached, if it doesn't continue, the resulting pain has been narrated as an intense hellish suffering! This is the domain of **Power** (*Qudrah*) and the command **Be!** (*Kun*) originates from here; this is the dimension of **knowledge**, where the mind and its functions are completely obsolete! This is the essence of the land of **wisdom** (*hikmah*)! The **mind** can only watch the activities that take place in the land of wisdom, where only **consciousness** can actively participate!

The dimension of Acts (*af'al*) in comparison to this plane (the dimension of Power) is a totally **holographic** (shadow) state of existence. All the activities of the entire parallel and multiple universes and all their inhabitants, i.e. natural resources, plants, animals (humanoids) and the jinni, are **governed** by the *Mala-i A'la* (the Exalted Assembly of angels) in this plane, depending on the perception capability of the perceiver.

Rasuls and their successors, the saints, are like the vocal expressions of the *Mala-i A'la*, that is, the forces (potentials) of the Names, on earth! And all of this is part of the **observation** taking place in the **dimension of Knowledge**! The essence of **man**, in this sense, is **angelic** and he is invited to **remember his angelic nature and to live accordingly**. This is an in-depth and intricate topic... Those who are not acquainted with this knowledge may find my words regarding the **observation** taking place from various dimensions to be contradictory. However, the reality I experienced when I was 21 years of age in 1966, which I have penned in my book *Revelations*, has been verified time and time again throughout the 45 years that followed it, and I have shared it all without expecting any tangible or intangible return. The knowledge I share is not a pass-down to me, rather it is the direct blessing of Allah for which I am eternally grateful! As such, there is no contradiction in my words. If it appears that way, it is probably due to the inability to make the correct connections, resulting from an inadequate database.

So, if this is the reality as I have observed, how should the topic of the **Names of Allah** be approached?

The Names of Allah are initially expressed through pure consciousness (revelation) without the interference of one's consciousness, which tries to evaluate them later. The Names are cosmic universal qualities (not in the galactic sense).

The Most Beautiful Names belong to Allah. The structural qualities they denote pertain to the Absolute Self-Sufficient One. The Names look to the quantum potential beyond time and place; the Names signify the **point**. As such, the Names and their meanings belong to Allah alone and are free from becoming conditioned by human concepts.

"Exalted (Subhan – beyond) **is Allah what they attribute to Him."** (Quran 23:91)

"And to Allah belongs the most Beautiful Names, so turn to Him through the meanings of His names. And leave the company of those who practice deviation (fall into duality) **concerning His Names. They will be recompensed for what they have been doing."** (Quran 7:180)

That is, leave the company of those who restrict the Names with their humanly values, and fail to recognize the reality of the Beautiful Names and who do not know Allah is respect of His *Akbariyyah*!

"And believes in (confirms) **the Most Beautiful** (Names) (to be his essential reality)**, we will ease him towards ease."** (Quran 92:6-7)

Even the consequence of **good** is related to the Names:

"For the doers of good (*ihsan*) **is the Beautiful** (Names) **and more** (pleasure). **No darkness** (egotism) **will cover their faces** (consciousness)**, nor derogation** (which results from deviating from one's essence). **Those are companions of Paradise; they will abide therein eternally."** (Quran 10:26)

Allah's Absolute Essence (*dhat*) cannot be likened to anything in existence. With His greatness (*Akbariyyah*) He is free from becoming limited or conditioned by His creation or the attributes denoted by His Names, which constitute one point amongst infinite others. In other words, what is referred to as the **Dimension of Names** is like a multidimensional holographic single frame. And, despite the fact that it is perceived as the **realm of multiplicity**, this realm of activity is essentially a unified field of existence created with the compositional qualities in His knowledge.

To summarize before going further...

The qualities and attributes that we have come to acquire through revelation as the Names of Allah (singular in nature) are the very structural compositions that manifest the totality of all the universal dimensions, from nothingness into this shadow (holographic) existence. This reality, of which earthly vicegerency aspires to become aware, is far beyond the reach of the cruel and ignorant.

The Dimension of Names is the 'exalted, magnificent, and perfect attributes and qualities' with all its sub-dimensions and inner-existence!

Let us now ponder on the world perceived by humanity... and then **"raise our gaze to the heavens and observe"** as the Quran states, without dogmatic views and bigotry, with the understanding of universality formed by proficient knowledge!

What value does a world based on our miniscule perception have in comparison to the magnificence, glory and perfection of the universe?

I hope, in the light of this understanding, we can approach the **Names of Allah** with the awareness that their revelation depends on the purging of the individual consciousness (based on its limited perception and conception of the Book of Knowledge) and that **their effects pertain to the whole of the cosmos**, constantly manifesting new meanings and expressions.

I would also like to take this opportunity to express one of my concerns. I do not feel the knowledge I shared through previous articles has been correctly understood. Let me restate that the meanings, qualities and attributes denoted by the **Names of Allah are only one point among infinite others in the sight of Allah**. Also, the quantum potential expressed as the **Reality of Muhammad** or the **Angel named Spirit** is not only pre- and post-eternal, but it is also the reality I refer to as the 'multi-dimensional single frame' picture! Because this has not been well understood, Allah is still perceived *as the one God out there*! Whereas the whole **observation** and all that has been articulated pertain only to a **point**: Allah is just Allah, Allah is *Akbar*! *Subhanahu min tanzihiy* (HU is beyond comparability)!

Please be aware that what I write and share with you can never be taken as the final conclusion; in fact, it can only be an introduction! It is not possible to openly disclose through publication matters that are deeper than this. Anyway, the people of this path will recognize that even what we have already shared are things that have never been shared in this much detail and this openly before. This is a very sensitive topic as the reader may very easily fall into the misconception of either an external God or worse, confine the reality to his Pharaoh-like 'I'ness and animalistic bodily self!

I tried to shed some light on the topic of the Names (*al-Asma*). Let us now take a look at the qualities and attributes denoted by these exalted, magnificent and perfect Names (*al-Husna*)... As much as simple words allow of course...

THE TRIGGER SYSTEM

All of the qualities and attributes pertaining to the Names are entirely present at every point of existence! However, depending on the desired manifestation, some attributes gain precedence over others, like the channels in an equalizer, to make up the specific formation. Also, qualities denoted by **certain Names naturally and automatically trigger the expressions of certain other Names**, in order to generate a new manifestation. This system is known as '*sunnatullah*' and entails the **universal laws of Allah** (or the laws of nature as those with limited perceptive ability would say) and the mechanics of His system.

This is a glorious mechanism beyond description; all beings from pre-eternity to post-eternity subsist with all their inter and inner dimensions and perceivable units within this system!

All **thoughts** and **activities** projecting from consciousness, whether through the universe or a single person's world, are all formed within and according to this system.

In short, we may refer to this mechanism, where qualities of Names trigger one another, as the **trigger system**.

As I warned above, consider the entire universality of existence (which is ONE by essence) as the plane of manifestation of these Names. The trigger system applies to every instance of perception by a perceiver in every plane of existence within this universality. Since the entire sequence of certain qualities triggering other qualities is a *known*, it is said that the pre- and post-eternal knowledge of everything that has and will happen at all times is present in Allah's knowledge!

The following verses and the Name *Hasib* allude to this trigger system:

"...Whether you show what is within your consciousness (your thoughts) **or conceal it, Allah will bring you to account for it with the Name *Hasib*..."** (Quran 2:284)

"Whoever does an iota's weight of good will see it." (Quran 99:7)

Evidently, the consequence of an action or thought is inevitably experienced within this system. **This is why every thought or action of gratitude or ungratefulness we may have output in the past would have most definitely caught up with us, or is bound to in the future**. If one seriously contemplates on this many doors will open and secrets will reveal themselves. The **mystery of fate** is also pertinent to this mechanism!

Let us now follow these signpost-like Names to discover the secret lands they point to:

ALLAH

ALLAH... Such a name... It points to *Uluhiyyah*!

Uluhiyyah encompasses two realities. HU which denotes **Absolute Essence** (*dhat*) and the realm of infinite points in which every single point is formed by the act of **observing knowledge through knowledge**. This act of observing is such that each point signifies an individual composition of Names.

By respect of His absolute essence, Allah is **other than**, but in terms of His Names, Allah is the **same as** the **engendered existence** (*sh'ay*) yet nevertheless **far and beyond** (*Ghani*) **from the worlds and any similitude!** This is why Allah, who created the engendered existence (*sh'ay*) and the acts with His Names, uses the plural pronoun 'We' in the Quran. For, in essence, the engendered existence (everything in creation) is none other than Allah! Please note that by engendered existence (*sh'ay*) we are referring to the Dimension of Names that constitute existence. One can ponder and contemplate the essence of creation and existence, but **one cannot contemplate the Absolute Essence of Allah**. It is inconceivable and inappropriate; indeed, it is absolutely impossible! This is because one that has been created with the expressions of Allah's Names cannot fully comprehend the Absolute Essence of Allah! Even if this knowledge is revealed by **divine inspiration** – which is impossible – it is inconceivable. This is why it is said 'the path of such pursuit ends in nothingness'.

HU

HU'Allahulladhiy la ilaha illa HU!

Whether via revelation or through consciousness, HU is the inner essence of the reality of everything that is perceived... To such extent that, as the reflection of *Akbariyyah*, first **awe** then **nothingness** is experienced and, as such, the Reality of Hu can never be attained! **Sight cannot reach HU!** HU denotes absolute obscurity and incomprehension! As a matter of fact, all names, including Allah are mentioned in connection with HU in the Quran!

"HU ALLAH is AHAD."

"HU is RAHMAN and RAHIM."

"HU is AWWAL, AKHIR, ZAHIR and BATIN."

"HU is ALIY and AZIM."

"HU is SAMI and BASIR."

And also the last three verses of Chapter *al-Hashr...*

It is also important to note that using HU as a prefix to other Names is first to establish incomparability (*tanzih*) and then to denote similarity (*tashbih*) in reference to the given Name. This should be remembered at all times.

AR-RAHMAN

Ar-Rahman signifies the materialization of the essence of every iota with Allah's Names in His knowledge. In modern terms, it designates the quantum potential. It is the potential of the source of the entire creation. It is the name of the **Dimension of Names!** All things obtain their **existence** at the level of **knowledge and will** with the attributes denoted by this name.

As signified by the verses "*ar-Rahmanu ala'l arsh'istiwa*" (Quran 20:5) and "*ar-Rahman Allamal Quran, Khalekal Insan, Allamul bayan*" (Quran 55:1-4). *Rahman* is the reality that manifests in **consciousness!** The 'mercy' is in the act of 'manifesting it into existence.'

The narration of Muhammad (saw) that **'Allah created Adam in the image of *Rahman*'** means the knowledge aspect of man reflects the qualities of *Rahman*, i.e. the qualities of the Names.

The essence (*dhat*) of man is also related to the name *Rahman*. As such, the polytheists are not able to comprehend the notion of prostrating to *Rahman* (Quran 25:60) and Satan (the mind, illusion) rebels against *Rahman* (Quran 19:44). These verses indicate the manifestation of the essence of 'Man'.

AR-RAHIM

Ar-Rahim is the Name that brings the infinite qualities of *ar-Rahman* into engendered existence. In this sense, it is the 'observation' of the potential. *Ar-Rahim* observes itself through the forms of existence, by guiding the conscious beings to the awareness that their lives and their essential reality are comprised of and governed by the Names.

"...And is ever He, *Rahim* to those who believe in their essential reality" (Quran 33:43).

Ar-Rahim is the source of the plane of existence referred to as 'heaven'.

Ar-Rahim is the producer of the angelic state.

AL-MALEEK

The Sovereign One, who manifests His Names as he wishes and governs them in the world of acts as He pleases. The one who has providence over all things.

"Subhan is He in whose hand (governance) **is the Malakut** (the force of the Names) **of all things, and to Him you will be returned** (the illusory self – ego will come to an end and the Absolute Reality will be discerned). (Quran 36:83)

The Sovereign One who has no partners!

He who is blessed with this awareness will find himself only in absolute submission to *al-Maleek*! Objection and rebellion will cease. *Al-Maleek* is the foremost quality pertinent to the phenomenon known as its manifestations through a continuum (*arsh-i istiwa*).

"Whatever is in the heavens and whatever is on the earth glorify (tasbih, with their unique dispositions) **Allah, *the Maleek, the Quddus, the Aziz, the Hakim* (to manifest whatever meanings He desires)."** (Quran 62:1)

AL-QUDDUS

The One who is free and beyond being defined, conditioned and limited by His manifest qualities and concepts! Albeit the engendered existence is the disclosure of His Names, He is pure and beyond from becoming defined and limited by them!

AS-SALAM

One who enables a state of peace by emancipating individuals from the conditions of nature and bodily life and endows the experience of 'certainty' (*yakeen*). One who facilitates the comprehension of Islam for the believers, and enables the heavenly state of existence called '*Dar'us-Salam*' (the explicit manifestation of our implicit potentials). (Quran 36:58)

This name is triggered by the name *ar-Rahim*:

"**'*Salam*,' a word from a '*Rahim*' Rabb shall reach them** (they will experience the manifestation of the Name Salam) **!**"

AL-MU'MIN

The One who enables the awareness that He, by respect of His Names, is beyond what is perceived. This awareness reflects upon us as **'faith'** (*iman*). All believers, including Rasuls and angels, have their faith rested upon this awareness, which frees the mind from the enslavement of illusion. While illusion can deter the mind, which uses comparison to operate, it becomes powerless and ineffective in the sight of faith.

The inherent quality of the Name *al-Mu'min* manifests itself directly from Awareness in one's consciousness, thereby rendering obsolete the effect of illusion.

AL-MUHAYMIN

The One who maintains and protects the manifestations of His Names with His own system (*al-Hafidhu war-Rakiybu ala kulli shay*)!

Al-Muhaymin also designates the One who safeguards and protects (the trust).

The root word of *al-Muhaymin* is *amanah* (trust), mentioned in the Quran as the trust from which the heavens, the earth and the mountains refrained, but which 'Man' (the twin brother of the Quran) accepted. Essentially, it indicates the consciousness pertaining to the knowledge of the Names, symbolized as the angel 'SPIRIT', which is then passed on to Man, the vicegerent on earth. That is, the 'trust' signifies living with the awareness that your essence is comprised of the Names. This works in conjunction with the name *al-Mu'min*. The angel (force) named SPIRIT also possesses a form since it is also a manifestation, and as such, it is *Hayy* and *Qayyum* due to the perfection of its 'faith' in the infinite qualities of the Names.

AL-AZIZ

The One who, with His unchallengeable might, disposes as He wishes. The One whose will to do as He likes, nothing can oppose. This name works in parallel with the name *Rabb*. The *Rabb* attribute carries out the demands of the Aziz attribute!

AL-JABBAR

The One whose will is compelling. The corporeal worlds (engendered existence) are compelled to comply with His demands! There is no room for refusal. This '*jabr*' (compelling) quality will inevitably express itself and apply its laws through the essence of beings.

AL-MUTAKABBIR

The One to whom the word 'I' exclusively belongs. **Absolute 'I'ness** belongs only to Him. Whoever, with the word 'I', accredits a portion of this Absolute 'I'ness to himself, thereby concealing the 'I'ness comprising his essence and fortifying his own relative

'I'ness, will pay its consequence with 'burning' (suffering). Majesty (Absolute 'I'ness) is His attribute alone.

AL-KHALIQ

The ONE Absolute Creator! The One who brings individuals into the existence from nothingness, with His Names! Everything *al-Khaliq* creates has a purpose to fulfill, and according to this unique purpose, possesses a natural predisposition and character. Hence it has been said:**"characterize yourselves with the character of Allah"** (Tahallaku biakhlakillah) to mean:Live in accordance with the awareness that you are comprised of the structural qualities of the Names of Allah!

AL-BARI

The One who fashions all of creation (from micro to macro) with unique functions and designs yet all in conformity with the whole, like the harmonious functioning of all the different organs in the body!

AL-MUSAWWIR

The fashioner of forms. The One who exhibits 'meanings' as 'forms' and devises the mechanism in the perceiver to perceive them.

AL-GAFFAR

The One who, as requisites of divine power or wisdom, 'conceals' the inadequacies of those who recognize their shortcomings and wish to be freed from their consequences. The One who forgives.

AL-QAHHAR

The One who executes the effects of His Name '*Wahid*' and renders invalid the seeming existence of the relative 'I'ness.

AL-WAHHAB

The One who bestows and gives unrequitedly to those He wishes, oblivious of deservedness.

AR-RAZZAQ

The One who provides all necessary nutrition for the survival of any unit of manifestation regardless of its plane of existence.

AL-FATTAH

The One who generates expansion within individuals. The One who enables the recognition and observation of Reality, and hence, that there is no inadequacy, impairment, or mistake in the engendered existence. The One who expands one's vision and activity, and enables their proper usage. The One who enables the recognition and use of the unrecognized (overseen).

AL-ALEEM

The One who, with the quality of His knowledge, infinitely knows everything in every dimension with all its facets.

AL-QABID

The One who exercises His verdict by retaining the essence of an individual's Name reality. The One who restrains and enforces withdrawnness.

AL-BASIT

The One who opens and expands; the One who enables dimensional and in-depth sight.

AL-KHAFID

The One who abases. The One who capacitates a state of existence which is far from reality. The creator of the '*asfali safileen*' (the lower state of existence). The former of the vision of **'multiplicity'** to conceal the reality.

AR-RAFI

The One who exalts. The one who elevates conscious beings to higher states of existence; to enable the realization and observation of their essential reality.

AL-MU'IZZ

The Giver of Honor. The One who bestows honor to whom he wishes and holds them in esteem over others.

AL-MUDHILL

The One who exposes dishonor in some and degrades below others. The One who deprives from honorable qualities and compels to humiliation with the veil of 'I'ness (ego).

AS-SAMI

The One who perceives His manifestations at every instance. The One who enables awareness and comprehension.

This name triggers the Name *al-Basir*.

AL-BASIR

The One who is constantly observing His manifestations and evaluating their outputs.

AL-HAKAM

The Absolute Judge whose judgment (verdict) is irresistibly applied.

AL-ADL

The One who provides each of His manifestations their due right in consonance with **their creation program**. The One who is absolutely free from unjustness or tyranny.

AL-LATIF

The One who is subtly present in the depths of every manifestation. The One whose favors are plentiful.

AL-HABIR

The One who is aware of the manifestations of His Names at all times. The One who allows his manifestations to discern the level of their comprehension via their outputs.

AL-HALIM

The One who refrains from giving sudden (impulsive) reactions to events, but rather evaluates all situations in respect of their purpose of manifestation.

AL-AZIM

The magnificent glory beyond any manifestation's capacity of comprehension.

AL-GHAFUR

The One who's Mercy should never be doubted or given up on. The One who enables necessary cleansing and triggers the name *Rahim* to bestow blessings.

ASH-SHAKUR

The One who allows the proper use of His bestowals in order that He may increase them. The One who enables the due evaluation of resources such that more can be attained. This name triggers the name *al-Karim*. If this name is not activated in one's life, one will be obstructed from a connection with Allah and not able to duly use his resources, turning his attention to other things and hence becoming veiled from the blessings of Allah. This leads to 'ungratefulness', which is defined as the inability to adequately evaluate and use blessings. Eventually this results in total deprivation.

AL-ALIY

The Highest (or the Sublime). The sublime One who observes existence from the point of reality (essence).

AL-KABIR

The magnitude of the worlds He created with His Names are incomprehensible.

AL-HAFIZ

The One who provides all requirements to preserve and maintain existence.

AL-MUQEET

The One who facilitates the expression of the Name *al-Hafiz* by providing the necessary material and spiritual platform for it.

AL-HASIB

The One who maintains individuality by holding them to account of their behavioral output through the mechanics of 'consequence'

In doing so, an indefinite flow of formation is established.

AL-JALIL

The One who, with His magnificent comprehensiveness and perfection, is the sultan of the world of acts.

AL-KARIM

The exceedingly generous and bountiful One who bestows His bounties even upon those who deny His existence. The ability to READ (*iqra*) is only possible through the activation of this Name, which lies dormant within the essence of every individual.

AR-RAQIB

The One who watches over and keeps under control the manifestations of His Names, with His names, at all times.

AL-MUJIB

The One who unequivocally responds to all who turn towards Him (in prayer and invocation) and provides their needs.

AL-WASI

The All-embracing. The One who embraces the whole of existence with the expressions of His Names.

AL-HAKIM

The One whose power of knowledge appears under the guise of 'causes', hence creating causality and leading to the perception of multiplicity.

AL-WADUD

The creator of attraction. The creator of unconditional and unrequited love. The essence within every beloved!

AL-MAJEED

The One whose majestic glory is evident through His magnificent manifestations!

AL-BAITH

The One who constantly transforms new dimensions of existence. As a requisite of the mechanism denoted by the verse **"Everything in the heavens and earth asks from Him; at every instance HU** (the Absolute Essence of Existence) **manifests Himself in yet another way! "**(Quran 55:29), *al-Baith* continually creates new experiences.

The expression of this name in respect to humanity is depicted in *'amantu'*(Comprises the six fundamentals of belief in Islam. It consists of belief in Allah, His angels, His books, His Rasuls, Doomsday [life after death] and destiny [*qadar*], that all good and evil are from Allah.) as 'to believe in life (resurrection) after death' (*bath'u badal mawt*) and the verse **"That you will certainly change dimensions and transform into bodies befitting those dimensions!"**.(Quran 84:19)

We said *ba'th* (resurrection) is to **taste** death and to commence a new state of life after death... However, resurrection is also possible here on earth in this plane of existence. Like the resurrections of *wilayah* (sainthood), *nubuwwah* (prophethood), and *risalah* (the personification of Allah's knowledge)! As all of these stations comprise new states of life.

To give an example, we may say *ba'th* is like the germination of a seed to sprout its plant, or 'give shoot to new life'. Similarly, life emerges from **death** (dormant inactive potential). In relation to the new state of existence, the previous state is considered as a 'grave' (*qabir*).

"That Hour (death) **will definitely come – there is no doubt about it. And Allah will definitely resurrect the beings** (individual forms of consciousness) **in their graves** (bodies) (to continue their lives through new bodies)**!"** (Quran 22:7)

ASH-SHAHID

The One who witnesses His existence through His own existence. The One who observes the disclosure of His Names and witnesses His manifestations! The enforcer of the reality that there is no other observer but Himself.

AL-HAQQ

The absolute and unequivocal reality! The source and essence of every function in manifestation!

AL-WAKIL

The One who provides the means for self-actualization. The One who advocates and protects those who place their trust in Him, providing them with the most auspicious outcomes. He who believes in the potential of the name *al-Wakil* in his own essence, will have confirmed his faith in all the Names (all his potentials). The source of the mystery of **vicegerency** lies in this Name!

AL-QAWWI

The One who transforms His power into the enabling potential for the manifestation of existence (hence comprising the force of the whole of existence).

The One who forms the angelic state.

AL-MATIN

The One who sustains the world of acts, the steadfast, the creator of robustness and stability, the provider of strength and resistance!

AL-WALIYY

The One who guides and enables an individual to discover their reality and to live their life in accordance to their essence. It is the source of *risalah* (personification of Allah's knowledge) and *nubuwwah* (prophethood), which comprise the pinnacle states of sainthood (*wilayah*). It is the dispatcher of the perfected qualities comprising the highest point of sainthood, *risalah*, and the state one beneath that, *nubuwwah*. While the expression of *nubuwwah* is indefinitely functional, the expression of *nubuwwah* applies only to earthly life. A *Nabi* continues to live at the same state of perfection after death, but his explicit role as a *Nabi* is no longer active. On the other hand, due to its inherent saintly qualities, *risalah* continues infinitely (as it does with saints).

AL-HAMID

The One who observes and evaluates His universal perfection on worldly forms manifested by His Name *al-Waliyy*.

Hamd belongs only to Him.

AL-MUHSI

The creator of the 'forms' (micro to macro) comprising the seeming multiplicities, each equipped with unique qualities and attributes, within UNITY.

AL-MUBDI

The One who originates the whole of creation in the corporeal worlds, all with exclusive and unique qualities.

AL-MU'ID

The One who restores life to those who turn back to their essence.

AL-MUHYI

The One who enlivens and enlightens! The One who enables the continuation of the individual's life through the application of knowledge and the observation of one's essential reality.

AL-MUMIT

The One who enables a 'taste' (experience) of death. The One who allows a transition between one state of existence to another.

AL-HAYY

The source of names! The One who gives life to the Names and manifests them. The source of universal energy, the essence of energy!

AL-QAYYUM

The One who renders Himself existent with His own attributes, without the need of anything. Everything in existence subsists with *al-Qayyum*.

AL-WAJID

The One whose qualities and attributes are unfailingly abundant. The manifest One. The One, from which nothing lessens, despite the abundance of His manifestations.

AL-MAJID

The magnificent and glorious One with unrestricted, infinite generosity and endowment (benevolence).

AL-WAHID

The One and only! 'ONE'ness far beyond any concept of multiplicity. The ONE, that isn't composed of (or can be broken into) parts (as in pantheism). The 'ONE'ness that renders duality obsolete! The 'ONE'ness that no mind or intellect can fully comprehend!

AS-SAMAD

The Pure Whole One! Free from the concept of multiplicity! Not formed of adjoining parts. Far from conceptualization and limitation. The self-sufficient One, in need of nothing!

An authentic hadith narrates: "*As-Samad* **is such that it bears no space or emptiness within it** (all, whole, one)."

AL-QADIR

The One who creates (discloses, manifests) and observes His knowledge with His power without depending on causality. The One who is absolutely boundless!

AL-MUQTADIR

The Determiner. The absolute possessor of all power pertaining to creation, governance, and disposition.

AL-MUQADDIM

The One who expedites (or prioritizes) the manifestation of Names according to their purpose of creation.

AL-MU'AKHKHIR

The One who delays manifestation in consonance with His name *al-Hakim*.

AL-AWWAL

The first and initial state of existence, the essential Name.

AL-AKHIR

The infinitely subsequent One, to all creation.

AZ-ZAHIR

The self-evident One, the explicit, unequivocal and perceivable manifestation.

AL-BATIN

The unperceivable reality within the perceivable manifestation! The source of the unknown (*Awwal*, *Akhir*, *Zahir*, *Batin*, *HU*!)

AL-WALI

The One who governs according to His own verdict.

AL- MUTA'ALI

The limitless, boundless Supreme One, whose supremacy encompasses everything! The One whose reality can never be duly reflected by any engendered, conceptualized existence. The One who is beyond being limited by any mind or intellect.

AL-BARR

The One who eases the actualization of individual temperaments and natural dispositions.

AT-TAWWAB

The One who guides individuals to their essence by enabling them to perceive and comprehend the reality. The One who allows individuals to repent, that is, to abandon their misdoings and to compensate for any harm that may have been caused. The activation of this Name triggers the name *Rahim*, and thus benevolence and beauty is experienced.

AL-MUNTAQIM

The One who makes individuals live the consequences of their actions that impede in the realization of their essence. To 'avenge' (*zuntiqam*) is to make one 'pay the price' i.e. face the consequence of their doings without exception or pity. Allah is beyond being bound by concepts such as revenge. When used in conjunction with 'severe in retribution' (*Shadid al-Iqab*) (Quran 59:4), *al-Muntaqim* denotes the force that most severely avenges individuals for failing to recognize their essence, by making them live out the consequences of their own obstructive actions in a most severe and intense way.

AL-AFUW

The One who forgives all offences except for 'duality' (*shirq*); the failure to recognize the reality of non-duality prevents the activation of the name *al-Afuw*. Note that to forgive an offence does not mean to compensate the losses of the past, for in the system of *sunnatullah* there is no compensation of the past!

AR-RA'UF

The compassionate and pitying One who protects individuals who turn to Him from all kinds of behavior which may cause harm or trouble to them.

AL-MAALIK'UL-MULK

The One who governs His Sovereignty as He wishes without having to give account to any individual.

"Say, 'Allah, the sovereign of all sovereignty... You give sovereignty to whom You will and You take sovereignty away from whom you will. You honor whom You will and You abase whom You will. In Your hand is all good. Certainly, you are Qadir over all things.'" (Quran 3:26)

DHUL-JALALI WAL-IKRAM

The One who makes individuals experience their 'nothingness' by enabling them to comprehend the reality that they were created from 'naught' and then bestowing them 'Eternity' by allowing them to observe the manifestations of the Names comprising their essence.

AL-MUQSIT

The One who applies justice, as the requirement of His *Uluhiyya*, by endowing every individual their due, based on their unique creation purpose.

AL-JAMI

The One who observes the whole of existence as a multi-dimensional single frame in His Knowledge. The One who gathers creation according to the purpose and function of their creation.

AL-GHANI

The One who is beyond being labeled and limited by the manifestations of His Names, as He is Great (Akbar) and beyond all concepts. The One who is infinitely abundant with His Names.

AL-MUGHNI

The One who enriches individuals and raises them above others in wealth and emancipates them. The One who enriches with His own riches. The One who grants the beauty of infinity (*baqa*) which results from '*fakr*' (nothingness).

"And did We not find you poor (faqr, in nothingness) **and made you rich** (with infinity – baqa, i.e.)**?** (Did we not make you a servant of the Ghani? Did we not enrich and emancipate you?)" (Quran 93:8)

"And indeed, it is HU who enriches and deprives." (Quran 53:48)

AL-MANI

The One who prevents those from attaining things they do not deserve!

AD-DARR

The One who afflicts individuals with various distressing situations (sickness, suffering, trouble) in order to make them turn to Himself!

AN-NAFI

The One who prompts individuals to engage in good thoughts and actions to aid them towards beneficent and auspicious outcomes.

AN-NUR

The Knowledge that is the source and essence of everything! The essence of everything is *Nur*; everything is comprised of knowledge. Life subsists with knowledge. Those with knowledge are the ever-living ones (*Hayy*), while those who lack knowledge are like living dead.

AL-HADI

The guide to the truth. The One who allows individuals to live according to their reality. The articulator of the truth. The guide to reality.

AL-BADEE

The incomparable beauty and the originator of beautiful manifestation! The One who originates innumerable manifestations, all with unique and exclusive qualities, and without any example, pattern, specimen etc.

AL-BAQI

The Everlasting. The One who exists beyond the concept of time.

AL-WARITH

The One who manifests under various names and forms in order to inherit and protect the possessions of those who abandon all their belongings to undergo true transformation. When one form is exhausted, He continues His existence with another form.

AR-RASHID

The guider to the right path. The One who allows individuals, who recognize their essential reality, to experience the maturity of this recognition!

AS-SABUR

"And if Allah were to hold responsible the people for their wrongdoings and enforce the consequences upon them at once, He would not have left upon the earth any creature (DABBAH, i.e. earthling, in human 'form' – not human), but He defers them until a specified time. And when their time comes, they can neither fall behind it nor precede it by even an hour." (Quran 16:61)

The One who waits for each individual to execute his creation program before rendering effective the consequences of their actions. Allowing the tyranny of the tyrant to take place, i.e. activating the Name *as-Sabur*, is so that both the oppressor and the oppressed can duly carry out their functions before facing the consequences in full effect. Greater calamity forces the creation of increased cruelty.

A FINAL REMINDER

Obviously the meanings of the Names of Allah cannot be confined to such a narrow scope. This is why I refrained from going into this topic for many years. For I know it is impossible to duly cover the comprehensiveness of this topic. However, my own experience of the reflections of this knowledge has compelled me to cover this topic to some extent. I ask Allah's forgiveness. Many books have been written in this field. I only touched upon it based on my understanding today and in a way that is easy to remember. Perhaps I have unveiled only the tip of the iceberg!

SubhanAllahu amma yasifun! (Quran 23:91)

I feel I need to reiterate the importance of the following point before concluding this topic:

Everything that I have shared with you here must be observed and experienced within one's consciousness, after becoming cleansed from the restraints of the illusory identity ('I'ness) and the density of the bodily state of existence. **If this cleansing involves the automated repetitions of certain words and phrases without experiential confirmation, the results will be no different from a**

computer running a program, and hence, ineffective. Sufism is a way of life! Those who narrate and repeat the words of others (hence gossip!) squander their lives, finding solace in Satan's adorned and embellished games!

The evidence of having attained the reality of this knowledge is the end of suffering! That is, if you are no longer bothered or troubled by anything or anyone, if no situation or person can upset you anymore, it means this knowledge has become your reality! **As long as one is bound by value judgments attached to conditionings and lives his life centered around emotions and behaviors resulting from these, his life will continue and mature as an 'earthling' (not a human) and be subject to 'causality', both here and in the afterlife.**

Knowledge is for application. So, let us begin with the application of: 'knowledge that is not applied is a weight on one's shoulders!'

Let us ask ourselves at the end of each day:

"Am I ready to embark on a 'one-way' journey tonight in my sleep?"

"Are worldly matters still bothering me and causing me to suffer? Or am I living my servitude in peace and happiness?"

If your answer is 'Yes', glad tidings to you my friend! If it is 'No', then many tasks await you tomorrow! In this case, when you wake up in the morning, ask yourself "What must I do today in order to go to bed in total peace and happiness tonight?"

Glory be to the One who allows us to live our days with the awareness that everything we own will perish...

Wassalam...

A special thank you to the honorable imam of Istanbul Kanlica Mosque, Hasan Guler Hodja, a venerable scholar and an exemplary man of knowledge, for sharing his valuable insight with me and for assisting me with '*Decoding The Quran*'.

Ahmed Hulusi
03 February 2009
North Carolina, USA

39

SPECIAL DHIKR RECOMMENDATIONS

"**The hearts** (consciousness) **finds contentment only in the remembrance of Allah** (dhikrullah; to remember one's essential reality, or original self, i.e. Allah, as comprising the essence of all things with His Names)**!**"

Why is this so?

Because man is created with the capacity to deliberate on the infinite, yet infinity and limitlessness are attributes of Allah!

When the Rasul of Allah (saw) says, "La uhsi thana'an 'alaika, Anta kama athnaita 'ala Nafsika," which means "It is not possible to duly praise You, only You can praise Yourself as only You have true knowledge of Yourself," he is referring to the reality that the limitless infinite Being can never be truly comprehended.[165]

So, what must we do in this situation?

Get to know Him to the extent He allows us to!

Observe and know ourselves in His mirror!

Become awed by His infinite, limitless perfection and sublime qualities and wisdom...

---

[165] Ibn Abi Shaybah, al-Tirmidhi.

Perhaps this is the reality the Rasul (saw) was referring to when he said, "O Allah, increase my bewilderment!"[166]

Dhikr is the tool to knowing Allah. Dhikr is done either with the name Allah as it encompasses the Absolute Essence, Divine Attributes and all the other Names, or with specific Names. As we have explained many times before, man is a composition of the divine Names. Every person comprises a different composition of all of the divine Names, collectively referenced by the name 'Allah'. We call these compositions 'man'. Allah calls these compositions 'man'.

Man's Rabb is the divine power designated by the Names of Allah that comprise him. Each person being different to the other is due to the varying levels of power with which the Names of Allah constitute him.

When one repeats the name Allah in their dhikr, it strengthens all of the names that comprise him equivalently; thus, all his qualities develop equally.

But, performing dhikr of *specific* Names of Allah helps in the development of specific qualities. For example, performing dhikr with the name Mureed, which points to Allah's attribute of willpower, strengthens this quality in one's unique composition of names. Thus, the person's willpower will become more active, enabling him to overcome things that he previously couldn't overcome.

Or the name Hakim, for example, will enable the person to understand the wisdom and reason behind events, why and how things happen... Things that previously seemed irrelevant and disconnected will now make sense and the person will be able to comprehend their relevant place in the system.

So, while the name Allah strengthens all of the Names in one's composition at an equal rate, specific names activate specific qualities, leading to profound progress in the person... Hence, those who want effective progress are advised to perform dhikr of specific names.

---

[166] Futuhat al-Makkiyya.

These dhikr recommendations have nothing to do with sects, tariqahs or factions!

Whether one is from a particular school of thought or not, engaging in these dhikrs will bring results within as little as a few months.

Let me stress the importance of the fact that Allah is not a physical entity or being who is outside ourselves, rather an infinite, limitless Oneness whose presence must be experienced internally and in every iota of existence! All thoughts to the contrary are satanic based provocations of the jinn!

There is only one tariqah, one way to knowing and finding Allah and that is the way of the Rasul of Allah (saw).

Anything that isn't based on or goes against the teachings of the Rasul (saw) will inevitably lead one astray!

This is why we say…

If you perform these dhikrs you will not be lead away from the path of knowledge! Do not heed ideas and thoughts that go against the Quran and hadith! Do not abandon what is mandatory (fardh), no matter what the justification may be! Do not heed any thought or idea suggesting you may be a saint, sheikh, Mahdi, etc. The biggest game of the jinn is to induce such ideas to those who have attained sensitivity and whose receptors have strengthened, in order to lead them astray by entertaining them with thoughts of being 'special' or 'chosen'! Let it be known with certainty that there is no higher rank than being a servant to Allah! This is the rank to which we should all aspire!

Do not believe in anything if you like… Or if you like, be of those who only believe in Allah and attend the Friday prayer once a week, it does not matter, the following formula is what I recommend initially:

100 x ALLAHUMMA A'INNEE ALA DHIKRIKA WA SHUKRIKA WA HUSNU IBADATIK

O Allah, enable me to remember You, to benefit from You and to engage optimally in the necessary practices thereupon.

300 x ALLAHUMMA INNEE ASALUKA HUBBAKA WA HUBBU MAN YUHIBBUKA

O Allah, bestow upon me Your love and the love of those who love You.

300 x LA ILAHA ILLA ANTA SUBHANAKA INNEE KUNTU MINAZ ZAALIMEEN

There is no deity-God (I as this person do not exist) only You (the meanings of the names that comprise my essence). I invoke You (as the manifestations of Your names necessitate me to). Indeed, I have wronged my self (by failing to realize and experience my reality).

500 x QUDDUS'UT TAHIRU MIN KULLI SOOIN

Cleanse me from all humanly impurities.

100 x YA NURA QULLI SHAY'IN WA HADAHU AKHRIJNI MINAZ ZULUMATI ILAN'NUR

O, source of light and guidance for all! Save me from the darkness of ignorance and enlighten me with Your knowledge.

3,600 x **MUREED**

2,700 x **HALIM**

1,800 x **MU'MIN**

2,700 x **RASHID**

3,600 x **QUDDUS**

3,600 x **NUR**

1,800 x **HAKEEM**

2,700 x **FATTAH**

You may start with only a few in the beginning and increase it gradually. If you find it difficult to keep count, you may keep track of time instead. If this is difficult too, then begin with only repeating the names Mureed, Nur and Quddus without keeping count at all.

If you don't have time to complete all of the names on the list, you may reduce their number of repetition, though it may take a little longer to see results. The important thing is that you begin these dhikrs in the morning and complete it before going to bed at night. You may do them everywhere and at all times, whether you have ablution or not, it does not matter.

If you make nine repetitions each time you draw a bead, and you have a set of beads that's one hundred beads long, then one full rotation will lead to nine hundred repetitions. You may prefer to complete the nine repetitions by three sets of three; For example: Mureed-Mureed-Mureed, Mureed-Mureed-Mureed, Mureed-Mureed-Mureed...

If you have a slender physique, or if your fingers are long and thin and your fingertips are pointy and oval shaped, or if you have a wide forehead and a pointy chin then you should also add the following:

300 x **ALLAHUMMA THABBIT QALBI ALA DEENIK**

If you frequently feel distressed and find it hard to enjoy life, then you should also add the following:

100 x **Chapter Ash-Sharh**

300 x **RABBISH RAHLI SADRI WA YASSIR LEE AMRI**

300 x **ALAM NASHRAH LAKA SADRAK** + 1,800 x **BASIT**

If you start seeing the benefits after a few months and your time permits and you choose to take it further, then you may also add the following:

300 x **ALLAHUMMA ALHIMNI RUSHDI WA-A'IDHNI MIN SHARRI NAFSI**

300 x **RABBI ZIDNI ILMAN WA FAHMAN WA IYMANA**

3,600 x **RAHIM**

2,700 x **SAMI**

2,700 x **BASIR**

2,700 x **ALEEM**

2,700 x **AZIZ**

2,700 x **WAKIL**

2,700 x **WAHHAB**

2,700 x **JAMI**

In applying the first list I provided above, if the person has passed the age of 40, then after a few months of repeating the name

MUREED 4,500 times and seeing its benefit, he may reduce it to 3,600.

Besides these, if one has time for more, I strongly recommend the salawat taught by Hadhrat Fatma (r) 100 times a day:

Rabbi innee ẓalamtu nafsee ẓalman katheeran lakal utba hatta tardha

If one is afflicted by any form of worldly affair, repeating the following prayer 500 times a day will have an enormous effect in a very short time:

Hasbiya Llaahu laa ilaaha illaa huwa ʽalayhi tawakkaltu wa huwa rabbu l-arshi l-ʽAdheemi. Sayajʽalu Allahu baʽda ʽusrin yusra.

Hasbiya Allahu wani'mal wakeel; wa kafaa billahi waliyyan wa kafaa billahi naseera

If you read up on and study Sufism and other sources informing of the reality of the system while engaging in these dhikrs you'll find your ability to understand to be much enhanced. For, whether you like it or not, these practices will activate a new capacity in your brain, enabling you to understand and comprehend new information with ease.

Additionally, I've included a prayer below that can be done in the last prostration of a two rakat salat performed during the night. Of course, using these exact words isn't necessary, so long as one makes a heartfelt prayer pointing to the same meaning.

"O Allah, the Rabb of the Throne and all of the angels... I plead to You with the comprehension that in Your sight I am helpless, powerless, needy and nonexistent... Please forgive me for all of my mistakes and all of the actions I did either inadvertently or by succumbing to my ego.

O Allah, the Rabb of our Master Muhammad (saw), ease for me the path of those whom You have blessed and protect me from becoming of those who have truly deviated. Make me of those whom You have honored by choosing for Yourself, make me close to Your most beloveds among those who are currently living on earth, and make their deeds easy and pleasant for me too!

O Allah, besides whom there is no other, O Allah who creates everything with perfection, O Allah who can never be fully comprehended, O HU, ya men HU! For the sake of Your Absolute Essence, save me from the blindness of my sight, make me comprehend the absolute truth, and make the truth easy for me to bear and understand. Enable me to reach such a state of certainty that all disbelief and duality is removed thereafter!

O Allah, I seek refuge in You from all things that prevent me from living in a state of absolute certainty... I seek refuge in You from You... I seek refuge in You from being in Your presence with my sense of 'self' (ego-identity)... You are the protector and Your power is sufficient over all things... You are the Azeem Rabb of the worlds, all dimensions of life...

Please grant as many blessings upon Your Rasul as there are in Your sight, who has informed us of these truths, as he deserves, we are incapable of duly discerning him."

I would like to provide some additional information in regards to the Names that have been recommended for dhikr, especially for those who want to be conscious of what they're repeating so it may be more beneficial.

The name MUREED points to Allah's attribute of will! Our being is comprised firstly of Allah's attributes. Although we have come to life with the attribute of life and our bodies are renewed with the name Baith according to the dimension it occupies, life will continue indefinitely... Based on the name Aleem, we are conscious beings with knowledge...

As a result of the name Mureed, Allah's attribute of will becomes manifest in us and we become perceived as beings with will. We gain perceptivity with the attribute 'Sami' and sight and comprehension with the attribute 'Basir'... The attribute 'Kalam' gives us the ability of expression and all of this is the manifestation of the attribute of 'Power'.

The secret of the name Mureed, as far as I'm aware, has been disclosed for the first time to us. I've not encountered this dhikr in any previous teaching; in fact, many have not even heard of this name before, as it usually isn't listed among the other divine names and attributes. Surely this is also due to divine wisdom...

As far as our observations are concerned and as a result of certain practices in which we have engaged, the name Mureed possesses a certain type of power that enables the most speedy progress and development in man.

In terms of intellectual knowledge, most of us are cognitively aware of many things, but when it comes to putting our knowledge into practice, we generally fail. There is only one cause for this, a weak power of will. The repetition of the name Mureed is a profoundly effective solution in strengthening one's willpower. When one begins to engage in this dhikr, his willpower begins to strengthen and thus he finds it much easier to practice the things that he previously could not. For example, one may have an addiction problem or find it difficult to pray, or perhaps he can't devote himself to study and higher learning as he would like to; in any case, this name strengthens one's willpower and enables him to achieve these things.

However, I would like to add an important note... Just as medicine is taken in certain dosages, so too the dhikr of divine names must not exceed a specific number, for the dhikr of divine names continually supplements the brain. In the same way that a diabetes patient needs additional sugar if the level of insulin is insufficent, and if no additional sugar is provided, the metabolism goes back to its default state. As long as dhikr is performed, whether its meaning is known or not, whether one believes it or not, it will fulfill its function. From experience, it takes no more than fifteen days for the metabolism to return to its normal state after abandoning dhikr.

The important point is to be mindful of the fact that you're not performing dhikr to a god in space, but that you're activating certain divine names and attributes of Allah, the infinite, limitless existence who is totally present in every iota of your being! And you can only know Allah to the degree that you're able to perceive Him, whether in yourself or your surroundings.

This is why, in my opinion, the name Mureed is the fastest way to knowing Allah. Though one must always ask that the process of 'getting to know Allah' is enabled with an ease of comprehension lest the inability to grasp and digest this information leads to other handicaps!

As for the name MUMIN... This name allows one to reach the light (nur) of faith... What does the light of faith mean?

Man spends his whole life based on the logic he forms with his conditionings. He rejects and refuses everything that goes against his conditioning-based logic. But when one begins to obtain the light of faith, he stops rejecting the things that go against his logic and begins to research its possibility... He begins to realize that certain things may be beyond his mental capacity. He abandons thoughts, such as, 'Things are the way I know them to be, I know everything, anything that goes against my logic is obsolete,' and expands his perception to greater and newer information...

This expansion of perception is what the light of faith is. Indeed, it is this very quality that allows one to remain open to and perceive new and different possibilities.

The name FATTAH triggers new insights. Not only does it aid in resolving external complications, but it also unblocks and clears internal issues, enabling one to experience inner self-conquest!

The name QUDDUS is beneficial in the area of cleansing one from his ego-identity, for man, due to his nature, thinks he is the mind-body... Imagine someone sitting in a 1958 Chevrolet thinking he is the car... You ask him, who are you? He answers, "I'm a 58 Chevy" unaware of the fact he's not the automobile and that he's going to, at some point, step out of it!

If one looks at the mirror and thinks he's the image reflecting back at him, not realizing at some point he's going to leave this body and continue his life in another dimension with another form, there is a serious situation!

The name Quddus enables one to realize this truth – that man is essentially a divine being, that he is consciousness beyond matter and spirit!

The name RASHID gives spiritual maturity and direction.

Spiritual maturity, in terms of the physical body, begins with adolescence, when the hormones of sexuality are activated and the intellect is strengthened through increased mental activity. These hormones also affect the biochemistry of the brain causing negatively charged energy, what we call 'sin' in religious terminology, to be uploaded to the spirit, a holographic radial body... According to another understanding, however, spiritual maturity begins at the age of 18.

It begins to form when one begins to ponder life after death and channels his life accordingly. The manifestation of the name Rashid begins at this point and may continue up to the state of 'self-conquest' (fath), which is the actualization and fruition of the divine attributes.

As for the name HAKEEM... The root of denial lies in the inability to comprehend. One denies what one cannot understand and fathom. Once we understand why something is the way it is, and why and how something is formed, all of our evaluations change! This name expands one's capacity to understand the underlying reason and wisdom behind all happenings.

The name HALIM activates tolerance and placidity, collectivity and the ability to control impulsive behavior... The first thing one must be able to control to strengthen spiritually is impulsive and reactive behavior. This kind of conduct will destroy not only the person's external world, causing his life to become depressive and stressful, but also his internal world, pulling a pitch-black curtain between himself and Allah. The name Halim brings order to one's internal and external worlds, enabling him to remain open to new understandings with tolerance and maturity, and rids him of anger, stress and impulsive behavior in a short time.

The name WADUD increases and strengthens one's sense of love, enabling the person to approach the whole of existence with love and to feel the love of Allah everywhere and in everything... It transforms his life to one full of love...

The name NUR increases one's comprehension and strengthens the spirit.

The name BAITH is generally understood as resurrection into a new body at the place of gathering (mahshar) after death. However, this is a great misconception and a very primitive understanding. The name Baith is active and observable at all times. Resurrection occurs at every instance... When death occurs, the person is separated from their biological body and is immediately resurrected into their radial-spirit body, thus continuing life without interruption. More information on this can be obtained in Imam Ghazali's book, *Asma'ul Husna*, or in the section on death in my book *Muhammad's Allah*.

In short, the name Baith helps us to both understand the reality of resurrection and add advanced qualities to our renewed existence at every instance, our constant and continual resurrection...

The name RAHMAN subjects us to divine grace and protects us from destructive behavior. For, it is the grace of Rahman that ceases the fire of destruction. The manifestations of this name vary greatly in those who are at advanced levels, though that's another topic altogether.

Also, some people ask whether they should add 'O' (Al or Ya) to the names while doing dhikr, as in Ya Mureed, Al Quddus, etc... Since we are not addressing a deity-god, there is no need for this.

The meanings and effects of the names not mentioned here can be found in the chapter the *Beautiful Names*.

40

SALAT AL-TASBIH – TASBIH PRAYER

This profoundly valuable prayer was taught by the Rasul of Allah (saw) to his uncle Abbas (ra), son of Abdullmuttalib.

One day Abbas (ra) asked Rasulullah (saw), "O Nabi of Allah, I have become quite old, my youthful years have passed… Teach me something that will compensate for all the years I have wasted, so I do not enter the presence of Allah empty handed."

The Rasul of Allah (saw) said, "O Abbas, my dear uncle! **Shall I give you a gift? Shall I show you something by means of which Allah will forgive your sins, the first and the last of them, the past and recent, the unintentional and the intentional, the small and the great, the secret and the open?**" Rasulullah (saw) then taught him the Salat al-Tasbih.[167]

The method of this salat based on this hadith is as follows:

- After beginning the salat by saying Allah-u-Akbar recite the tasbih *Subhaanallaahi walhamdu lillaahi walaa ilaaha illallaahu wallaahu akbar* 15 times, followed by chapter al-Fatiha and a short chapter, and then the above tasbih 10 times again.

---

[167] Abu Dawud.

- Then bow down (ruku) and after reciting the usual tasbih for ruku recite the above tasbih 10 times.

- After standing up from ruku recite the above tasbih 10 times.

- Then prostrate, and after reciting the usual tasbih for prostration, recite the above tasbih 10 times.

- Then sit up and recite the above tasbih 10 times between the two prostrations.

- Then prostrate again, and after reciting the usual tasbih for prostration, recite the above tasbih 10 times.

This adds up to 75 tasbihs in one rakah. Do the same for the remaining 4 rakat so it adds up to a total of 300 tasbihs.

The Rasul of Allah (saw) advised that this prayer be offered daily, if possible. If not, then every Friday or once a month or once a year or at least once in one's life time.[168]

Depending on one's speed, this prayer takes between 20-30 minutes to perform. If the rewards of such a prayer are seriously considered, performing it at least once a week, especially on Friday nights, should not be so burdensome.

The Sufi aspirants who wish to progress and advance spiritually are advised to perform this prayer every night either before going to bed or when they wake up during the night. The spiritual strength gained by this prayer can only be truly appreciated by those who actually experience it.

---

[168] Al-Tirmidhi.

41

VERY SPECIAL PRAYERS TAUGHT BY THE RASULULLAH (SAW)

اَللَّهُمَّ اَعِنِّى عَلَى ذِكْرِكَ وَ شُكْرِكَ وَ حُسْنِ عِبَادَتِكَ

Allahumma a`inni `alaa dhikrika wa shukrika wa husni `ibaadatika[169]

Oh Allah, with ease and abundance, allow me, to remember You, to thank You and to serve You in the best way possible.

I consider this prayer to be very valuable; therefore, I place it in the forefront of all my dhikr formulas.

Rasulullah (saw) taught this prayer through Muaz Bin Jabal, who was a most beloved and close companion of the Rasul (saw).

Muaz Bin Jabal explains:

"One day Rasulullah (saw) held my hand and said, "Oh Muaz... I swear by Allah I love you dearly! Let me recommend something to you that you may read at the end of each salat (before giving salam) and never refrain from reading it... Say –"*Oh Allah, with ease and*

---

[169] Abu Dawud, al-Hakim.

abundance, allow me, to remember You, to thank You and to serve You in the best way possible."

In reflecting on how Rasullullah (saw) taught this prayer and advised it be consistently read to his beloved companion, especially by verifying and testifying his love through giving an oath! Given the above, you be the judge of how important this prayer is!

اَللَّهُمَّ اَلْهِمْنِى رُشْدِى وَاَعِذْنِى شَرَّ نَفْسِى

Allahumma l-himni rushdi wa a`idhni sharri nafsi[170]

Oh Allah, please inspire me my spiritual direction. I seek refuge in You from the evil acts of my identity (ego).

Upon becoming Muslim, Imran Bin Husayn (ra) came to the Rasul of Allah (saw) and reminded him:

"Oh Rasulullah, you had promised me that if I was to become a Muslim you would teach me some words (that will significantly benefit me)."

Rasulullah (saw) replied,

"Husayn, supplicate this as your prayer: Oh Allah, please inspire me my rushd (maturity). I seek refuge in You from the evil acts of my identity-self soul (ego-nafs)."

Following the direction of this hadith, I practice and find benefit from this prayer and so I recommend this prayer be included in the general prayer list and be repeated at least 300 times a day

---

[170] Al-Tirmidhi.

اَللَّهُمَّ اِنِّى اَسْأَلُكَ حُبَّكَ وَ حُبَّ مَنْ يُحِبُّكَ

Allahumma inni as-aluka hubbaka wa hubbi man yuhibbuka

Oh Allah, I ask for Your love, and to love those who love You.

Ebu Derda reports that:

"The Rasul of Allah (saw) said 'from among humankind, David (as) was the most esteemed in worship' then he continued and said 'This was the prayer of David; O Allah, I ask for Your love, and to love those who love You. I ask for the love towards the acts that will draw me to Your love, Oh Allah, let Your love be dearer to me than my own self and my family, let Your love be dearer to me than cool water."[171]

Hence, there is not much more I can say other than that this prayer is also one that I have included in my daily prayer list and one that I recommend to everyone.

اَللَّهُمَّ اِنَّا نَسْأَلُكَ مِنْ خَيْرِ مَا سَأَلَكَ مِنْهُ نَبِيُّكَ مُحَمَّدٌ (صَلَّ اللهُ عَلَيْهِ وَ سَلَّمَ) وَ نَعُوذُ بِكَ مِنْ شَرِّ مَااسْتَعَاذَ مِنْهُ نَبِيُّكَ مُحَمَّدٌ (صَلَّ اللهُ عَلَيْهِ وَ سَلَّمَ) وَأَنْتَ مُسْتَعَانٌ

Allahumma inna nasaa'luka min khayr maa saa'laka minhu nabee'uka Muhammadin wa n-`audhu bika min sharri maa s-t`aadha minhu nabee'uka sallallahu `alayhi wa sallam wa anta l-must`aan

---

[171] Al-Tirmidhi.

Oh Allah, whatever good Your Rasul Muhammad (saw) wanted from You, I too want that, and whatever evil from which he sought refuge in You , I too seek refuge in You from them... For You are Musta'anu (helper).

Ebu Umame (ra) narrates:

One day the Rasul of Allah (saw) made a very long prayer and we could not memorize any of it. Upon this we said...

"Oh Rasul of Allah, you made such a long prayer that we were not able to memorize any of it."

The Rasul of Allah (saw) replied:

"Shall I show you a prayer that encompasses all of this prayer? Pray like this: Oh Allah, whatever good Your Rasul Muhammad (saw) wanted from You, I too want that, and whatever evil from which he sought refuge in You, I too seek refuge in You from them... for You are Musta'anu (helper). All ends meet with You, power and strength is only by Allah."[172]

Again, it was the Rasul of Allah (saw) who taught us this comprehensive prayer that encompasses all needs, desires and protection...

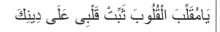

Ya muqalliba l-quluba thabbit qalbi `alaa deenika[173]

O the One who turns the hearts, turn my heart to stay stable upon Your system.

---

[172] Al-Tirmidhi.
[173] Al-Tirmidhi.

It was asked from Ummu Salama (ra):

"Oh mother of the believers, when Allah's Rasul was with you, which prayer did he make the most?"

The blessed wife of the Rasul of Allah (saw) explained:

"The prayer that Rasulullah made most was: O the One who turns the hearts, turn my heart to stay stable upon Your religion. So I asked him 'why do you mostly make this prayer?' To which he answered: O Ummu Salama, the truth is there is no one who is not between the two fingers of Allah, He will secure whom He wills and let slip whom He wills!"

Those whose rising or moon sign is in Gemini, Sagittarius, Virgo or Pisces are seriously recommended to read this prayer.

اَللَّهُمَّ اِنَّا نَجْعَلُكَ فِى نُحُورِهِمْ وَنَعُوذُ بِكَ مِنْ شُرُورِهِمْ

Allahumma inna naj`aluka fee noorihim wa na`udhubika min shuroorihim[174]

Oh Allah, I ask that You face them and that You protect (me) **from their evils.**

This is a highly important prayer that our master Rasulullah (saw) taught us. It is a prayer that deserves our full and serious attention. Why is this so?

It is absolutely normal that in the face of danger man will strive to respond with their personal ability.

Likewise, it is normal that they may turn to and ask for help from Allah.

---

[174] Abu Dawud, al-Nasai.

However, there is a fine point in this prayer that needs attention. Our Master, with this prayer, is asking the divine power to respond instead of the 'person self'. This divine power may express itself from outside and stand up against the danger or it may manifest from one's own being.

Furthermore, we may better comprehend this prayer if we look at such situations in the light of the verse **"And you threw not** (the arrow) **when you** (illusory self; ego) **threw, but it was Allah who threw!"**[175]

Hence, in the same way, prayer is made for the divine to defend... But I do not want to open this any further, whoever wants to understand in a deeper way may themselves show effort to do so.

اَللَّهُمَّ اَخْرِجْنِى مِنْ ظُلُمَاتِ الْوَهْمِ وَاَكْرِمْنِى بِنُورِ الْفَهْمِ

Allahumma akhrijni min zhulumaati l-wahmi wa akrimini bi noori l-fahmi

Oh Allah, take me out of the darkness of doubt and bless me with Your Nur (Light).

Those who follow the path of Sufism will know that the worst problem for mankind is to be trapped in DOUBT. The thickest veil that separates man from Allah is the veil of DOUBT.

Immediately, unity with Allah will be reached when the veil of DOUBT is lifted and understanding will be bestowed with the Nur of Allah. One will attain awareness! Only those who have reached and tasted this state will truly understand how great a blessing this is!

---

[175] Quran 8:17.

If, indeed, while still alive in this world you want to be freed from DOUBT and reach AWARENESS, then continue to read this prayer at least 100 times a day.

رَبِّ زِدْنِى عِلْمًا وَفَهْمًا وَيَقِينًا صَادِقًا

Rabbi zidnee `ilman wa fahman wa eemanan wa yaqeenan saadiqa

My Rabb, increase my knowledge, understanding, faith and loyalty with certainty (yakeen).

This is a comprehensive prayer that encompasses a few very important factors. Rasullullah is commanded in the Quran to say 'Increase my knowledge' and throughout hadith we find he has asked for understanding, faith, loyalty and divine closeness or certainty (yakeen).

Strengthening of faith is very important since the degree of one's faith determines their freedom from the mind barriers formed by conditionings. For whatever cannot be accepted due to the conditionings of the mind, can be reached through a strengthened level of faith. There is expounded information on this subject in both my written book and audio recordings titled *Mind and Faith* (Akil ve Iman). You can find, in this text, descriptive information on the point up until which you can use the mind, and then from which point you need to revert to faith to gain greater understanding.

As for certainty (yakeen), there is a state of certainty that leads to disbelief (kufur) or 'covering of the truth'... Then there is a state of certainty that results in loyalty and reunion! 'Certainty' is the experiential living of the truth 'Allah is Eternal'.

May Allah make it easy!

Those who recite this prayer at least 100 times a day will encounter many of its benefits within a few months.

وَأَنزَلَ اللهُ عَلَيْكَ الْكِتَابَ وَالْحِكْمَةَ وَعَلَّمَكَ مَا لَمْ تَكُنْ تَعْلَمُ

Wa anzala l-Llahu `alayka l-kitaaba wa l-hikmata wa allamaka maa lam takun t`alamu[176]

Allah revealed (from the dimension of Names to your consciousness) **the Book** (knowledge of the reality) **and Wisdom** (the knowledge of religion and sunnatullah) **to you, and taught you that which you did not know...**

If we continue to recite this verse of the Quran, which came to the Rasulullah, at least 300 times a day, we will surprisingly notice that our ability to know and understand Allah's system will increase and expand astonishingly.

عَلَّمَ الْإِنسَانَ مَا لَمْ يَعْلَمْ

`alama l-insaana maa lam y`alam[177]

Taught man that which he knew not.

Those who have read this verse at least **300 times** a day have experienced immense development. But it must not be forgotten that **Certainty of Allah** is attained through knowledge.

---

[176] Quran 4:113.
[177] Quran 96:5.

245

وَكَذَلِكَ أَوْحَيْنَا إِلَيْكَ رُوحاً مِنْ أَمْرِنَا مَا كُنتَ تَدْرِي مَا الْكِتَابُ وَلاَ الْإِيمَانُ وَلَكِن جَعَلْنَاهُ نُوراً نَهْدِي بِهِ مَن نَشَاء مِنْ عِبَادِنَا وَإِنَّكَ لَتَهْدِي إِلَى صِرَاطٍ مُسْتَقِيمٍ

Wa kadhalika aw haynaa ilayka roohan min amrinaa maa kunta tadree maa l-kitaabu wa la l-leemaanu wa lakin ja`alanahu nooran nahdee bihi man nashaa man `ibaadinaa wa innaka latahdee ilaa siraatin mustaqeemin[178]

Thus We have revealed to you a spirit (the sensing of the meanings of the Names in your consciousness) **by Our command... And you did not know what the knowledge of the reality and sunnatullah was, or what faith meant! But We formed it** (the spirit) **as Nur** (knowledge) **by which We guide to the reality whom We will among Our servants! And indeed, you guide to the reality** (the straight path).

This verse aids to strengthen one's spirit, to sharpen one's insight, for better appreciation and use what's been granted, and to be better able and more useful to one's environment.

For those whose conditions are suitable, under the guide of a mentor and if possible while fasting this verse is advised to be read one thousand times a day for forty or eighty days. I have benefited much from this practice and so advise it without hesitation.

كَمَا أَرْسَلْنَا فِيكُمْ رَسُولًا مِنْكُمْ يَتْلُو عَلَيْكُمْ ءَايَاتِنَا وَيُزَكِّيكُمْ وَيُعَلِّمُكُمُ الْكِتَابَ وَالْحِكْمَةَ وَيُعَلِّمُكُم مَّا لَمْ تَكُونُوا تَعْلَمُونَ

---

[178] Quran 42:52.

Kamaa ar-salnaa feekum rasoolan minkum yatloo `alaykum aayaatinaa wa yuzakeekum wa yu`allimukumu l-kitaaba wa l-hikmata wa yu`allimukum maa lam takoonoo t`alamoona[179]

We revealed a Rasul from within you (to disclose the reality), **reciting** (teaching) **to you Our verses** (signs pertaining to our reality within the core of all existence) **and purifying you and teaching you the Book** (of the reality and sunnatullah) **and wisdom** (the system and mechanics of creation) **and that which you do not know.**

These verses, Bakara 151 and Ash-Shura 52 the verse previously listed, were taught to me by the eminent **Abdulkareem al-Jii.** By constantly reciting these two verses with the determining of Allah, I have acquired endless benefits... Such as in **READing the BOOK**, in attaining wisdom and acquiring insight on things that I had never imagined. We are transient, soon we will leave this abode, but we would like to be the cause for many others to benefit from this good and reach enlightenment and wisdom, in hope they may say **'May Allah be pleased with you'** and send the blessing of Ikhlas and Fatiha.

For this reason, I'm revealing these important verses to you here, and advising that they should be read at least one hundred times a day.

What's even better is if the first verse is recited one thousand times a day, as explained above, for forty or eighty days whilst fasting and thereafter reduce it to one hundred daily repetitions. Then, this second verse should be done in the same manner, that is to recite one thousand times a day for forty or eight days while fasting and thereafter to continue by reading it one hundred times a day.

With certainty, we should know that these two verses are of the most valuable jewels in the Quran!

May Allah make it easy!

---

[179] Quran 2:151.

42

THE SPECIAL 19 FORMULA PRAYER OF NEED

I'd like to provide a potent formula in this section, one that is very effective in delivering one from any state of hardship or affliction, or in aiding in the attainment of a desired state.

I have personally witnessed that many people who have applied this formula reached the outcome they desired within nineteen days!

But let me make it very clear that if you apply this with the intention to unjustly cause harm to others or with any other ill intention, you will never be able to escape adversity and the effects of the formula will revert and afflict you instead.

Here is the prayer:

FARDUN HAYYUN QAYYUMUN HAKAMUN ADLUN QUDDUSUN

First, memorize these six names which in Arabic have nineteen letters in total.

After the fardh of every salat, repeat these six names nineteen times after repeating Allahuakbar ten times!

After the nineteenth day, if there is still a hardship, add the verse **Sayaj`alu Allahu ba`da `usrin yusra** (Allah will bring about ease after hardship)[180] to the names, such that:

"Ferdun, Hayyun, Qayyumun, Hakamun, Adlun, Quddusun... Sayaj`alu Allahu ba`da `usrin yusra"

Continue to recite this nineteen times after every prayer for nineteen days.

If you are not after deliverance from a difficult situation, but have other requests, then you may replace the verse above with any of the verses below, depending on your situation.

For Knowledge

Quran 3:48 – **Yu`allimuhu alkitaba wa alhikmata** – He will teach (program – embed into existence) the Book (the knowledge of the reality), Wisdom (the operation mechanism of the system and order formed by the Names of Allah in the worlds)...

For Self-Conquest (Fath)

Quran 48:1 – **Inna fatahna laka fathan mubeenan** – Indeed, we have given you the Clear Conquest (fath; the clear observation of the system of the reality)!

Quran 5:52 – **Fa`asa Allahu an ya'tiya bil-fathi** – Perhaps Allah will bring clarity or a verdict from Himself (HU)...

---

[180] Quran 65:7.

Quran 4:75 – **Wa Aj`al lana min ladunka naseeran** – Grant us a patron and victory from Your Self.

For Victory Over The Enemy

Quran 5:56 – **Inna hizba Allahi humu al-ghaliboon** – Whoever befriends Allah, the Rasul of HU, and the believers (should know) the allies of Allah are the ones who will prevail!

Quran 40:12 – **Faalhukmu lillahi al`aliyyi al-kabeer** – The judgment belongs to Allah, the Aliy, the Kabir (the One whose judgment of His manifest forces you cannot refuse)!

For Protection From The Enemy

Quran 9:129 – **Hasbiya Allahu la ilaha illa hu** – Sufficient for me is Allah! There is no god, only HU!

Quran 3:173 – **Hasbuna Allahu wa ni`ma al-wakeelu** – Allah is sufficient for us, and how excellent a Wakil He is!

Quran 8:40 – **Ni`ma almawla wa ni`ma an-naseeru** – An excellent Protector (owner) and an excellent Helper (giver of victory He is)!

For Prosperity And Abundance Of Provision

Quran 2:212 **Wa Allahu yarzuqu man yashao bighayri hisabin** – Allah gives provision (both limited sustenance for the corporeal life and infinite life sustenance pertaining to the realization of one's inner reality and its benefits) to whom He wills without account.

Quran 33:31 – **Wa a`tadna laha rizqan kareeman** – We have prepared a generous – abundant – life sustenance for them.

Quran 57:24; 60:6 – **Inna Allaha huwa al-ghaniyyu al-hameedu** – Indeed, Allah is the Ghani, the Hamid.

May Allah enable us all to be of those who duly evaluate the blessing of prayer. Amen.

43

THE PRAYER OF NEED

لاَ اِ لَ اِلاَّ اللهُ الْحَلِيمُ الْكَرِيمُ
سُبْحَانَ اللهِ رَبِّ الْعَرْشِ الْعَظِيم
الْحَمْدُ للهِ رَبِّ الْعَالَمِينَ
اَسْأَلُكَ مُوجِبَاتِ رَحْمَتِكَ وَعَزَاإِم مَغْفِرَتِكَ وَالْغَنِيمَةَ مِنْ كُلِّ بِرٍّ وَالسَّلاَمَةَ مِنْ
كُلِّ اِثْم لاَتَدَعْ لِى ذَنْبًا اِلاَّ غَفَرْتَهُ وَلاَ هَمًّا اِلاَّ فَرَّجْتَهُ وَلاَحَاجَةً هِىَ لَكَ رِضًا اِلاَّ
قَضَيْتَهَا يَاأَرْحَمَ الرَّاحِمِينَ*

La ilaha illa Allahu l-haleemu l-ikareemu Subhaana Allahi rabbi l-
`arshi `adheem.

Al-hamdulillah rabbi l-`alameen. As'aluka mujibati rahmatika, wa
`aza'ima maghfiratika, wal ghaneemata min kuli birr, was-salamata
min kulli ithm. La tada` li dhanban illa ghafartahu, wala hamman illa
farajtahu, wala hajatan hiya laka ridan illa qadaytaha ya arhama ar-
rahimeen.

**There is no god. Only Allah, the Halim, the Kareem. I declare
the incomparability (tanzih) of Allah, the Azim Rabb of the
Throne. Hamd belongs to Allah, the Rabb of the worlds. O
Rabb, subject me to what Your grace and mercy necessitate and
every good and bring me out to a state of salam** (emancipation
from the conditions of bodily life and the experience of 'certainty' of

Allah) **from every sin and mistake. Let there be no sin or mistake left to be forgiven and no affliction left from which to be delievered. Amen, O the most merciful Rahim.**

This prayer of need, which is read to present one's need or difficulty to Allah and to ask for deliverance, is recommended to us by the Rasul of Allah (saw), in his words:

"He who is need of something from Allah or from someone should take ablution, perform two rakahs of salat, make repentance, bring salawat to Allah's Rasul and then read this prayer."

If anyone who is suffering from hardship and difficulty reads this prayer and then recites a thousand times the following verse from chapter Talaq, which was mentioned earlier, he would have sought the greatest refuge in Allah:

Wa man yattaqi llaaha yaj`al l-lahu makhrajan wa-yarzuqhu min haythu laa yaḥtasibu wa man yatawakkal `alaa Allahi fahuwa ḥasbuhu

Whoever protects himself from Allah, He will open a way out for him. And He will provide sustenance for him from where he does not expect. He who places his trust in Allah, Allah will be sufficient for him (he who believes in the forces pertaining to the qualities of the Names comprising his essence and complies with their requirements, those forces will be ever sufficient for him). **Indeed, Allah will fulfill His word!**

In any case, reciting this verse one thousand times daily until reaching one's desired state or object is proven to be very effective.

The biggest advice given by saints and the enlightened ones to those who are in need is repentance. For it is said that if a person is unable to reach the degree to which he has been assigned in

the sight of Allah via his own means then Allah subjects him to various afflictions until he reaches that degree.

Repentance is the most effective tool to raise one's degree and erase his mistakes. Thus, those who are in difficulty should first resort to the prayers provided in the section on repentance. It is especially recommended to read the prayer named 'Sayyid al istighfar' every morning and evening or after every salat with the condition that it is not merely read, but felt and contemplated.

44

ISTIKHARAH: THE GUIDANCE PRAYER

اَللَّهُمَّ إِنِّي اَسْتَخِيرُكَ بِعِلْمِكَ وَ اَسْتَقْدِرُكَ بِقُدْرَتِكَ وَ اَسْأَلُكَ مِنْ فَضْلِكَ الْعَظِيم فَإِنَّكَ تَقْدِرُ وَ لاَ أَقْدِرُ وَتَعْلَمُ وَ لاَ أَعْلَمُ وَأَنْتَ عَلاَّمُ الْغُيُوبِ اَللَّهُمَّ إِنْ كُنْتَ تَعْلَمُ أَنَّ هَذَا الْأَمْرَ خَيْرٌ لِي فِي دِينِي وَمَعَاشِي وَ عَاقِبَةِ أَمْرِي فَاقْدُرْهُ لِي وَيَسِّرْهُ لِي ثُمَّ بَارِكْ لِي فِيهِ وَإِنْ كُنْتَ تَعْلَمُ أَنَّ هَذَا الْأَمْرَ شَرٌّ لِي فِي دِينِي وَمَعَاشِي وَ عَاقِبَةِ أَمْرِي فَاصْرِفْهُ عَنِّي وَاصْرِفْنِي عَنْهُ وَاقْدُرْ لِي الْخَيْرَ حَيْثُ كَانَ ثُمَّ أَرْضِنِي بِهِ* (قَالَ وَيُسَمَّى حَاجَتَهُ).

Allahumma inni astakhiruka bi'ilmika. wa astaqdiruka bi-qudratika, wa as'aluka min fadlika al-adheem fa-innaka taqdiru wala aqdiru, wa ta'lamu wala a'lamu, wa anta `allamu-l-ghuyub. Allahumma, in kunta ta' lamu anna hadhaI amra khayrun lee fee deeni wa ma'ashi wa aqibati amri (or 'ajili amri wa'ajilihi) faqdirhu lee wa ya s-sirhu lee thumma barik lee fee-he, wa in kunta ta'llamu anna hadha-l-amra sharrun lee fee deeni wa ma'ashi wa-aqibati amri (or fi'ajili amri wa ajilihi) fasrifhu annee was-rifnee'anhu. Wa aqdir leel-khaira haithu kana thumma ardini bihi [181]

O Allah, I seek Your guidance (in making a choice) **by virtue of Your knowledge, and I seek ability and strength by virtue of Your power, and I ask from Your great bounty that You inform**

---

[181] Sahih al-Bukhari, al-Tirmidhi.

me of whatever is best for me. For You are powerful, I am powerless. And You have knowledge, I know not. You know all the secrets of the unknown...

O Allah, if in Your knowledge, this [the subject matter should be specifically mentioned here] is good for me both in terms of my religion my livelihood and my affairs, my life in this world and in the Hereafter, then ordain it for me, make it easy for me, and bless it for me.

And if in Your knowledge this matter [which should be specifically mentioned here] is bad for me and for my religion, my livelihood and my affairs, both in this world and the next, then turn me away from it (and turn it away from me), and ordain for me the good wherever it may be and make me pleased with it.

Istikharah is a very important notion in Islam. It is a profound opportunity to be able to ask guidance from Allah, the knower of the unknown, regarding a specific matter.

This is why the close companions of the Rasul of Allah (saw) said, 'Rasulullah used to advise us to do istikharah regarding all our affairs."

Istikharah is narrated to us by many eminent companions of the Rasul of Allah (saw), including Abu Bakr (ra), Ibn Masud (ra), Abu Ayyub al-Ansari (ra), Abu Said al-Hudri (ra), Sa'd bin abi wakkas (ra) Abdullah bin Abbas (ra) and Abu Hurairah (ra):

"If any one of you is concerned about a decision he has to make, then let him pray two rakahs of non-obligatory prayer, then recite... (the prayer above)."

Chapter al-Qafirun shuld be recited after the Fatiha in the first rakah of salat and chapter al-Ikhlas should be recited after the Fatiha in the second rakah, those who do not know al-Qafirun can recite al-Ikhlas instead.

If a clear sign is not received that night, it should be repeated for seven nights until a clear and definite sign is received. The Rasul of Allah (saw) told Anas bin Malik:

"O Anas, when you attempt to do something, do istikharah seven times and then look at your heart and its inclination, for the heart inclines towards what is good."

What about if it's an urgent situation and there is no time for this?

Then the best thing to do is to pray two rakah salat, make repentance and then make the following prayer:

"O Allah, You are the knower of all things, the unknown, the past and the future... You also know the situation I'm currently in... Please do not leave me to my own accord, do not leave me to my self, make me incline towards what is good and ease it for me. Protect me from choosing what is harmful and close to me the way to harm. You have no partner in Your sovereignty, You are powerful over all things, I am Your servant and You are my Rabb, the Rabb of the Great Throne. Please show me the best way, inspire me to do the right thing."

After this, place your trust in Allah and act according to how you genuinely feel.

If you happen to see a dream on the night you make istikharah where you see religious leaders and saints, or colors such as white and green, it is a positive sign, but if you see colors, such as black, blue or yellow, it is generally a negative sign.

Istikharah is especially recommended to Sufi aspirants to protect them from knocking on the wrong doors.

Some even make istikharah to ask about their spiritual state, somewhat like an auto-control to keep themselves in check.

However, let us never forget that:

There are things that seem good for us, that we may want with an utmost desire, yet they may actually be harmful for us...

And there are things that seem harmful, that we resist with persistence, but they may actually be good for us in the reality... Only Allah knows, we know not...

One who asks Allah will never feel regret.

45

PROTECTION FROM AFFLICTIONS

اَللَّهُمَّ اِنِّى اَعُوذُ بِكَ مِنَ الْكَسَلِ وَالْهَرَمِ وَالْمَأْثَمِ وَالْمَغْرَمِ وَمِنْ فِتْنَةِ الْقَبْرِ وَعَذَابِ الْقَبْرِ وَمِنْ فِتْنَةِ النَّارِ وَعَذَابِ النَّارِ وَ مِنْ شَرِّ فِتْنَةِ الْغِنَى وَاَعُوذُ بِكَ مِنْ فِتْنَةِ الْقَبْرِ وَاَعُوذُ بِكَ مِنْ فِتْنَةِ الْمَسِيخِ الدَّجَّالِ اَللَّهُمَّ اغْسِلْ عَنِّى خَطَايَاىَ بِمَاءِ الثَّلْجِ وَالْبَرَدِ وَ نَقِّ قَلْبِى مِنَ الْخَطَايَا كَمَا نَقَّيْتَ الثَّوْبَ الْأَبْيَضَ مِنَ الدَّيْنِ وَ بَاعِدْ بَيْنِى وَبَيْنَ خَطَايَاىَ كَمَا بَاعَدْتَ بَيْنَ الْمَشْرِقِ وَالْمَغْرِبِ

Allahumma innee a'oodhu bika minal-kasali walharami wal-ma'thami wal-maghrami wa min fitnatil-qabr wa 'adhabil-qabri, wa min fitnatin-nar wa 'adhabin-nar wa min sharri fitnatil-ghana wa a'oodhu bika min fitnatil faqri wa a'oodhu bika min fitnati masihid-dajjali... Allahumma aghsil `annee khatayaya bima'ith-thalfi wal-barad, wa naqqi qalbi minal-khataya kama naqqaytath-thawbal-abyadha mina addeeni wa ba'id bayni wa bayna khatayaya kama ba'adta baynal-mashriqi wal-maghrib.[182]

O Allah, protect me by virtue of the meaning of the letter B, from laziness, senility, sin (succumbing to bodily desires), fear, debt, the provocation of the grave, the suffering of the grave, the provocation of the fire, the suffering of the fire, and the danger of the trial of wealth... I seek refuge in You from the trial of

---

[182] Fath ul-Bari fi Sharh Sahih al-Bukhari.

The

poverty, the provocation (trial) **of the antichrist... O Allah, please wash the dirt of my sins** (arising from the illusion that I am this body) **with** (untouched) **snow water and hail... Like purifying a white garment from dirt, purify my heart from sins** (arising from mistakenly thinking I am this body) **and make the distance between my sins and I as vast as the distance between the East and the West.**

This prayer, narrated by Hadhrat Aisha (ra), summarizes that which the Rasulullah (saw) knows to be a threat to man and teaches us to seek refuge from it in Allah.

Laziness is a disease that eliminates the function of the concept of humanity... Senility is also a disease that hinders man's consciousness and renders man dysfunctional... Fear is the greatest evil in impeding the progress of man, preventing him from putting his thoughts into action.

Can you imagine the initial shock and horror you would feel being buried alive, totally conscious and able to perceive your surroundings, and having to come face to face with the creatures of this new dimension of life? How scary and shocking it must be! And what if you're not prepared for this dimension, how dreadful it would be to have to cope with and adapt to a totally new dimension and condition of life while completely unprepared!

If, due to your lack of knowledge, your logic remains incapable of fathoming this truth, then perhaps you won't fear the provocation and suffering of the grave... Though the Rasul of Allah (saw) warns us about this! Whether you take heed or not, the consequences will be binding upon you...

The provocation of the antichrist... He is blind of the right eye, in other words, he is veiled from perceiving the truth, he will possess extraordinary powers that will make mankind deify and serve him when he claims to be the great lord.

First, the Mahdi will emerge... The Mahdi will invite mankind to believe in Allah, he will remind people that Allah is the infinite, limitless One, and that there is no god to deify, that Allah is the Oneness beyond all form, color and all conceptual understandings, that He is the possessor of sublime knowledge and power, beyond the universe, beyond energy, etc... Then, the antichrist will emerge and convince mankind that he is god, the one they've been deifying and worshipping for centuries...

Those who have comprehended the concept of Allah, as described by the Mahdi, will not succumb to the antichrist no matter how extraordinary and supernatural his displays may be, they will remain loyal to the teachings of the Quran and Muhammad (saw) and pass on to the next dimension in this state of faith.

But those who have not grasped the chapter Ikhlas in the Quran, and thus haven't quite understood the concept of Allah, thinking he is an external god, are going to be awed by and submit to this 'god' who appears before them, unaware of the bitter consequence of their failure to take heed of the warning they were given.

The only way to escape the provocation of the antichrist is by truly understanding the concept of Allah as explained in chapter Ihklas.

We seem to hear more and more of extraterrestrial visits, UFOs and aliens these days, and those who claim the god of mankind is to come to earth... These could be important signs...

We don't know when the Mahdi will come, we can't know when the antichrist will come... These are in the knowledge of Allah; however, we can prepare ourselves, increase our knowledge and warn the generation to come after us, for the signs show us these days are not too far...

The collection of hadith called *Qutubu Sittah* contains important information regarding the Mahdi and antichrist. Those who wish to obtain more information can resort to it, especially the hadith narrated by Ibn Maja, Muslim and Bukhari.

According to these hadith, the antichrist is going to be able to fly from one side of the earth to the other, travel the earth in 40 days, leave no house unvisited, be sighted in many places around the world at once... Of course, centuries ago when the concept of airplanes and television didn't exist, this was the kind of language that had to be employed... I suggest we look further than the literal meaning of these warnings...

The Rasul of Allah (saw) emphasizes the importance of the antichrist with his words, "Humanity has not seen such provocation (fitnah) since its creation."

This is because the antichrist is going to possess such extraordinary powers and display such supernatural things that everyone except those under the protection of Allah are going to believe in him.

Jesus (as) is going to be the only person to remove the antichrist from earth. There are endless theories as to whether Jesus is going to come back or not and in what form, etc... According to the knowledge and insight bestowed to me by Allah, my understanding is as follows:

Before departing from earth Jesus is said to have said, "I will come back to earth two thousand years later."

All authentic hadith books record that the Rasul of Allah (saw) has stated that Jesus (as) will definitely come back to earth and remove the antichrist.

According to my observation, Jesus (as) is currently in his spirit body freely corresponding with the other Rasuls and other eminent individuals who have attained self-conquest (fath) in the realm of barzakh.

Discovery (kashf) is the state of communication with the spiritual realm while still connected to the physical realm and body.

Self-conquest (fath) is when the holographic spirit body gains its independence, which in Sufism is referred to as dying before death.

So, those who have attained self-conquest, who have died before death, who have attained the ability to live with their radial-spirit body can densify and materialize into a physical body when they like…

Hidhr (as) is an example of this reality. He can switch to and from the radial-spirit body and physical body if and when he chooses…

It is also based on this reality that people like Abdulqadir Jilani are seen in different places at the same time.

So, Jesus' return will also be an event of this sort where he will materialize his spirit body and appear with a physical body of a biological age of thirty-three. Only Allah knows the truth.

This is the observation bestowed by my Rabb… I admit my inability to duly thank Him…

اَللَّهُمَّ ارْزُقْنَا اِيمَانًا دَآئِمًا وَيَقِينًا صَادِقًا وَقَلْبًا خَاشِعًا وَلِسَانًا ذَاكِرًا وَعَمَلاً مَقْبُولاً وَرِزْقًا وَاسِعًا وَعِلْمًا نَافِعًا وَدَرَجَةً رَفِيعَةً وَتَوْبَةً نَصُوحَةً قَبْلَ الْمَوْتِ وَرَاحَةً عِنْدَ الْمَوْتِ وَمَغْفِرَةً بَعْدَ الْمَوْتِ وَاَمْنًا مِنْ عَذَابِ الْقَبْرِ

Allahumma'arzuqna eemanan daaeman wa yaqeenan sadiqan wa qalban khashian wa lisanan dhakiran wa amalan maqbolan wa rizqan wasian wa ilman'n nafian'wa darajatan rafeyatan wa tawbatan nasuhatan qabl-al mawti wa rahatan 'indal-mawti wa maghfiratan badal mawti wa amnan men aathabil qabr.

O Allah, give us steadiness in faith, certainty (yakeen) **of the truth, a heart full of awe** (not fear) **a tongue that is engaged in constant dhikr, the ability to perform beneficial deeds, a comprehensive provision, knowledge that will be eternally beneficial to me, with the worthiness of high rank, the ability to make genuine repentance before dying, comfort at the point of death, repentance after death, and safety from the suffering of the grave.**

This prayer and the previous one taught to us by the Rasul of Allah (saw) is relevant to all facets of life, their comprehensiveness and effectiveness are beyond our imagination.

The first prayer I provided outlines the most important things from which we should refrain and seek refuge in Allah, while the second one reveals the most urgent and important things we should request from Allah.

Please consider carefully the importance of these prayers and then if you agree on the importance of them, make it a habit to read these two prayers every morning and evening. Don't forget you will only attain the results of what you do. There is no god in space to send you something. Allah has established a system and it is not subject to change.

اَللَّهُمَّ اَسْلَمْتُ نَفْسِي اِلَيْكَ وَوَجَّهْتُ وَجْهِي اِلَيْكَ وَفَوَّضْتُ اَمْرِى اِلَيْكَ وَاَلْجَأْتُ ظَهْرِى اِلَيْكَ رَغْبَةً وَرَهْبَةً اِلَيْكَ لاَ مَلْجَأَ وَلاَمَنْجَأَ مِنْكَ اِلاَّ اِلَيْكَ ءَامَنْتُ بِكِتَابِكَ الَّذِى اَنْزَلْتَ وَ نَبِيِّكَ الَّذِى اَرْسَلْتَ

Allahumma aslamtu nafsi ilaika, wa wajjahtu wajhiya ilaika wa fawwadtu amri ilaika, wal-ja'tu thahri ilaika, raghbatan wa rahbatan ilaika, la malja'a wa la manja minka illa ilaika, amantu bikitabik-alladhi anzalta, wa binabiyyik-alladhi arsalta[183]

O Allah, I have submitted myself to You, only You exist in my consciousness, I refer all my affairs to You, I place my trust in You and seek only You and fear what is to come from You. I have no place of refuge other than You and there is none to protect me but You. I have believed in the book You have disclosed and the Rasul You have sent.

---

[183] Sahih al-Muslim, al-Tirmidhi.

Bukhari narrates that Bara bin Adhib (ra) says the Rasul of Allah (saw) made this prayer when he went to bed before going to sleep.

The Rasul of Allah (saw) says, "If someone makes this prayer before going to bed and dies that night, he will have died upon the fitrah (disposition) of Islam."

46

THE PRAYER OF NEED
(Salat al-Haajat)

اَللَّهُمَّ اِلَيْكَ اَشْكُوا ضَعْفَ قُوَّتِي وَقِلَّةَ حِيلَتِي وَهَوَانِي عَلَى النَّاسِ! يَا اَرْحَمَ
الرَّاحِمِينَ! اَنْتَ رَبُّ الْمُسْتَضْعَفِينَ، اَنْتَ اَرْحَمُ بِي مِنْ اَنْ تَكِلَنِى اِلَى عَدُوٍّ بَعِيدٍ
يَتَجَهَّمُنِى اَوْ اِلَى صَدِيقٍ قَرِيبٍ مَلَّكْتَهُ اَمْرِى. اِنْ لَمْ تَكُنْ غَضْبَانَ عَلَىَّ فَلَاأَبَالِي.
غَيْرَ اَنَّ عَافِيَتَكَ اَوْسَعُ لِى. اَعُوذُ بِنُورِ وَجْهِكَ الَّذِى اَشْرَقَتْ لَهُ الظُّلُمَاتُ وَصَلَحَ
عَلَيْهِ اَمْرُ الدُّنْيَا وَالْآخِرَةِ اَنْ يَنْزِلَ بِى غَضَبُكَ اَوْيَحِلَّ عَلَيَّ سَخَطُكَ، وَلَكَ
الْعُتْبَى حَتَّى تَرْضَى، وَلاَ حَوْلَ وَلاَ قُوَّةَ اِلاَّ بِكَ*

Allahumma ilayka ashku dha'fa quwwati, waqillata hilati, wahawani ala an-nas. Ya arham ar-rahimin, anta rabb ul-mustadh'afina wa anta arhamu bey min antaqelane ila aduween ba'idin yatajahhamuni, aw ila sadeeqkan qareeban mallaktahu amri. In lam takun ghadbana alayya fala ubali, ghayra anna 'afiyatuka awsau' li. A'oodhu binuri wajjhika alladhi ashraqat lahudh thulumatu wa saluha alayhi amru ud-dunya wal-akhira an yanzila biy ghadabuka, aw yahilla alayya sakhatuk. Laka al-'utba hatta tardha, wa lahawla wala quwwata illa bika [184]

---

[184] Al-Tabarani *Kitab-ud-Dua*.

O Àllah, You can see that I have become helpless and inadequate in strength, and have become contemptible in the sight of people. O the most Rahim of all Rahims, You are the Rabb of those who are considered weak and who are oppressed. You are so Rahim as to not abandon me to those who are bad-tempered and ill-behaved, and in fact not even to a friend among the relatives to whom You have placed me as trust. O Allah, if You are not angry with me, then all the pain and suffering I am subject to means nothing to me... But I also know Your field of protection is wide enough to not subject me to such things. O Allah, I seek refuge in Your NUR, which enlightens all forms of darkness and leads all affairs pertaining to the world and the afterlife to a state of salam (security) **from being subject to Your wrath or displeasure... O Allah, I ask that You forgive me until You are pleased with me. Strength and power is from You alone.**

The Rasul of Allah (saw) had gone to the city of Taif during his early years of Risalah to spread the message of the reality...

Despite his sincere effort and strife to awaken the people of Taif, he was unfairly criticized and assaulted by them to the point where the children stoned him out of the city, leaving him with bleeding feet.

Though hurt and offended, he was finally able to escape from this ruthless attack when he reached the farm of one of his relatives... He had gone there totally without any personal interest, only to spread the truth, but he was assaulted and stoned in return... Involuntarily, he made the prayer above with teary eyes...

That's when the angels who had been appointed in charge of the mountains came to the Rasul and told him they could join the two mountains and destroy the city of Taif.

But the Rasul of Allah (saw) was not after vengeance! He prayed, "Perhaps Allah will bring about believing people from the generations to come from them"[185] and returned to Makkah.

---

[185] Sahih al-Bukhari.

Allah accepted his prayer. Some time after, the Nur of faith spread in the city of Taif and the entire city became Muslim.

Anyone who is afflicted with great adversity, or subject to injustice and suffering, should definitely read this prayer, especially after completing or during prostration of the night prayer, or after every salat during the day... Hopefully, they will reach salvation and security in a very short time.

اَللَّهُمَّ اِنِّى اَعُوذُ بِرِضَاكَ مِنْ سَخَطِكَ وَبِمُعَافَاتِكَ مِنْ عُقُوبَتِكَ وَاَعُوذُ بِكَ مِنْكَ لَأُحْصِى ثَنَآءً عَلَيْكَ اَنْتَ كَمَا اَثْنَيْتَ عَلَى نَفْسِكَ

Allahumma inni a`oodhu biridhaka min sakhatika wa bimu`aafaatika min `uqubatika wa a`oodhu bika minka la uhsi thanaa'an alayka anta kamaa athnayta `alaa nafsik [186]

I seek refuge in Your pleasure from Your displeasure, in Your forgiveness from Your recompense, In You from You. I admit my inability to praise You as You praise Yourself.

We have been informed via various sources that the Rasul (saw) made this prayer during prostration of the night prayers.

This is a wonderful prayer; especially the last two lines point to the levels of the reality and gnosis in Sufism, the qualified must evaluate this. I advise the qualified ones to take special consideration of these messages to try and grasp the essence of what the Rasul (saw) wanted to teach us.

---

[186] Ibn Abi Shaybah, al Tirmidhi.

47

PRAYERS FOR THE INCREASE OF PROVISION AND REDUCTION OF DEBTS

اَللَّهُمَّ اَكْفِنِى بِحَلاَلِكَ عَنْ حَرَامِكَ وَاَغْنِنِى بِفَضْلِكَ عَمَّنْ سِوَاكَ

Allahumma'kfni bi halaalika `an haraamika wa aghnini bi fadlika `amman siwaak[187]

O Allah, suffice me with Your legitimate (provision) **not from Your illegitimate and bestow me with wealth such that I shall be in need of no one other than You.**

When the Rasul of Allah (saw) taught this prayer he said:

"Even if one was in as much debt as a mountain, on continual recitation of this prayer, Allah will enable him to pay his debt off..."

Those who are in debt and are having difficulty paying it are advised to read this prayer 300 times a day

---

[187] Al-Hakim.

اَللَّهُمَّ رَحْمَتَكَ اَرْجُو فَلَاتَكِلْنِى اِلَى نَفْسِى طَرْفَةَ عَيْنٍ وَاَصْلِحْ لِى شَأْنِى كُلَّهُ لَآاِلَهَ اِلاَّ اَنْتَ

Allahumma rahmataka arjoo falaa takilni ilaa nafsi tarfat `aynin wa aslih-lee sha`nee kullahu la ilaha illa anta [188]

O Allah, I seek Your grace, do not leave me to my self not even for a blink of an eye, correct me every instance, there is no god, only You.

The Rasul of Allah (saw) says "those who are in hardship and necessity should read this prayer" at least forty times a day.

---

[188] Abu Dawud.

48

SOME VERY POWERFUL PRAYERS

اَعُوذُ بِوَجْهِ اللهِ الْكَرِيم وَ كَلِمَاتِ اللهِ التَّآمَّاةِ الَّتِى لاَ يُجَاوِزْهُنَّ بَرٌّ وَلاَفَاجِرٌ مِنْ شَرِّ مَا يَنْزِلُ مِنَ السَّمَاءِ وَمَا يَعْرُجُ فِيهَا وَ مِنْ شَرِّ مَا ذَرَأَ فِى الْلأَرْضِ وَمَايَخْرُجُ مِنْهَا وَمِنْ فِتَنِ اللَّيْلِ وَالنَّهَارِ اِلاَّ طَارِقًا يَطْرُقُ بِخَيْرٍ يَا رَحْمَانُ!

A`aoodhu bi wajhi l-llahil kareem wa kalimaati l-ta'ammatillati la yujaawiz huna barun wa la fa'ajirun min sharri maa yanzilu mina s-samaa-i wa maa y`aruju feeha wa min sharri maa dhara fee-l ardhi wa mayakhrujoo minha wa min fitanil layli wan nahari illa tariqan yatruku bikhayrin ya Rahman[189]...

I seek refuge in the countenance of Allah, the Kareem (the exceedingly generous and bountiful), **and in all of His Names, nothing good or bad can attack them. I seek refuge in RAHMAN from that which ascends to the heavens** (provocative illusory thoughts) **and that which descends from the heavens** (thoughts that conjure doubt and suspicion), **from that which is produced from the earth** (that which emanates from corporeality) **and grows out of it** (bodily demands and desires), **from the provocations of the day** (our internal life) **and the night** (the outside world), **and**

---

[189] Musnad of Ahmad ibn Hanbal.

from that which knocks on the door at night (instinct)**, except with good.**

There was a man known as Haji Osman Efendy from Madina, whom was said to be living in Beykoz, a suburb in Istanbul. He had spent fifty years of his life in Madina. He was a man who had not left a book unread in Madinan literature! Sayyid Mehmed Osman Akfirat... May Allah have mercy and increase his Nur (light) with grace... When I kissed his hand in early 1960 he was eighty-six years old and I was around eighteen. He introduced me to the one who opened the doors to understanding, first the external then the internal world, that is, it was he who introduced Rasullullah (saw) to me... What's more, I witnessed his spiritual guidance during the most important events of my life. May he forever be bestowed grace from Allah's decree, may he be presented with perfection eternally!

It was Haji Osman Efendy from Madina who taught me this prayer of Rasulullah (saw). He would recommend that this prayer be written on a paper and carried by those who are experiencing various struggles... Therefore, I also recommend it. Because...

Among the jinn there are those known as Ifrit who are very strong. When the Ifrit received the news that the Rasul of Allah (saw) ascended during the event of Miraj, they became very worried, thinking "If Muhammad ascends to the heavens and unites with Allah, nothing will be able to proceed him" so with all their might they attacked the Rasul of Allah (saw). In that moment, Gabriel (as) revealed this prayer to the Rasul of Allah (saw) and taught him to be protected through this prayer. When the Rasul of Allah (saw) read this prayer, all the jinn were burnt... Now, knowing how this prayer emerged from such an event, we are free to value it as we like.

يَاحَىُّ يَاقَيُّومُ يَا ذَا لْجَلَالِ وَاللاِكْرَامِ اَسْأَلُكَ اَنْ تُحْيِي قَلْبِى بِنُورِ مَعْرِفَتِكَ اَبَدًا يَا اَاللهُ يَا اَاللهُ يَابَدِيعَ السَّمَوَاتِ وَالْأَرْضِ

Yaa Hayyu Yaa Qayyoom Yaa dha l-jalaali wa l-ikraam asaluka an tuhyeeya qalbi binoori m`aarifatika abadan Yaa Allah Yaa Allah Yaa Allah Yaa Badee`u s-samawaati wa l-ard

(Oh the) **Absolute Alive, Perpetually Self Sufficient, Exhaulted Giver! I ask** (enlgihtenment) **from You,** *eternally awaken my heart with the light (nur) of gnosis***! Oh Allah, who brings together the heavens and earth with none like it in existence!**

Those who read this prayer 40 times just before praying the morning salat, and who repeat this for 40 days, will immediately start to see its benefits.

What is meant by "**eternally awaken my heart with the light (nur) of gnosis**" is this: In Islamic terminology, the word '**heart**' is used to refer to '**consciousness**'. The heart/conciousness can only be awakened through the 'light (nur) of gnosis'... so then, what is the **light (nur) of gnosis**?

With the **light (nur) of belief and faith**, one can surpass the boundaries of the mind (and reach awareness), yet with the **light (nur) of gnosis,** one can attain the capacity to further evaluate the realities that are beyond the minds boundaries (and reach enlightenment).

Consistently, throughout our entire life, may Allah never, not even for one moment, deprive us of the **light (nur) of belief and faith** nor of the **light (nur) of gnosis**...

Since the one who is deprived of the **light (nur) of belief and faith** will live blindly with a blocked mind and the one deprived of the **light (nur) of gnosis** will never be able to comprehend, contemplate or evaluate the realities beyond the boundaries of the mind.

For this reason, at every oppurtunity, we should ask Allah to bestow us with the **light (nur) of belief, faith and gnosis,** eternally and without cease.

رَبِّ اِنِّى مَغْلُوبٌ فَانْتَصِرْ وَاجْبُرْ قَلْبِى الْمُنْكَسِرْ وَاجْمَعْ شَمْلِى الْمُدَّثِرْ اِنَّكَ اَنْتَ الرَّحْمَانُ الْمُقْتَدِرُ اِكْفِنِى يَا كَافِى فَأَنَا الْعَبْدُ الْمُفْتَقِرُ وَكَفَى بِااللهِ وَلِيًّا وَكَفَى بِااللهِ نَصِيرًا اِنَّ الشِّرْكَ لَظُلْمٌ عَظِيمٌ وَمَا االلهُ يُرِيدُ ظُلْمًا لِلْعِبَادِ فَقُطِعَ دَابِرُ الْقَوْمِ الَّذِينَ ظَلَمُوا وَالْحَمْدُ لله رَبِّ الْعَالَمِينَ

Rabbi inni maghloobun faantasir wajbur qalbi l-munkasir wajm`aa shamli l-muddathir innaka anta r-rahmaanu l-muqtadir ikfini yaa kaafee fa'anaa l-`abdul muftaqiru wa kafaa billahi l-waliyyan wa kafaa billahi l-naseera, inna ashshirka lathulmun adheem wa maa Allahu yureedu thulman lil-`ibaadi, faquti`a daabiru l-qawmi l-ladheena thalamoo wa l-hamdu lillahi rabbil `alameen

My Rabb, I am defeated; allow me to succeed with Your Help... My heart (the faculty with which I feel the reality) **has parted to pieces; restore it to wholeness, unity and oneness... Restore and collect my shattered heart** (scattered cognitive perception that is unable to percieve unity)**, which has been veiled** (from its original state)**, for You, yes You are the Absolute Muqtadir and You are the Rahman** (the source of all potentials)**. Help me, O Qafi** (Sufficient One)**, for I am Your servant who has nothing** (I, with all my being am owned by You and fully dependent on You)**. As Wali, the One denoted through the name 'Allah'** (one's essential reality) **is enough! As Nasr** (protector from enemies) **the One denoted through the Name 'Allah'** (one's essential reality) **is enough!.... Surely shirq** (duality) **is a great injustice! And Allah does not will injustice upon His servants.**

Those who inflict injustice are severed! Hamd belongs to the Rabb of all the worlds.

I have included this significant prayer, which was taught by the eminent Ghawth al-Azam (great spiritual pillar) Abdulqadir Jilani, for the good fortune of this book. Gaws Azam Abdulqadir Jilani, a great saint from whom believers throughout the ages have sought spiritual strength and guidance, has recommended this prayer to whoever finds themselves in difficulties. It is to be read seven times in the morning and night. InshaAllah, we will be of those who benefit from this prayer.

49

SOME SALAT PRAYERS

SUBHANAKA

سُبْحَانَكَ اللَّهُمَّ وَبِحَمْدِكَ وَتَبَارَكَ اسْمُكَ وَتَعالَى جَدُّكَ (وَجَلَّ ثَنَاؤُكَ) وَلاَ إِلَهَ غَيْرُكَ!

Subhaanaaka l-lahumma wa bi hamdika wa tabaaraka s-muka wa t'aala jaduka (wa jalla thanaa'uka) wa laa ilaha ghayruka

Allah, You are Perfect with Your hamd! Blessed is Your Name! Exhaulted and Great is Your Existence (Your Praise is unprecievably great). **There is none besides You in possession of Uluhiyyah.**

AT-TAHIYYATU

اَلتَّحِيَّاتُ لِلهِ وَالصَّلَوَاتُ وَالطَّيِّبَاتُ؛ اَلسَّلاَمُ عَلَيْكَ اَيُّهَا النَّبِىُّ وَرَحْمَةُ اللهِ
وَبَرَكَاتُهُ؛ اَلسَّلاَمُ عَلَيْنَا وَعَلَى عِبَادِ اللهِ الصَّالِحِينَ؛ اَشْهَدُ اَنْ لاَ اِلَهَ اِلاَّ اللهُ
وَاَشْهَدُ اَنَّ مُحَمَّدًا عَبْدُهُ وَرَسُولُهُ!

At-taheeyatu lillahi wa s-salawatu wa t-tayyibatu as-salaamu `alayka
ayyuhaa n-nabiyu wa rahma tullahi wa barakaatuhu as-salaamu
`alayna wa `alaa `ibaadi l-Llahi his-saliheen ashhadu anna
Muhammadan `abduhu wa rasooluhu

**All reverence, prayers and appeals and the purest worship is
for Allah and all is according to Allah's Uluhiyyah. Oh Nabi!
Salam! May Allah's grace and propserity be upon you! May
Salam be upon us and the righteous servants of Allah. I bear
witness that there is no God! There is only Allah!... And I bear
witness that Muhammad is Allah's servant and Rasul!**

SALAWATS (SALLI – BARIK)

اَللّٰهُمَّ صَلِّ عَلٰى مُحَمَّدٍ وَ عَلٰى اٰلِ مُحَمَّدٍ كَمَا صَلَّيْتَ عَلٰى اِبْرَاهِيمَ وَعَلٰى اٰلِ اِبْرَاهِيمَ اِنَّكَ حَمِيدٌ مَجِيدٌ*
اَللّٰهُمَّ بَارِكْ عَلٰى مُحَمَّدٍ وَ عَلٰى اٰلِ مُحَمَّدٍ كَمَا بَارَكْتَ عَلٰى اِبْرَاهِيمَ وَعَلٰى اٰلِ اِبْرَاهِيمَ اِنَّكَ حَمِيدٌ مَجِيدٌ*

Allahumma salli `alaa Muhammadin wa `alaa ali Muhammad kama sallayta `alaa Ibraheema wa `alaa ali Ibraheema Innaka Hamidun majid

Allahumma baarik `alaa Muhammadin wa `alaa ali Muhammad kama baarakta `alaa Ibraheema wa `alaa ali Ibraheema Innaka Hamidun majid

Oh Allah! As You bestowed Your salat to Abraham and to Abraham's family and household, so too bestow salat to Muhammad and Muhammad's family and household!

Indeed, You are Hamid and Majid.

Oh Allah! As You blessed Abraham and Abraham's family and household, so too bless Muhammad and Muhammad's family and household.

Indeed, You are Hamid and Majid.

103. AL-ASR

بِسْمِ اللهِ الرَّحْمنِ الرَّحِيمِ
وَالْعَصْرِ {1} إِنَّ الْإِنسَانَ لَفِي خُسْرٍ {2} إِلَّا الَّذِينَ آمَنُوا وَعَمِلُوا الصَّالِحَاتِ وَتَوَاصَوْا بِالْحَقِّ وَتَوَاصَوْا بِالصَّبْرِ {3}

A`oodhu biLlaahi min al-shaytaani l-rajeem
Bismi Llaahi l-rahmaani l-raheem

1. Wa l-`asri 2. Inna l-insaana lafee khusrin 3. 'Illaa l-latheena 'aamanoo wa `amiloo l-ssaalihaati watawaasaw bi l-haqqi watawaasaw bi l-ssabri

By the one who is denoted by the name Allah (who created my being with His Names in accord with the meaning of the letter 'B'), **the Rahman, the Rahim.**

1. By that time (the life span of man),

2. Indeed, mankind is in loss!

3. Except for those who have believed (in their essential reality) **and fulfilled the requisites of faith, advised each other the Truth, and advised patience upon one another!**

105. AL-FIL

بِسْمِ اللهِ الرَّحْمنِ الرَّحِيمِ
أَلَمْ تَرَ كَيْفَ فَعَلَ رَبُّكَ بِأَصْحَابِ الْفِيلِ {1} أَلَمْ يَجْعَلْ كَيْدَهُمْ فِي تَضْلِيلٍ {2}
وَأَرْسَلَ عَلَيْهِمْ طَيْرًا أَبَابِيلَ {3} تَرْمِيهِم بِحِجَارَةٍ مِّن سِجِّيلٍ {4} فَجَعَلَهُمْ
كَعَصْفٍ مَّأْكُولٍ {5}

A`oodhu biLlaahi min al-shaytaani l-rajeem
Bismi Llaahi l-rahmaani l-raheem

1. Alam tara kayfa f`ala rabbuka bi'ashaabi l-feeli 2. Alam yaj`al kaydahum fee tazleelin 3. Wa arsala `alayhim tayran abaabeela 4. Tarmeehim bi-hijaaratin mmin sijjeelin 5. Faja`alahum ka`asfin maakoolin

By the one who is denoted by the name Allah (who created my being with His Names in accord with the meaning of the letter 'B'), **the Rahman, the Rahim.**

1. Did you not see how your Rabb dealt with the people of the elephant?

2. Did He not make their plan worthless?

3. And disclosed upon them the birds in flocks (the Common Swift).

4. Who threw upon them stones of hard clay.

5. Until they became like chewed straw.

106. QURAYSH

بِسْمِ اللهِ الرَّحْمنِ الرَّحِيم
لِإِيلَافِ قُرَيْشٍ {1} إِيلَافِهِمْ رِحْلَةَ الشِّتَاءِ وَالصَّيْفِ {2} فَلْيَعْبُدُوا رَبَّ هَذَا
الْبَيْتِ {3} الَّذِي أَطْعَمَهُم مِّن جُوعٍ وَآمَنَهُم مِّنْ خَوْفٍ {4}

A`oodhu biLlaahi min al-shaytaani l-rajeem
Bismi Llaahi l-rahmaani l-raheem

1.'Li'eelaafi quraysh 2. 'eelaafihim rihlata l-shshitaa'i wa l-ssayfi 3.
Faly`abudoo rabba haatha l-bayti 4. Alathee 'at`amahum-mmin
joo`in wa 'aamanahum-mmin khawfin

By the one who is denoted by the name Allah (who created my
being with His Names in accord with the meaning of the letter 'B'),
the Rahman, the Rahim.

**1. In order to establish acquaintanceship and respect for the
Quraysh,**

**2. For the safety and comfort of their winter and summer
journeys.**

3. Let them serve the Rabb of this city (as those who
acknowledge the Truth of non-duality)!

4. Who fed them (saving them from hunger) **and secured them
from fear.**

107. AL-MA'UN

بِسْمِ اللهِ الرَّحْمنِ الرَّحِيمِ
أَرَأَيْتَ الَّذِي يُكَذِّبُ بِالدِّينِ {1} فَذَلِكَ الَّذِي يَدُعُّ الْيَتِيمَ {2} وَلَا يَحُضُّ
عَلَى طَعَامِ الْمِسْكِينِ {3} فَوَيْلٌ لِّلْمُصَلِّينَ {4} الَّذِينَ هُمْ عَن صَلَاتِهِمْ سَاهُونَ
{5} الَّذِينَ هُمْ يُرَاؤُونَ {6} وَيَمْنَعُونَ الْمَاعُونَ {7}

A`oodhu biLlaahi min al-shayṭaani l-rajeem
Bismi Llaahi l-raḥmaani l-raḥeem

1.'Araayta l-lathee yukaththibu bi-ddeeni 2. Fathalika l-lathee yadu`u`u l-yateema 3. Wa laa yaḥuḍḍu `alaa ṭa`aami l-miskeeni 4. Fawaylun li-l-muṣalleena 5. Allatheena hum `an ṣalaatihim saahoona 6. Allatheena hum yuraa'oona 7. Wa-yamna`oona l-maa`oona

By the one who is denoted by the name Allah (who created my being with His Names in accord with the meaning of the letter 'B'), **the Rahman, the Rahim.**

1. Did you see the one who denies his religion (the sunnatullah)?

2. Who scolds the orphan - pushing and shoving him,

3. And who does not encourage feeding the needy (stingy, selfish)!

4. So, woe to those who pray (out of custom),

5. Who are heedless (cocooned) **of** (the experience of the meaning of) **their salat** (which is an ascension [miraj] to their innermost essential reality; their Rabb).

6. They are the ones who make show off their deeds!

7. And prevent good!

108. AL-KAWTHAR

بِسْمِ اللهِ الرَّحْمنِ الرَّحِيمِ
إِنَّا أَعْطَيْنَاكَ الْكَوْثَرَ {1} فَصَلِّ لِرَبِّكَ وَانْحَرْ {2} إِنَّ شَانِئَكَ هُوَ الْأَبْتَرُ {3}

A`oodhu biLlaahi min al-shayṭaani l-rajeem
Bismi Llaahi l-raḥmaani l-raḥeem

1. Innaa ‘a`aaṭaynaaka l-kawthara 2. Faṣalli li-rabbika wa-anhar 3. Inna shaani’aka huwa l-‘abtaru

By the one who is denoted by the name Allah (who created my being with His Names in accord with the meaning of the letter ‘B’), **the Rahman, the Rahim.**

1. Indeed, We gave you the Kawthar!

2. So, experience salat for your Rabb and sacrifice (your ego)!

3. Indeed, it is the one who resents you that is cut off (whose progeny has been made discontinuous)!

109. AL-KAFIRUN

بِسْمِ اللهِ الرَّحْمنِ الرَّحِيمِ
قُلْ يَا أَيُّهَا الْكَافِرُونَ {1} لَا أَعْبُدُ مَا تَعْبُدُونَ {2} وَلَا أَنتُمْ عَابِدُونَ مَا أَعْبُدُ
{3} وَلَا أَنَا عَابِدٌ مَّا عَبَدتُّمْ {4} وَلَا أَنتُمْ عَابِدُونَ مَا أَعْبُدُ {5} لَكُمْ دِينُكُمْ وَلِيَ
دِينِ {6}

A`oodhu biLlaahi min al-shaytaani l-rajeem
Bismi Llaahi l-rahmaani l-raheem

1.Qul yaa 'ayyuha l-kaafiroona 2. Laa 'a`abudu maa t`abudoona 3.
Wa laa 'antum `aabidoona maa 'a`abudu 4. Wa laa 'anaa `aabidun
mmaa `abadttum 5. Wa laa 'antum `aabidoona maa 'a`abudu 6.
Lakum deenukum waliya deeni

By the one who is denoted by the name Allah (who created my
being with His Names in accord with the meaning of the letter 'B'),
the Rahman, the Rahim.

1. Say, "O those who deny the knowledge of the reality!"

2. "I do not deify that which you deify!"

3. "Nor are you worshippers of (in servitude to) **what I
worship."**

4. "Nor will I worship (serve) **that which you deify."**

5. Nor will you worship (serve) **what I serve."**

6. "For you is your (understanding of) **religion and for me is**
(my understanding of) **religion!"**

110. AN-NASR

بِسْمِ اللهِ الرَّحْمنِ الرَّحِيمِ
إِذَا جَاءَ نَصْرُ اللهِ وَالْفَتْحُ {1} وَرَأَيْتَ النَّاسَ يَدْخُلُونَ فِي دِينِ اللهِ أَفْوَاجًا {2}
فَسَبِّحْ بِحَمْدِ رَبِّكَ وَاسْتَغْفِرْهُ إِنَّهُ كَانَ تَوَّابًا {3}

A`oodhu biLlaahi min al-shaytaani l-rajeem
Bismi Llaahi l-rahmaani l-raheem

1.'ithaa jaa'a nasru L-laahi wal-fath 2. Wara'ayta l-naasa yadkhuloona fee deeni L-laahi 'afwaajan 3. Fasabbih bi-hamdi rabbika wa'astaghfirhu 'innahu kaana tawwaaban

By the one who is denoted by the name Allah (who created my being with His Names in accord with the meaning of the letter 'B'), **the Rahman, the Rahim.**

1. When the help (of Allah) **and the conquest** (absolute clarity - conscious observation) **has come,**

2. And you see the people entering the religion of Allah in masses,

3. Glorify (tasbih) **your Rabb as his Hamd and ask forgiveness of Him! Indeed He is the Tawwab.**

111. AL-MASAD

بِسْمِ اللهِ الرَّحْمنِ الرَّحِيمِ
تَبَّتْ يَدَا أَبِي لَهَبٍ وَتَبَّ {1} مَا أَغْنَى عَنْهُ مَالُهُ وَمَا كَسَبَ {2} سَيَصْلَى نَارًا
ذَاتَ لَهَبٍ {3} وَامْرَأَتُهُ حَمَّالَةَ الْحَطَبِ {4} فِي جِيدِهَا حَبْلٌ مِّن مَّسَدٍ {5}

A`oodhu biLlaahi min al-shayṭaani l-rajeem
Bismi Llaahi l-raḥmaani l-raheem

1. Tabbat yadaa 'abee lahabin wa-tabba 2. Maa 'aghnaa 'anhu maaluhu wa maa kasaba 3. Sayaṣlaa naaran thaata lahabin 4. Wa'amra'atuhu ḥammaalata l-ḥaṭabi 5. Fee jeedihaa ḥablun mmin mmasadin

By the one who is denoted by the name Allah (who created my being with His Names in accord with the meaning of the letter 'B'), **the Rahman, the Rahim.**

1. May the hands of Abu Lahab be ruined... And ruined he is!

2. Neither his wealth nor his earnings availed him!

3. He will be subject to a blazing Fire!

4. His wife as well... As a wood-carrier!

5. With a rope of palm-fiber around her neck!

112. AL-IKHLAS

بِسْمِ اللهِ الرَّحْمنِ الرَّحِيمِ
قُلْ هُوَ اللَّهُ أَحَدٌ {1} اللَّهُ الصَّمَدُ {2} لَمْ يَلِدْ وَلَمْ يُولَدْ {3}
وَلَمْ يَكُن لَّهُ كُفُوًا أَحَدٌ {4}

A`oodhu biLlaahi min al-shaytaani l-rajeem
Bismi Llaahi l-rahmaani l-raheem

1. Qul huwa Llaahu 'ahadun 2. Allaahu l-ssamadu 3. Lam yalid walam yoolad 4. Walam yakun llahu kufuwan 'ahadun

By the one who is denoted by the name Allah (who created my being with His Names in accord with the meaning of the letter 'B'), **the Rahman, the Rahim.**

1. Say: "Allah is Ahad (One)." (Allah is the infinite, limitless and indivisible, non-dual ONENESS.)

2. "Allah is Samad" (Absolute Self-Sufficient One beyond any need or defect, free from the concept of multiplicity, and far from conceptualization and limitation. The one into whom nothing can enter, and the One from whom no other form of existence can come out!),

3. "He begets not. (No other form of existence has ever originated from Him, thus, there is no other.) **Nor was He begotten."** (There is no other god or form of existence from which He could have originated.)

4. "There is none like unto Him!" (Nothing – no conception – in the micro or macro planes of existence is equivalent to or in resemblance of Him.)

50

FAREWELL

Although it was not planned, due to the persistent request of my significantly close friends, I started to write this book just fifteen days ago. Gracefully, Allah did not humiliate me and allowed me to complete this work...

I could not turn down the request of my friends who persistently asked, "What is the power of prayer and dhikr? Why is it important? What will one lose if they neglect it? And what will be the gain of those who revere it? Only you can write and explain these in a way that the next generation can understand." Seeking refuge in Allah's grace and mercy, I sat before the typewriter and began....

If, indeed, I have been able to explain what the power of prayer and dhikr is, why it is important and how it should be practiced, it is only because Allah has willed and permitted it, and Allah desires that this information be available to people.

If, on the other hand, I have not been successful, then the fault is due to my own limitations.... In this case, may my good intentions be considered and my faults be forgiven...

I plead to Allah, the Azim and Karim Rabb of the heavens, earth and all the worlds, that for the love of the beloved Muhammad Mustafa (saw), Allah's graceful mercy and blessing be showered upon me for being the vehicle for this knowledge, upon the reader and those who cause it to be read! May Allah grant the light of faith and the light of gnosis, may He grant true closeness and protect from all kinds of divergence, discord and hypocrisy. May He grant praise and blessings from us to the Rasul of Allah!

May Allah allow us all to benefit from this book! Amen Amen Amen.

ABOUT THE AUTHOR

Ahmed Hulusi (Born January 21, 1945, Istanbul, Turkey) contemporary Islamic philosopher. From 1965 to this day he has written close to 30 books. His books are written based on Sufi wisdom and explain Islam through scientific principles. His established belief that the knowledge of Allah can only be properly shared without any expectation of return has led him to offer all of his works which include books, articles, and videos free of charge via his web-site. In 1970 he started examining the art of spirit evocation and linked these subjects parallel references in the Quran (smokeless flames and flames instilling pores). He found that these references were in fact pointing to luminous energy which led him to write *Spirit, Man, Jinn* while working as a journalist for the Aksam newspaper in Turkey. Published in 1985, his work called '*Mysteries of Man (Insan ve Sirlari)*' was Hulusi's first foray into decoding the messages of the Quran filled with metaphors and examples through a scientific backdrop. In 1991 he published *The Power of Prayer (Dua and Zikir)*' where he explains how the repetition of certain prayers and words can lead to the realization of the divine attributes inherent within our essence through increased brain capacity. In 2009 he completed his final work, '*Decoding the Quran, A Unique Sufi Interpretation*' which encompasses the understanding of leading Sufi scholars such as Abdulkarim al Jili, Abdul-Qadir Gilani, Muhyiddin Ibn al-Arabi, Imam Rabbani, Ahmed ar-Rifai, Imam Ghazali, and Razi, and which approached the messages of the Quran through the secret Key of the letter 'B'.

56639107R00186

Made in the USA
Columbia, SC
29 April 2019